The Pocket Hercules

The Pocket Hercules

Captain Morris and the Charge of the Light Brigade

M J Trow

But they that fought for England,
Following a falling star,
Alas, alas for England
They have their graves afar.

G K Chesterton, 'Elegy in a Country Churchyard'

Pen & Sword
MILITARY

This book is dedicated to John

First published in Great Britain in 2006 by
Pen & Sword Military
an imprint of
Pen & Sword Books Ltd
47 Church Street
Barnsley
South Yorkshire
S70 2AS

Copyright © M J Trow 2006

ISBN 1-84415-378-9
    978-1-84415-378-7

A CIP catalogue record for this book is
available from the British Library

Typeset in 11/13pt Plantin by Mac Style, Nafferton, E. Yorkshire
Printed and bound in England by CPI UK

Pen & Sword Books Ltd incorporates the Imprints of Pen & Sword Aviation,
Pen & Sword Maritime, Pen & Sword Military, Wharncliffe Local History,
Pen & Sword Select, Pen and Sword Military Classics and Leo Cooper.

For a complete list of Pen & Sword titles, please contact
Pen & Sword Books Limited
47 Church Street, Barnsley, South Yorkshire, S70 2AS, England
E-mail: enquiries@pen-and-sword.co.uk
Website: www.pen-and-sword.co.uk

Contents

Plates

The only known photograph of Morris, probably taken at home, either in 1848 or in 1855.

Anonymous painting of Morris, probably painted before he left the 16th Lancers in 1847.

The church of St Michael's, Sandhurst, where Morris married Amelia Taylor in April 1852.

The various awards, medals and decorations which Morris acquired during his service in India and the Crimea.

Lord Raglan's headquarters at Khutor-Karagatch, drawn by William Simpson.

Lord Cardigan.

Captain Louis Nolan.

Lord Lucan.

Lord Raglan.

A panoramic view of the Charge, as recorded by William Simpson.

The climax of the Charge, as portrayed by Christopher Clark.

The aftermath of the Charge, by Caton Woodville.

The sword presented to William Morris at Great Torrington, Devon, in 1856, with detail of the inscription.

The Casual and Squad Roll Book of Captain Morris, 17th Lancers.

Pages from the Squad Book, showing details of some of the men who rode behind Morris in the Charge of the Light Brigade.

The monument erected in 1860 in memory of William Morris on Hatherleigh Moor, North Devon.

The bas-relief of Morris being carried semi-conscious from the 'Valley of Death' by Surgeon James Mouat and men of the 17th Lancers.

Introduction: Tony Richardson's
The Charge of the Light Brigade

There had been rumours about a film, following the events of the Crimean War far more closely than Errol Flynn's epic of 1936, throughout the 1960s. At one point, it was to star Laurence Harvey and be called, after Tennyson and Mrs Woodham-Smith, *The Reason Why*. The first script was by John Osborne working in collaboration with director Tony Richardson and the redoubtable Mollo family as military/historical advisers. The Mollos set up the Historical Research Unit in 1964 and produced a fascinating collection of archive work on the uniforms of the period. The result was my favourite historical film, a Woodfall/United Artists Release, in 1968. Trevor Howard played Lord Cardigan, John Geilgud Raglan, David Hemmings Captain Nolan and Vanessa Redgrave Clarissa [sic] Morris.

The film is a wonderful evocation of the 1850s, contrasting the class-obsessed dilettant life of officers and their ladies with the grim squalor of other ranks and their women. The hero of Richardson's *Charge* is Louis Nolan, for reasons of simplicity and storyline gazetted to the 11th Hussars (he actually served in the 15th) at the start of the film. Before joining, he meets again his old Indian Army chum, William Morris (played by Mark Burns) and his soon-to-be-bride, Clarissa.

There has never been a film which so accurately captures the life of a regiment. The late Norman Rossington is quite superb as RSM Corbett, filling the heads of raw recruits with stirring tales of his regiment's history, teaching them left from right and being broken to the ranks for refusing to obey Cardigan's orders to spy on fellow officers. The quiet dignity he displays as the farrier's cats bite into his torn flesh during a flogging in the riding school speaks for the thousands of men who really suffered that way.

And the screenplay by Charles Wood (who took over from Osborne) sums up the mental mind-set of the officer class. Nolan is appalled that floggings are standard practice and Riding Master Mogg (Alan Dobie) rounds on him with 'Would you have them fight like fiends of Hell for money? Or ideas? That would be unchristian.'

Nolan soon falls foul of the petulant, impossible Cardigan, who despises the man as an 'Indian officer', one of that band who was professional and had seen action. The only action Cardigan witnessed before the Crimea was on manoeuvres at Chobham Ridges.

The Charge itself is a very small part of the film, perhaps fifteen minutes in its entirety; and the end – by contrast to the patriotic, flag-waving beginning – is brutish and almost silent; the drone of flies buzzing around the smashed corpses of horses and men.

Despite the meticulous planning of John Mollo, Richardson insisted on equipping the entire Light Brigade (and not merely the 11th Hussars) in crimson overalls. Conversely, the scarlet-jacketed Heavy Brigade wore a uniform of light cavalry blue. Theirs, as Richardson and Tennyson might have chorused, not to reason why.

Historical accuracy was sacrificed elsewhere. Thus Captain Henry Duberly, who was in fact Paymaster of the 8th Hussars, becomes a friend of Nolan's in the 11th, and his wife, Fanny, whose journal is often quoted in this book, has a quirky, not to say kinky seduction scene with Cardigan on board his yacht! Crucially to the Morris ménage, Amelia had to become Clarissa, as screenwriter Charles Wood admitted to me, 'so that she could have an affair with Nolan' and thus create some love interest. An old uncle of Monty Morris of Johannesburg (whose document collection forms the core of this book), on seeing the film in South Africa was so outraged at this that he leapt to his feet shouting 'Bloody rubbish!' and had to be reminded it was only a story!

Such liberties did not detract, however, from a fine film. Who can forget the bristling lion that is Britain in the *Punch*-style cartoons of animator David Williams, furious at the cruelty of the Russian bear to defenceless Turkey, feathers flying in all directions? Or the grey faces of the cholera-struck army marching out from Varna and writhing in the agony of their vomiting under a merciless sun? Or the look of horror and disbelief on the faces of Raglan and his staff as the Light Brigade moves off down the 'valley of death'?

The film was not a box-office success and Charles Wood's deliberately stilted dialogue jarred a little, but today it has taken its place among the truly great achievements of the cinema, echoing perhaps our emotive response to the events it was portraying.

Richardson's targets were the 'nest of noodles', the officer class whose amateurish attempts to cope with warfare would lead to disaster. But he himself was a Communist and bisexual – neither facet tending to acceptance anywhere at the time outside the traditionally bizarre world of films.

The character of William Morris was portrayed by Mark Burns, tall, blond, good-looking, every inch a good officer, dutiful husband and faithful friend. As such he is something of a cardboard cut-out and every time I watch the video I wince at the accolade he gives to Nolan – 'It is at natives and kaffirs you put your men; you Indians ...'. It was of course Morris himself who was the

'Indian'. We knew that in the film his wife was having an affair with his best friend behind his back, a swipe at the hypocrisy of the period, but in the film, Morris knew nothing of it, trusting to the last. It is Morris's wedding in the sunny church at Sandhurst; his home at Fishleigh in Devon and the numbed expression on his blood-covered face as he stumbles back from the Charge that are among the film's most memorable moments.

Acknowledgements

Many thanks to Rupert Harding and his team, and to everyone who contributed to the production of this book, especially to Carol Trow, my long-suffering typist, and Monty Morris, owner of the Morris Papers, without whom this book would not have been possible.

Chapter One

The Morrises of Fishleigh

The enormous family tree drawn up by Monty Morris of Johannesburg – the owner of the papers that form the framework of this book – traces the Morris family back to around 930, but the name 'Morys' first appears, as a Christian name, in 1510 when Morys of Clanelly [sic], Caernarvon, married Ellen, daughter of Jevan ap Griff-dduy, who was descended from the same house as her husband. Their children, the eldest of whom seems to have been born in 1538, were apparently the first to use the name Morys as a surname. P H Reaney's *Dictionary of British Surnames* gives the original derivation as 'Moorish, dark and swarthy'. The grandfather of this book's subject, also called William Morris, claimed in a document dated 22 June 1785 to be fifth in line of descent from Sir William Morice born in 1602 of 'an equestrian family of Clenelly[1] [sic] County Caernarvon'.[2] He was a scholar and statesman of repute, his mother coming from a Devon family. Morice seems to have bought land in and around Plymouth and other parts of Devon, establishing the family's connection with the county. Between 1648 and 1653, Morice was elected several times for parliament for the boroughs of Newport in Cornwall and Plymouth itself. He did not actually take his seat until 1660 and seems to have been excluded from the House, first under Pride's Purge[3] and second because he did not have the approval of Cromwell's council.

The restoration of Charles II was a difficult time. The new king was setting foot on English soil for the first time since he had left it as a hunted fugitive, and in tackling parliament he was in effect dealing with the institution, if not the actual men, who had cut off his father's head 'with the crown upon it'. For his part in these delicate negotiations Morice was made Colonel of a Regiment of Foot by General Monck (establishing a somewhat tenuous link between the Morris family and the Army), was knighted by Charles II and in May 1660 was sworn in as Secretary of State and Privy Councillor. Eclipsed by more ruthless politicians, he retired to his estates in 1668, spending his declining years studying literature and building up a fine library.

The earliest actual documents which have survived relating to the Morris family concern the William Morris who was born in 1738 and died in 1796. The Morris clan was large by this time, but the various estates both in England and the West Indies must have brought in a steady income.

Barbados, to which the Morrises moved, was first colonized by the British in 1627. Like all the West Indian Islands, it carried its share of deadly diseases for white men and was subject, along with the other Windward Isles, to hurricanes and earthquakes. As the white man settled and the plantations were hacked out of the jungle, a massive slave population was put to work to produce cotton, tobacco, indigo, coffee and arrowroot. The most profitable commodities, however, were sugar and rum. By the time William Morris arrived in Barbados the native Carib Indians were all but extinct and the slave population was African. By the time Morris's children were born, a humanitarian backlash, both at home in Britain and in the Indies was beginning to challenge the right of individuals to buy and sell slaves as cattle.

Morris married twice. His first wife was Anne Maria Moore, the daughter of William Moore, Solicitor General of Barbados, and he augmented whatever landed income he may have had in two ways. First, he practised law; and second, he ran the estates of landowner William Baker, probably between 1780 and 1786.

By the time of William Morris's second marriage, to Judith Mary Cholmley, probably the daughter of Montague Cholmley[4] of Barbados, his assets were quite considerable. In 1784, whether on a visit to England or through a broker by long distance, he had bought various estates in Devon, which were valued in October 1790 at £12,000, then a very respectable sum indeed. The lands amounted to approximately 2,500 acres and included the Manors of Inwardleigh, Gorhuish and Cleve and the parishes of Northlew and Hatherleigh. By 1792, his total assets in England amounted to £22,206. 1s. 3$\frac{1}{2}$d., while the value of assets in Barabdos was £3,619. 10s. 1$\frac{1}{2}$d., including £210 which represented the value of six of his slaves.

It is not clear why Morris should have decided to return to England when he did (1795) but perhaps he came home to die and to give his new family a chance to grow up in the land of their fathers.

William Morris of Barbados died in Exeter and was buried in Westminster Abbey on Tuesday, 23 February 1796. A codicil to his will demanded that land should be obtained for the family adjacent to an existing estate. Accordingly, on 25 August, the house and estate of Fishleigh, Hatherleigh was purchased for £1,700.

The settling of the Morris family at Fishleigh was largely undertaken by William Baker. Perhaps he felt he owed a debt of gratitude to the man who had managed his estates in Barbados. Perhaps he realized how hard it was for a woman to struggle on alone in what was very much a man's world. The

Inwardleigh estates in particular were in chaotic disrepair and large tracts of timber had to be cut to pay for repairs to houses on the land.

By this time, William Cholmley Morris was eleven and there was a need to attend to his schooling. In keeping with the traditions of the time, his sisters would have been educated at home, probably by governesses, to fulfil the needs of the Georgian social round and make good and dutiful wives. On 27 October 1808, when William Cholmley was fifteen, William Baker, acting as the boy's guardian, chose Charterhouse.

The entrance fee was eight guineas and the annual fee for boarding £64. Various disciplines were priced separately – Mathematics, French, Drawing and Dancing cost one guinea per quarter with an additional entrance fee of one guinea. It was probably at Charterhouse that the young William Cholmley decided on a career in the Church, one of the surprisingly few professions open to young men of his class.

Originally, it seems to have been the young man's intention to join Queen's College, Oxford, but he changed his mind and entered Christ Church in October 1812. First called Cardinal College, and doubling as both a college and a cathedral, with a Dean who is head of both, it is an odd foundation. Its Fellows (teaching staff) were referred to, confusingly, as Students, and discipline was carried out by two Censors.

While at Christ Church, perhaps deterred by the religiosity of the place,[5] William Cholmley transferred his energies to a career in law. No letters have survived to confirm whether or not he was ever called to the Bar or actually practised as a lawyer. On 11 October 1816 a bond of marriage was drawn up between William Cholmley and Jane Mallett Veale, of Passaford in Hatherleigh. It seems at least reasonable to suppose that the couple had known each other since childhood.

The Veales emerge on a par with the Morrises from the point of view of property and status and the documents which have survived lay emphasis on cash settlements. The sum of £1,000 was offered by the Veales in the form of a dowry, but it was a dowry with strings. William Cholmley had to agree that in the event of his death £2,000 should be payable to his widow and any children they might have. The eldest of these, Louisa, known in the family as Missy, was born in 1819, and the second, William, the subject of this book, in 1820.

There is some confusion over the exact date of William Morris's birth. One account refers to 15 October, but the usual date is given as 18 December. The relevant page in the Baptismal Register for Hatherleigh has the entry that William was baptized on 20 December (No. 415) and this would be in keeping with a birth either in October or December. What is interesting is that the ceremony was private, implying that it took place not in the Church of St John, but elsewhere, presumably at Fishleigh. Accordingly, the entry has been squeezed in the slot reserved for 11 December because it was 'not inserted in due time'.[6] The ceremony was performed by the Reverend C Glascott and the private baptism was probably a family tradition. Morris's parents are listed as William C and Jane and his father's 'Quality, Trade or Profession' listed as 'Gentleman'.

The world into which William Morris was born was a turbulent one. About a month before he was conceived, Arthur Thistlewood and a group of conspirators had been apprehended while plotting the assassination of the Prime Minister, Lord Liverpool, and his cabinet. These Cato Street Conspirators were duly hanged and were the last felons in British history to be decapitated after the event – such was the inaccuracy of the art of hanging. It was generally believed, wrongly, as we see with hindsight, that Cato Street was merely the tip of the iceberg, that lurking not far below the surface of society was a national conspiracy of vast proportions, ready to topple the state. Twenty-two years of warfare, first against Revolutionary France and then Napoleon, had left their mark on society. Everywhere there seemed to be plots, sedition and dangerous talk. The advent of peace in 1815 brought a brief burst of prosperity – the boom that inevitably follows a return to a peacetime economy – but by 1816, the economic problems of a recession added to the tense political situation. In 1812, the Prime Minister, Spencer Percival, had been shot dead in the lobby of the House. Radicals were writing explosive pamphlets, demanding something which would have been unthinkable even a few years earlier – universal suffrage. The Corn Law of 1815 kept foreign corn out of the country until an artificially high price for home-grown corn was reached. Elsewhere, though not perhaps in rural Devon, problems revolved around the demobilization of 300,000 soldiers after Waterloo – the typical demand of parliament in peacetime – and the first horrors of an unplanned and uncontrollable Industrial Revolution.

How much of this unrest – some historians estimate that the period 1815–22 marks the closest to revolution in Britain in modern history – reached the Morris estate at Fishleigh, it is impossible to say. The tradition of the deferential tenant who knew his place was bound to remain stronger and longer in the country, but it is likely that economic problems would have been there and along with them, underlying tension.

When Morris was seven months old, George IV was crowned at Westminster. For the last time in history, the King's Champion, in full armour, clattered under the Gothic arch specially built at Westminster Hall and threw down his gage in the feudal tradition. Less elegant was the spectacle of the debauched Caroline of Brunswick, George's wife, hammering on the doors to be let in to take her rightful place. After years of riotous living with various opera singers in Italy, the cold shoulder was no more than she could expect.

Morris's childhood is virtually a closed book. Between 1819 and 1840, Jane Morris gave birth to ten children. How many of them survived to adulthood we do not know. The eldest was Louisa (Missy), who died in 1882; after

William came Cholmley, who died in 1869; Emma, born 1824; Jane, born 1827; James Veale, 1829–78; Westcott, 1830–88; Juliana Mary, born 1832; Montague Cholmley, born 1836; and Augusta Maria, referred to in various letters in the Morris Papers as 'Baby', born 1840. Jane Morris was twenty-two when William was born and forty-two at the birth of her last child. Effective contraception was of course unknown and the risks attendant on childbirth still great. Infant mortality, though lower among the gentry and in country areas than in other classes elsewhere, remained extremely high.

There were probably similar relationships among the Morris family as those which existed at the same time among the Taylors, across the bleak expanse of Exmoor, at Ogwell, near Newton Abbott. Reynell George Taylor, whose sister, Amelia, Morris was to marry in 1852, was born at Brighton in January 1822 and when he was ten moved with the family to his grandfather's estate at Ogwell. His biographer conjured up the delights of a country childhood:

> cricket and archery, bird nesting, butterfly catching ... a day with the hounds in winter, or long gallops over the moorlands in the hot summer sun ... In the summer, when the shadows began to creep slowly over the grass, the children, in company with their father, would often walk to the summerhouse ... in the park and watch the sun sink slowly to rest behind the great line of hills, while High Tor, Saddle Tor and Rippen Tor stood up in blue shadow against the clear sky and rich Devonshire valleys were bathed in thick mists.[7]

Morris's childhood would be a total blank were it not for the fact that a family friend was John Russell, the 'hunting parson', who grew up with a passion for riding to hounds. At Blundell's School in Tiverton, Russell established a 'scratch pack' with a friend and was in danger of being expelled before winning his headmaster's praise by obtaining a scholarship to Balliol College, Oxford. Needless to say, in the aristocratic circles of Oxford undergraduates, Russell found ample time to attend to hunting. His first curacy was at George Nympton near South Molton in Devon and his fame spread throughout the West Country. 'His stentorian "view-halloo" could be sworn to by every rustic between Dartmoor and Exmoor and sportsmen journeyed from afar to have a day with the classical Nimrod.'[8]

In the first year of his marriage (1827), Russell wrote:

> I was soon on the spot with about ten of my little hounds and found, standing around the earths, about a hundred fellows – the scum of the country – headed I am almost ashamed to say, by two gentlemen, Mr Veale of Passaford and his brother-in-law, Mr Morris of Fishley, the father of Colonel W Morris of the 'Light Brigade' – that

brilliant swordsman to whose memory a monument is erected on Hatherleigh Moor.[9]

They were out to destroy the foxes in their earths and Russell was appalled by this. They seem to have accepted his complaints and gone away, he having distributed 'a few shillings' among the 'hoi polloi by way of compensation.'

Russell's control of his pack was legendary, as was his never needing a whip. In 1828 he wrote:

> One evening, soon after the hounds had been fed, who should ride to our door at Iddesleigh but Billy Morris, a great chum of mine, then a small boy living with his father and mother at Fishley, but afterward a distinguished swordsman and one of the glorious Six Hundred in the Balaclava Charge.
>
> 'I've a holiday tomorrow, Mr Russell,' he said; 'and I've come to ask you if you will kindly bring out your hounds and show me a day's sport.'
>
> 'With all my heart,' I replied; 'but I have promised your father's tenant at Norleigh to kill a hare for him, so come and meet me there at ten o'clock.'
>
> 'I'll be there to a minute,' he said, thanking me warmly and then, galloping off on his pony, big with hope.
>
> It was a wretched morning – a regular downpour of rain – and no one came to meet me but dear little Billy and Lord Clinton's steward from Heanton.
>
> Having killed three hares 'Now,' said Billy, 'Just throw them into uncle's covers [Mr Veale of Passaford]; there's a fox there, I know.'
>
> 'Not on any account,' I replied, 'till I have his permission to do so.'
>
> 'But I'm sure you may,' he continued; 'for he told me so last night.'
>
> I begged him however to ride up to Passaford, half a mile off and bring me word, 'yea or nay' from his uncle; and I promised that I would wait an hour for his return. I did wait a full hour ... but I saw nothing of Billy.[10]

This rather engaging picture of the seven-year-old Morris is really the only first-hand account we have of his boyhood. Three things can be salvaged from it. First, his passion for horses and hunting, which in a sense made his choice of the cavalry as a career an obvious one. Second, his ability as a rider. He was still a very small boy, but was allowed to ride around the countryside on his own and to hunt with adults, which speaks volumes for his horsemanship. Third, since he had 'a holiday' the day of the hare coursing with Russell, it implies that he was kept hard at work most of the time.

Why Morris was educated at home by his father (there is no record of a tutor) is not clear. The pattern of education for a boy of this class was to be reared by a nanny until he was seven or eight. About that time, depending on aptitude, the boy would be taught by a governess or tutor, appointed by the parents and living in or not as the case may be. Presumably because William Morris senior was an Oxford man, with leanings both to the Church and the law, he took this on himself. Exactly what form Morris's education took is impossible to say, but if it followed the usual pattern, then apart from the basics of reading and writing, it would have been the Classics, a little Mathematics, perhaps some History (probably Ancient) and perhaps, because Morris seems to have loved flowers, some elements of Nature Study. His horsemanship was perhaps in the blood, but the social class to which he belonged and the wide open spaces of Exmoor created the right and inevitable climate for riding. Many witnesses testify to the fact that Morris was an excellent swordsman and it is not likely he learned this either in the Army or at Cambridge. Whether his father taught him at home or whether he had expert tuition is unknown. Certainly there were private academies – usually small and obscure – where fencing was part of the curriculum, but by Morris's day, it was in many ways an obsolete pastime, in that duelling in England had long been illegal and it was not yet a spectator sport.

By the age of twelve or thirteen it would have been quite in keeping for Morris to have attended public school. By 1832, the year in which he might have gone, there were a number of schools, each of varying standard and reputation and each intensely snobbish about their own prestige. It would have been perfectly natural for young Morris to have followed in his father's footsteps by going to Charterhouse, but for some reason he did not. Perhaps this was that the reputation of the public schools was no better than it had been in William senior's day; in some ways, it was rather worse.

There had been one rebellion at Charterhouse, before William senior had gone there, and, as usual, it was caused by the headmaster curtailing various abuses of power. By and large, the perpetrators of these rebellions were the sons of the *very* rich and the *very* powerful. In the 1820s, Charterhouse became popular, but there was a sudden catastrophic fall in 1835 to only ninety-nine pupils. Perhaps whatever caused the reversal in popularity had been building up for a while and perhaps it explains why William Cholmley did not want his son educated there. Perhaps it was the notoriety of the prefect-fagging system, which reached a national scandal in 1831 by appearing in the august pages of *The Edinburgh Review* following an incident at Winchester when a boy was beaten to death. Perhaps it was the reverse – the fact that at Charterhouse, the headmaster, John Russell (no relation to the parson) had abolished fagging and in fact opened the door to the worse abuses of unbridled bullying.

Morris's childhood was no doubt as careless and unaware as it was for most children of the leisured classes. Rural poverty and deprivation were in evidence all around him. Over-investment to pay for enclosure and subsequent high debts had ruined many farmers. The vicissitudes of the Corn Law and high rents combined to create a discontented landless labourer class long after the worst years following Waterloo. When Morris was eleven, the last Labourers' Revolt took place, and in the West Country, the riots led by the fictitious 'Captain Swing' merged with those over the Reform Bill and led to rick burning and cattle maiming as well as orchestrated attacks on property in village and town alike. There is no evidence to suggest that the Morris family were the targets of any of this. Between January 1830 and September 1832, Devon was only marginally affected by these disturbances. There were four cases of arson, seven 'Swing' letters, one wages riot, one tithe riot, one strike and three examples of machine breaking. In the same period, only one court case was heard and the defendant was acquitted.

In 1902, Lieutenant General White-Thomson KCB in his memoir on William Morris wrote:

> I believe that there are still living in Hatherleigh and this neighbourhood some who remember him riding well to hounds as a small boy on his pony and there is a tradition that he was one day discovered by his father astride the weathercock on the steeple of Hatherleigh church.[11]

Like much else in the story of William Morris, it belongs to legend.

Chapter Two
Schola Cantabrigiensis

We do not know why Morris chose Cambridge rather than the Oxford of his father. Perhaps Cambridge was the son's choice rather than the father's, as a deliberate and conscious desire to go it alone. Perhaps there were newer, local influences at work – a relative or family friend having been there recently.[1]

The College of St John the Evangelist was built on the site of an Augustinian hospital dating from 1135. Much of the college's prosperity was owed to John Fisher, Bishop of Rochester, who was executor to the Lady Margaret, Countess of Richmond and Derby, the mother of Henry VII. As benefactress, her name lived on in Morris's time in the form of a portrait in Hall and the rather exclusive Lady Margaret Boat Club. The official date of founding of St John's is 1511 and by the end of the century the college boasted two courts, the second, completed in 1602, notable for its brickwork. Its alumni before Morris's time were a famous if varied group: Roger Ascham, the tutor of Elizabeth; William Cecil, her Lord Treasurer; Thomas Fairfax, 'Black Tom' of the New Model Army, and, nearer to Morris in time, radicals like William Wilberforce, Horne Tooke and William Wordsworth.

Reforms were made in the eighteenth century, most notably under William Powell, who was Master between 1765 and 1775. Most of these were to do with the finances of the college and the restructuring and tightening of the internal examinations. The courts were improved and modernized; the gardens called the Wilderness which ran to the river were landscaped by the most famous gardener of his day, 'Capability' Brown. The college even had its own rat-catcher by 1795. By the same token, Powell remained stubbornly resistant to other moves. The staff and Fellows had to remain celibate, the introduction of university, as opposed to college, examinations was resisted, and there had to be total subservience to all the Thirty-Nine Articles. Despite an increase in the student intake – forty-six in the 1770s, as compared with thirty-one in the 1750s – the eighteenth-century pattern of patronage and influence still held sway. William Wood, Bursar in the 1790s, speculated with college money and the average students or 'poll men' were quite prepared to accept an ordinary degree rather than put in the effort necessary to obtain an honours degree with its large mathematical content.

William Craven, Master from 1789 to 1815, was very much a man of his time in that he would have nothing to do with 'Jacobins and infidels'. Others were more liberal. Horne Tooke, ordained in 1759, spent his life supporting rebellious causes; William Wilberforce brought home to an indifferent parliament the horrors of the slave trade; and William Wordsworth supported the new freedoms brought about by the French Revolution. A Fellow of the college, Henry Martyn, followed a different kind of liberalism in translating the prayer book into Hindustani.

There was by the end of the century greater diversity in undergraduates, not in terms of the social groups from which they came, which were increasingly narrowing to the sons of aristocracy and gentry, but in the professions into which they gravitated. In the latter instance, St John's mirrors Georgian society hit sideways by the twin impacts of revolution – French and Industrial. In the 1790s, just over half entered the Church (a drop from the 80 per cent of the early century); the number of doctors had dropped (perhaps because of the rise of the Scottish universities and the appalling reputation of the Cambridge medical school); lawyers had increased fourfold; and above all there was that steady drift towards the armed services and government and colonial offices which was the inevitable concomitant of a nation about to take its place at the head of the largest empire the world had ever seen.

As the railway did not reach Cambridge until 1845, Morris would probably have gone up in the October of 1839 across country from Okehampton by a series of coaches. The new buildings erected in the college after 1815 enabled each undergraduate to have three rooms – a sitting room, bedroom and scullery or pantry. College servants cooked, cleaned, laundered and directed mail. By the time Morris arrived St John's had been considerably enlarged. The largest building erected to that date of any college was completed by 1831, to the designs of Rickman and Hutchinson, across the river from 'the Backs'. It was linked by the 'Bridge of Sighs' which the young Queen Victoria found 'so pretty'. Its total cost was £78,000 and the debt incurred as a result was not cleared until 1857.

A new Master arrived in the same year as Morris – Ralph Tatham – though he was less distinguished than some of his predecessors. All lectures and teaching took place within the college and a Classical tripos introduced in 1824 was designed to modify the daunting mathematical element. At the same time, that element was broadened and if anything made more difficult, continuing the traditional division between the mathematical honours men and the classical 'hoi polloi'. Men on the different 'sides' did not meet academically until the final examination, apart from the lectures in Hebrew and the Sadlerian lectures designed to teach algebra to freshmen. Contemporaries noted that the standard of these lectures was rather like sixth-form lessons at inferior schools. It led the poll men to seek private coaching if they wanted to be sure of their degree and this of course cost extra.

When Morris arrived at St John's, it was still a pillar of the establishment. It was totally opposed to the Reform Bill (in fact a previous Master had banned political topics in the Students' Union as early as 1817), to Catholic Emancipation (which was already a reality by 1829), and decidedly anti-Semitic.

Both White-Thomson, a fellow officer in the 17th Lancers, and Fulford Williams, an antiquarian descended from the Veales of Passaford, cite letters written home by Morris from Cambridge. White-Thomson's memoir (1902) and Fulford Williams's unpublished typescript (1964) are among the Morris Papers. The first letter is to his sister 'Missy', dated May 1839:

> I was kept in chapel so long by the anthem that I was too late for the barge in which I was to have gone down the river.

Attendance in chapel, seven times a week, was compulsory. A new organ had just been installed, with three manuals and pedals. The choir was shared with St John's rival Trinity and other colleges and on Sundays cassocked boys must have been seen hot-footing it from one to the other. The barge had started, Morris goes on,

> and in trying to jump on it from the bank I cut my leg and hurt my shoulder so much that I can hardly lift my hand to my head, also cut and bruised my face a good deal, so that I am not very comfortable today.

The rest of the letter contains themes to which Morris often returns in his letters – horses and flowers:

> I will bring you a quantity of scented violet roots when I come home to plant about the grounds, and have scented violets at least at Fishleigh ... I cannot make out why you do not like Roger, as I am certain he is a very good pony. I think you must have mismanaged him some way. I mean to have something to ride when I come home, if I steal a horse from Hatherleigh Moor.

There is also a curious allusion to an incident which may have given rise to the nickname Morris acquired later in the 16th Lancers:

> I was very vexed to see in the paper you sent me that Bungaree, the Australian who fought the other day, was dead, as it was downright

falsehood. The man was as well as ever, and walking about Newmarket two days afterwards.[2]

There is no mention in the official history of St John's that undergraduates visited Newmarket, but the nearness of Charles II's racecourse and the proclivities of young country gentlemen like Morris would make such sprees inevitable. Cambridge men rode, drove dog carts, played cards and chess and held lavish parties after Hall and at breakfast, when ham, chops and pigeon pie were consumed. Newmarket also boasted bare-knuckle championships and Bungaree, the Australian, would have been just such a contender.

Morris's letter to Louisa also makes reference to the imminent visit of Prince Albert. The Master of Trinity had been given £1,000 to buy new furniture for his installation as Vice-Chancellor. Albert of Saxe-Coburg and his brother Ernst had arrived in England on 10 October 1839, to arrange a marriage with Victoria. Not content to wait the three or four years demanded by court etiquette and prompted by the ageing Prime Minister, Lord Melbourne, the details were somewhat rushed through by the Queen and the marriage took place on 10 February 1840. The Prince was intellectual, scientific and technological, with a passion for music and manly sports which made him ideal as a consort for the Queen. He was also ideal for Cambridge University, and Whewell, the Master of Trinity, probably courted the German's favour in the hope that he would protect the place, in Hermione Hobhouse's phrase 'from the hostile winds of change which were beginning to blow'.[3] Whewell's hope was pious. Within eight years Albert the Good had spearheaded reforms and brought about an astonishing widening of the curriculum which introduced Law, Modern History, Philosophy, Anatomy, Chemistry, Biology and Botany.

A second letter to Louisa, whose original is now lost, mentions the Lady Margaret Boat. It is dated June 1840 and confirms the fact that as a gentleman who paid full fees (as opposed to the poor sizars who relied on scholarships and prizes) Morris was eligible to join the exclusive boating club and the college cricket team. In the winter he huddled with the others around the single charcoal brazier in the Hall before Latin grace, taking dinner at the 'peculiar hour' of four o'clock rather than one or two. In the late eighteenth century and probably still in Morris's time, this meal consisted of a joint with vegetables and college-brewed beer. Sweets and other food could be bought from the kitchens and were expensive. Along with others of his social class Morris probably looked with contempt on the sizars who lived in the Labyrinth (the old hospital), whose patterns of study, prayer and eating were thought objectionable. The irony was that most of these men were gifted and extremely hardworking – the professionals in a world of amateurs, as was Morris himself for the rest of his life.

While Morris was at Cambridge his brothers and sisters were growing up. A letter from his father to his mother dated March 1841 (Jane was on holiday at

Plymouth) refers to Cholmley, who was nineteen, and James, twelve, who had been fishing. William at that time had flu and Louisa, the eldest in the family, was running the house in her mother's absence. Another letter, dated 17 September of the same year, from William to Jane concerns Cholmley's emigration to South Africa. There was no link between the Morris family and the Colonies at the Cape beyond the fact that Cholmley was a young man, probably without his elder brother's modest academic claims and above all suffering the rather unenviable position of being the second son of a landed family not as landed as all that. William stood to inherit the estate and that left little or nothing for the other boys. William Morris senior wrote from Evans Hotel, Covent Garden that he was seeing Cholmley off from Gravesend (from where William was to sail to India in the following year). Credit of £130 had been arranged for him with the bankers Messrs Borradaille Tompson and Pellam of Cape Town. Father and son would not meet again.

White-Thomson skates over Morris's leaving Cambridge in a kindly way – 'He was reading for his degree when he was gazetted.'[4] The truth was that Morris's academic performance, at best average, was steadily slipping over the nine terms he kept. He did not win prizes, but in his favour it should be noted that these were often restricted to men from certain schools (which automatically excluded him) or from certain parts of the country. In May 1840 he was placed in the second class. His texts for the year were Euclid, Books 4, 5, 6 and 11; Euripides' *Andromache*; St Matthew's Gospel; and work in logic, algebra and trigonometry. In December he was still there, continuing to wrestle with trigonometry, but adding geometry and conic sections. He read Paley's *Moral Philosophy and Evidences* as well as the *De Senectute* of Cicero. A year later he was in the third class, struggling with optics and hydrostatics as well as Newton, Butler's *Analogy*, Euclid, Xenophon and Horace's *Epistle ad Pisones*. By May 1842 the only mention of him is that he and a fellow student named Gilbanks were up before the Master and Seniors (the disciplinary body of the College) for not having prepared for the examination in the Greek New Testament. Gilbanks was re-examined in November, by which time Morris had set sail for India.

An incident in February 1840, when Morris was still a freshman, may perhaps shed some light on his failure at Cambridge. He and a fellow student named King were discovered scrambling out of college over a cloister wall at quarter past one in the morning. For this they were confined to walls by the Master and Seniors for the rest of term and had to take a daily imposition from the Dean. All we see here is a typical carousing young man of his times, off for a night on the tiles, but such young men rarely make good scholars and it is probably true to say that Morris's heart was never really in his work.

Three questions must be posed at this point: why did Morris join the Army? Why the cavalry? And why the 16th Lancers? No correspondence has survived in connection with this. There were surprisingly few careers into which a young man of Morris's class could go. Some professions such as the law and medicine had only recently gained an aura of respectability. Practitioners of both had been dubbed – not without justification – charlatans, quacks and tricksters in the eighteenth century. They were regarded much as actors were. And the mid-nineteenth-century antipathy towards professionalism, which smacked of 'trade', militated against a gentleman joining these professions too. It must be said, of course, that Morris had proved at Cambridge that he did not really have the academic ability for either medicine or the law (although the only medical examinations held at this time were orals conducted in Latin!). Another possibility was the Church. Traditionally this was reserved for the duffer of the family – the least talented or youngest son. Morris was neither and despite the fiercely equestrian example of Jack Russell, does not seem to have been at all motivated in this area. Politics might have provided a career, but since the Morris Papers give no hint at all of the political leanings of the family, it is likely that the subject was of secondary importance and would certainly not have led young William to the House. There is one vague reference to Morris campaigning on the political front in a speech made at Great Torrington in Devon in 1856, but the meaning of this is obscure. The most logical career for him was to inherit, as eldest sons usually did, his father's lands. Various members of the Light Brigade in the Crimea did this and resigned their commissions to manage their estates. In 1842 William Morris senior was not an old man and we must assume that William junior wanted to make his own mark in the world.

All that remained, if a man was to remain true to his class, was the armed forces. The Navy offered a challenge, but there was no tradition whatever of this in the Morris family. It is likely that Morris's devotion to horses and hunting led him naturally to the cavalry. Junior officers were expected to have courage and élan, but not a great deal more. Increasingly as the century wore on they were the products of the public schools (several of Morris's contemporaries among the officers of the Light Brigade were educated at Rugby, Eton and Harrow), and in the case of some, of the universities. What they were not, until much later in the century, was products of Sandhurst, the training school for officers. Morris did not join its Junior Department on leaving St John's, but he had been in India only weeks when he was writing to his father expressing his intention of joining the Senior Department. It is likely that Sandhurst was in his mind from the beginning.

There is no obvious reason for Morris's choice of the 16th Lancers. Invariably young men obtained their first commission and usually subsequent ones by purchase. This was originally a French system dating from the late seventeenth century, which ensured that only the wealthy controlled the Army by virtue of excluding the poor from the officer class. The system reeked of corruption and was already seen as an anomaly in an age of radicalism and working–class agitation by the time Morris bought his commission. It was also wide open to abuse. The Duke of York, Commander in Chief of the Army in 1809, had had to relinquish that post when it became known that his mistress, Mrs Clarke, was involved in a scandal selling Army commissions like auction lots to a long list of handsome young men who paid her court. Immensely wealthy men like George Bingham, later Lord Lucan, and James Brudenell, later Lord Cardigan, added to the corruption of the system by paying far over the regulation prices laid down by their lordships at the Horse Guards. The reason that this iniquitous system, which squeezed out and kept down many able soldiers, survived until 1871 and died a hard death in the Lords under Edward Cardwell, is that it *worked*. As Wellington said, it ensured that the men who protected the country had a stake in it. To a twenty-first-century society sadly used to colonels' and even corporals' coups in various parts of the world, the British Army of the eighteenth and nineteenth centuries is astonishingly loyal. Part at least of this loyalty was due to the purchase system. It also ensured that the social gulf which existed between gentleman and labourer, master and servant, was perpetuated between officer and ranker. Those few rankers promoted to a commission without purchase, invariably for valour on the field, were probably bitterly unhappy men. They were alienated from their friends in the ranks by virtue of their officer status and yet were not accepted as equals by the gentlemen officers.

It is likely that Morris's father wrote to the Horse Guards (the War Office in Whitehall) and the deal was arranged through Cox and Company who were the agents for various regiments including the 16th Lancers. The 16th had a vacancy for a cornet, the most junior officer in the cavalry regiments, and the commission was duly drawn up. The document is dated 5 November 1842 but not sealed until 7 September 1843:

> To our trusty and well-beloved William Morris, Gentleman, greeting. We do by these presents constitute and appoint you to be Cornet in the 16th Regiment of Light Dragoons from the 18th day of June 1842 ... Given at our court of Windsor ... in the 6th Year of Our Reign.

It is signed by Lord Stanley, who was Secretary for War and the Colonies under Robert Peel, the Prime Minister.

This must have been a time of whirlwind activity for Morris. The 16th Lancers were stationed at Meerut in Northern India and had been there since 1823. A small skeleton force – the depot troop – would probably have been stationed at Maidstone or a similar permanent cavalry barracks and Morris may have made contact with them there. He must have gone to London to be kitted out by the regimental tailors and would also have booked his passage east. As the journey took a staggering eight months he must have gone via the long route, sailing all the way round the Cape of Good Hope and into the

Indian Ocean. This year, 1842, for the first time officers received a baggage allowance to help pay for such journeys. What ship Morris sailed in is not recorded, but the length of the voyage would indicate that it was a sailing vessel.

The England he left, from Gravesend in July, was a rapidly changing one. It was a year of depression, notable for a second national Chartist petition and for the reintroduction of the hated income tax by Robert Peel. It was the beginning of the Hungry Forties, with chronic unemployment and a trade recession; the only bright spot the increasingly important railway boom. Gangs of highly paid navvies roamed the countryside building shanty towns with colourful names like Jericho and Batty Wife Hole. Isambard Kingdom Brunel was building his Great Western Railway; Robert Stephenson and George Hudson were planning and building others. There had been two attempts on the life of the Queen.

The India for which Morris sailed was changing just as rapidly.

Chapter Three

The Scarlet Lancers

The regiment to which William Morris was gazetted in June 1842 was eighty-three years old. It had been raised in 1759 by 'Gentleman Johnny' Burgoyne in response to the catalystic effects of the Seven Years War and was styled, after the fashion of the time, Burgoyne's Light Horse.

John Burgoyne was born in 1722, the son of a Baronet whose expensive lifestyle led to his death in a debtors' prison. John was educated at Westminster School and rose rapidly by purchase to a captaincy in the 1st Royal Dragoons. Hounded by creditors and those members of his new wife's family who disapproved of their elopement, the Burgoynes fled to France. It was not until 1756 on the outbreak of the Seven Years War that he returned, buying a captaincy in the 11th Dragoons. There can be little doubt that Burgoyne's wit, charm, his reputation as a dashing officer, poet, playwright and gambler won him an established place at the court of George II. It was this royal patronage – in an age when patronage was essential – that obtained for Burgoyne first a captaincy, then a lieutenant colonelcy in the 2nd Foot Guards. This exchange from regiment to regiment was very common as places were blocked in various regiments and gaps occurred in others. Neither was the transfer from Horse to Foot unusual in an age without real specialism. Wellington purchased his way through seven regiments in nine years, two of them cavalry. Morris himself, on leaving the 16th Lancers, toyed with a commission in the infantry.

The recruiting poster for the 16th, perhaps devised by Burgoyne himself, has justly been widely quoted, not merely because it smacks of Burgoyne, but because it reeks of the amateur spirit which was to survive in the cavalry up to and perhaps beyond the First World War.

> You will be mounted on the finest horses in the world, with superb clothing and the richest accoutrements; your pay and privileges are equal to two guineas a week; you are everywhere respected; your society is courted; you are admired by the Fair, which, together with the chance of getting switched to a buxom widow or bushing with a

rich heiress, renders the situation truly enviable and desirable. Young men out of employment or uncomfortable, 'There is a tide in the affairs of men which, taken at the flood, leads on to fortune'; nick in instantly and enlist.[1]

The privates who enlisted in Burgoyne's Light Horse had not yet acquired the nickname 'Tommy Atkins', but their reputation was the same. Wellington's famous lines of years later, that the common soldier was the scum of the earth, enlisted for drink, may well have been true, but as Wellington went on to say, the Army made men of them. In 1846, the year of Aliwal, a staff sergeant compiled the following statistics based on his experience of enlistment.

1. Indigent – Embracing labourers and mechanics out of employ who merely seek for support – 80 in 120
2. Indigent – Respectable persons induced by misfortune or imprudence – 2 in 120
3. Idle – who consider a soldier's life an easy one – 16 in 120
4. Bad characters – who fall back on the army as a last resource – 8 in 120
5. Criminals – who seek to escape from the consequences of their offences – 1 in 120
6. Perverse sons – who seek to grieve their parents – 2 in 120
7. Discontented and restless – 8 in 120
8. Ambitious – 1 in 120
9. Others – 2 in 120.[2]

The sergeant's figures may not be entirely accurate and his observations, particularly on the perversity of sons who seek to grieve their parents, are no doubt coloured by the fact that for years the Army had 'aided the civil power', and incidents such as the notorious Peterloo of 1819 became etched into the public mind and part of the working-class myth of the nineteenth century. That clash in Manchester, between a vast unarmed crowd of civilians on the one hand and the Manchester and Salford Yeomanry and the 15th Hussars on the other was lauded by the government of the Prince Regent, but did nothing at all for the reputation of the cavalry. Eleven people were killed and over four hundred injured.

In essence, the broad pattern of enlistment in the 1760s would have been true of the 1840s. Although those decades saw the impact of the Industrial Revolution in very different phases, such as the eccentric and sporadic effect of labour demand, there must invariably have been a high proportion of destitute labourers for whom the Army, at first anyway, seemed a viable alternative. Burgoyne's reference to 'young men out of employment or uncomfortable' only makes sense in this context.

To the agricultural labourer of the eighteenth century, the Army offered a suit of clothes, a permanent roof, regular meals and at least the prospect of daily pay. For the ambitious, adventurous or just plain foolhardy, it also offered travel and action which were impossible in civilian life. In reality, the 'bounty' offered by the recruiting sergeant or 'bringer' was whittled down by various 'expenses' once a recruit reached his barracks. Most the of 'Johnny Raws' of the eighteenth and early nineteenth centuries were illiterate, so Burgoyne's recruiting poster would need to be reinforced by the stirring tales of valour and free-flowing pints of the bringer, ever wandering the hiring fairs and ale houses in search of likely lads. As the regiment's career lengthened and it accumulated battle honours, such tales became more numerous and impressive. Worse than loss of the promised bounty, by far the largest amount of money the labourer was ever likely to see in one place in his life (by the 1840s about £8 or £9), was the harsh regime that pertained in most regiments, maintained always by the lash. It was not just to the colour of the uniform the American colonists were referring in the 1770s when they called the British troops 'Bloodybacks'.

Officers of British cavalry were, by 1759 (and the tradition was to continue for too many years) a reflection of the social status they held in civilian life. Within six months of the formation of the 16th Light Dragoons, there were three Baronets and three Honourables among their officers. Such men were very aware of the huge gulf which existed between themselves and their men. On their country estates, labourers pulled off their caps or tugged their forelocks in respect and the deferential tenant was expected to know and hold his place once in the ranks. This social gap was so wide that we are almost talking about the Army as two distinct professions. To the private soldier, it was a trade and a bloody one at that. To the officer, in peace and war, it was the natural calling of a gentleman. And as such, the only qualities required of an officer were courage and leadership. It is an interesting observation that Morris's only official comment on Cardigan's handling of the Light Brigade at Balaclava was that he 'led like a gentleman'.[3]

Burgoyne's views on the role of an officer were rather different. He issued a written Code of Instructions, itself a rarity among colonels, who usually thought of 'their' regiments in terms of private and fancy playthings, and he expected the code to be followed. Most radical among the notions expressed here was that Burgoyne played down the discipline prevalent in the British Army, in essence borrowed from the Prussian system, then the most highly esteemed in Europe. He also encouraged a degree of camaraderie between officers and men: 'There are occasions, such as during stable or fatigue duty, when officers may slacken the reins so far as to talk with soldiers; nay, even a joke may be used.'[4] All this was sound psychology, a pointer to the modern army and a tradition which appears to have been cherished in the 16th to Morris's time. Something else which would have gladdened the heart of a professional like Morris was Burgoyne's insistence on study of the profession of arms. Beyond the qualities already described, the Army as a whole demanded little of its cavalry or infantry officers. It was not until the obvious emergency of the Revolutionary War in the 1790s that a training school for officers was established (at High Wycombe) and even that (along with the 'Shop', the military academy at Woolwich for the Artillery) had made little impact on professionalism by the outbreak of the Crimean War. Burgoyne, however, expected his officers to read daily, particularly French, since that was the universal language of diplomacy, culture and the best military histories and discourses. And he encouraged mathematics, with its obvious links with fortification and gunnery. He also encouraged concise reporting, good judgement of distance and ground and an ability to sketch swiftly and accurately – 'this would be a talent peculiarly adapted to the light dragoon service.'[5] What no doubt came hardest of all was Burgoyne's insistence that horsemanship was a science in itself, that the officers of the 16th should 'sometimes' saddle their own horses and be familiar with the forage and care of the regiment's mounts. In this, Burgoyne was no doubt taking a leaf from the book of the Prussian Cavalry, who sponged their horses' nostrils, checked their hoofs and fed and watered them before they looked after themselves.

The new regiment under Burgoyne won its spurs in Portugal and Spain between 1762 and 1765 and on its return home, because of its success and the continuing popularity of its commander, was given the new title of the 16th, the Queen's Light Dragoons, in honour of Charlotte of Mecklenburg Strelitz, the Consort of George III. By 1768 the regiment had adopted the motto *Aut cursu, aut cominus armis* ('Either by speed or by close combat').

Less happy was the regiment's record in the War of American Independence. There can be little doubt that this was one of the worst planned campaigns on record as far as the British were concerned, with the amateur George III and the incompetent George Germaine trying to conduct a war whose operational front was three thousand miles away. They in turn were hampered by a succession of indifferent generals (arguably, Burgoyne among them) and an underestimation of the colonists bordering on stupidity. Not least among misapprehensions was that few troops were needed to contain the colonists' military strength. When, perhaps too late, reinforcements were sent, the 16th Light Dragoons were despatched to Boston, centre of anti-British hostilities. The crossing was appalling and a foretaste of similar crossings to India in the nineteenth century. The 16th's horses panicked in their makeshift hammocks below decks and as there were no firearms on board, men had to use their sabres to cut the throats of the fear-maddened animals before all the horses died in their lashings and rearings. With outbreaks of scurvy occurring during the three-month sailing voyage, it is nothing short of astonishing – and speaks volumes for the morale of the regiment – that the 16th were in action within a week of landing, at White Plains in October 1776.

This was not a war for cavalry. The country was heavily wooded, with steep ravines and sheer drops and the officers, senior and junior, were less than impressive. Three years were spent riding around the wilderness of Pennsylvania, in search of an enemy and forage that were equally elusive. After the turning point of Burgoyne's surrender at Saratoga in October 1777, horses began to dwindle in number and remounts were difficult to obtain. The 16th were sent home in 1779 before the final humiliation of Yorktown. There were no battle honours.

The 16th next took part in the largely ineffectual campaign of the 'Grand Old' Duke of York to the Low Countries in 1794, the expeditionary force responding to the European conflict created by the French Revolution. But the campaign was lacklustre in its execution and achievements and in any case William Pitt, the Prime Minister, had ideas of recreating his father's 'Blue Water' successes of the Seven Years War; the bulk of the British Army was sent to the West Indies where it suffered appalling casualties from yellow fever and other diseases. At least this time, the 16th returned with battle honours – Beaumont (26 April 1794) and Willems (10 May 1794) – before embarking for England in February 1796.

The rest of the 1790s and the early years of the next century were marked by home service, in many ways the least popular and certainly the least glorious of any regiment's life. For any officer who was less than Burgoyne's ideal, the social round of Georgian England and the opportunity to absent himself from duty were attractive propositions. Unfortunately, most people's view of cavalry officers of this period is coloured by the ludicrous figure of George Brummel, who resigned his commission in the 10th Light Dragoons rather than go on 'foreign service'. The regiment was posted to Manchester! So the 16th 'aided the civil power', acted as preventive officers against the smugglers along the Kent coast and coerced the Irish. It was not until April 1809 that they saw real service again, in the Iberian peninsula under the immediate command of Colonel the Honourable George Anson and the supreme command of Sir Arthur Wellesley, prominent at this stage in his career as the foremost of the Sepoy Generals, having distinguished himself in India in the years up to 1803.

Much of the information pertaining to the 16th in the Peninsular campaign comes from the diary of Cornet William Tomkinson. This was the first campaign to produce literate men, in the ranks as well as among the officers, who cared to describe their experiences. Unlike the Crimean campaign of the 1850s, however, Wellesley's troops did not perform under the watchful eye of a war correspondent. The arduous duties which the 16th carried out earned them new battle honours – Talavera, Fuentes d'Oñor, Salamanca, Vittoria and Nive. In common with many other regiments, the honour 'Peninsula' was also granted to them. Wellington, despite his time as an officer in two cavalry regiments, had the instincts of a foot soldier and constantly complained in the Peninsula that his cavalry 'got him into scrapes'. Certainly the British cavalry continued the reckless hell-for-leather traditions of Prince Rupert's horsemen of the Civil War and their fast, powerful thoroughbreds and hunters were better suited to it than the heavier breeds of the seventeenth century. On the other hand, the 16th's duties and those of many other cavalry regiments, often involved picquet and reconnaissance work in compliance with Wellesley's cautious advance through Portugal and Spain. They crossed the Pyrenees onto French soil and returned to the cavalry barracks at Hounslow once Napoleon had abdicated.

Waterloo has probably been the battle on which most ink has been wasted by British military writers. It was not Wellington's best and was certainly not the day for which to remember Napoleon. By the time the 16th arrived in Ostend, the Clothing Warrant of March 1812 had come into effect and the regiment looked very different from the horsemen who had come to a similar shore under the Duke of York years before.

The central action taken by the 16th on that wet Sunday, 18 June 1815, was to charge as part of Major General Sir John Vandeleur's brigade, comprising the 11th, 12th and 16th Lights. Ponsonby's Heavy Cavalry – the Royals, Greys and Inniskillings – had delivered a charge, but found themselves struggling back over the sticky mud of ploughed fields on blown horses, harried by fresh French Lancers. Vandeleur went in to cover their retreat, and at the end of the day the 16th clashed with various stubborn French units fighting rearguard actions. It won them the battle honour 'Waterloo'.

Thanks in part to the Congress of Vienna and the subsequent congresses that followed it, Britain embarked on 'the long peace'; a period of non-participation in European affairs in a military sense that only ended at the Alma in September 1854. In many ways this stagnation was bad for the Army because it gave little incentive for professionalism or the need for training and it also gave the 'feather-bed soldiers' a chance to neglect their duties as officers or to become obsessed with the fripperies of uniform. The 16th fared better than most in that respect because in 1822 it was posted to India.

In the interim a further change occurred in the status and dress of the regiment. While on duty in Ireland in 1816, they were equipped as and given the title of 16th The Queen's Light Dragoons (Lancers) and this clumsy term remained until the 1840s. The lance as a weapon of war had disappeared from European battlefields in the seventeenth century. One or two regiments carried it in the Civil War, but essentially it was an outmoded weapon, associated with chivalry (itself a largely dead concept) and with the practice rather than the reality of war. Napoleon's use of the Polish lancers of the Vistula under Marshal Poniatowski had revived interest in the weapon, however, and the British cavalry had seen at close quarters what these lances could do in the right hands, particularly in the narrow streets of Genappe in 1815.

The 9th, 12th, 16th and 23rd Light Dragoons were to be re-equipped and known as Lancers, just as several other Lights had become Hussars from 1805.

As the century wore on, the 'pure' Light Dragoon became an increasing rarity and had gone altogether by 1860. To try to save on expense (the National Debt had rocketed by 1816 and the country was gripped by economic and social depression) the new Lancer regiments were allowed to retain their Light Dragoon jackets and girdles. Contemporary paintings by Denis Dighton show the huge influence of Continental styles. The shako, itself a foreign import, was replaced by the Polish lance cap, or *schapska*, which was a leather contraption with a square trencher top, heavily festooned with lace for officers and carrying a huge plume of drooping cock's feathers (swan's from 1826). The mameluke sabre, light and curved, which had probably found its way westward after Bonaparte's campaign in Egypt in 1798, was carried by many officers of cavalry and infantry but it was specified for Lancer officers and those of certain Hussar regiments in levee dress of the 1820s. Lancers of this period wore very wide 'cossack' overalls and pantaloons, fitting under the instep with a leather strap. Unlike the Light Dragoons, Lancers now had lace loops on their upright Prussian collars. The lance itself was made of ash, sixteen feet long and tipped with iron. At first, the pennon was the Union flag but this was altered by 1820 to a strip of cloth, red over white, and in order to make the Pimlico Divisions of Lance Drill easier to manage, the length of the shaft was reduced to nine feet. Other Ranks were soon to be armed with the 1821 pattern three-bar hilt sword and the lance; they therefore lost their carbines. By 1842, non-commissioned officers of Lancer regiments were issued with pistols. As had always been the case, officers bought their own.

James Lunt in his book on the 16th/5th Royal Lancers implies that the 16th's loyalty to the appalling Caroline of Brunswick on her return to England for her husband's coronation is the reason for their being posted to India.[6] It was a fact, however, that regiments were posted to the subcontinent regularly throughout the century and politics was not necessarily involved. The political situation in India will be dealt with fully in the next chapter, but life there was vastly different from that of home service, both for officers and men. To begin with, the tour of duty was often prolonged. The 16th were there for twenty-two years. William Morris was an infant when they sailed from Gravesend; when he returned a month before they did after Aliwal, he was already an experienced young soldier. Only one officer, George McDowell, had survived those years – countless men had died in action and from heat and disease. Faced with this situation, officers had a choice. Those who wanted action and experience could transfer to a regiment that was posted. Others, who preferred the comfortable social round of Georgian society, could transfer out. Impecunious officers, unable to stand the financial pressure of life in England, could live much more cheaply in India, where the social round was very different. Life for the men was something approaching paradise because of the abundance of native labour. Sergeant Thomas of the 16th wrote: 'Each man has a syce [groom] to clean and saddle his horse. Each troop has two barbers, two shoe blacks, two belt cleaners and eight dhobis or washerwomen.'[7] And experienced men like Thomas were aware of the problems of idleness that this caused: 'At this time the men know not how to pass away the time unless by drinking or gambling; thus they are led to be drunkards or gamblers before they have been many years in India.'[8] It was not until the 1840s that regiments were encouraged to provide a daily ration of coffee for their men rather than rum, and the social benefits of schoolrooms and inter-regimental sports to provide soldiers with a profitable occupation belong to a much later generation. When William Morris joined the 17th Lancers in 1847, the regiment was something of a rarity in having its own library.

Officers and men alike took native women for partners. Although actual marriage was unlikely (for many years permission to marry had to be obtained even by junior officers from the commanding officer), close bonds often developed. It was part of that mutual understanding that was already being eroded by the time of the First Sikh War and which contributed perhaps to the Mutiny of 1857.

It was at Bhurtpore in 1826 that the 16th used the lance in battle for the first time, against the powerful Jat fortress known as the Bulwark of Hindustan. From there, they were transferred to Meerut, which effectively became their home until orders were received for England.

In the year which followed Bhurtpore, the whole subject of uniform was reviewed, especially considering the vast expense to which officers were now put. The Dress Regulations for Officers had first appeared in 1822, and in those of 1831 and 1834 the changes influenced by the new king, William IV, were affirmed. The sailor king decided to retain dark blue, the colour of Light Cavalry regiments, for the Navy only, so the 16th along with all other Lancer regiments, adopted scarlet coatees. It is from these regulations too that the notion of 'dress' and 'undress' for officers came about and all regular regiments adopted gold or yellow lace, whereas silver or white became reserved for yeomanry or militia. In 1840 it was decided to revert to dark blue for Light Cavalry, as scarlet had never been popular. For some reason it *was* popular with officers and men of the 16th and they sought and obtained permission to continue wearing the scarlet jacket. This in turn became the scarlet tunic in 1855 and remained until the effective end of full dress in 1914.

Chapter Four
'A Bloody War and a Sickly Season'

The sheer vastness of India accounted for its majesty, its fascination and its problems. It was a land of mysticism and of magic, of murder and mayhem, regulated by cruel extremes of temperature and climate and dismembered periodically by native and interloper alike. In the northern area of the Punjab, where the 16th Lancers fought the first Sikh War, the monsoon period is less obtrusive and slight frosts occur at night, but the midday sun, especially in the months between March and June, can often exceed 110°F. It was in temperatures like this, with the monotonous hot winds that accompanied them, that men went mad. The story is well attested of the Private of the 16th who, on the day the regiment was due to march to join the Bhurtpore Field Force in 1826, drew his pistol and killed himself. He was one of five who had committed suicide in that intolerably hot summer.

The history of British involvement in India begins with the East India Company, which received its charter in 1600, and the first English settlement or 'factory' of the Company was established at Surat on the West Coast twelve years later. Madras followed on the East Coast in 1639 and a third on the Hooghli near the Ganges mouth in 1640; the three later 'Presidencies' of the Company were formed – Bombay, Bengal and Madras.

What spurred on the Company to establish and extend its territory was the lure of fabulous wealth. Englishmen had never seen such extremes of wealth and poverty until they saw India. Life was 'brutish, nasty and short'. Epidemic disease was rife, starvation endemic. Very lucky was the white man who did not succumb to any one of the several indigenous illnesses before he had been in the country for more than a few days. On the other hand, the fabulous and ostentatious wealth of the native princes fascinated hard-bitten Englishmen of the 'middling sort' who hoped to strike it rich in India via trade and who came home as 'nabobs' (from the Hindi *Nawab*, a prince) laden with treasure.

The rather late arrival of the French Compagnie des Indes at Pondicherri in 1674 ensured that the British East India Company not only stayed, but did its best to seize potentially valuable markets before the French did. In this situation, it was necessary for the Company to create its own armies to assert itself against the French and any native rulers the French backed as a means to the end of removing the British. In the mid-eighteenth century the Company delivered fierce blows to the French and their Indian allies. By the time of Plassey (23 June 1757), probably the most famous of the victories of Robert Clive, British supremacy in India was assured and the way was paved for successive Governors General to annex and cede even more areas of India, a policy which was to continue under mounting tension until the Mutiny of 1857.

The post of Governor General was nominally filled by the directors of the East India Company at their headquarters in Leadenhall Street, London, but in fact from George II's reign, the Governor General was a royal servant, and empowered to overrule his Council, if he saw fit. The trading monopoly of the Company ceased in 1833, and thereafter trade and politics went their separate ways.

Opponents of the British in India have criticized the typical European ignorance of older, native sensibilities. The all-important caste structure, the religious sects, native costume and language were all dismissed as so much superstitious rubbish; and administrator, soldier and missionary alike set to recreate England east of the Indian Ocean. It is true that a deliberate westernization policy did take place, particularly under the Governor Generalship in Bengal of Lord William Bentinck (1828–33) when land revenue administration was reformed, the civil service's lower ranks were opened to Indians (which in turn meant that English had to be adopted as the official language of the various states), railways first appeared, a postal service developed and the Hindu custom of *suttee*, or the burning of widows, was abolished.

But before the system began to sour, there were often very close, harmonious relationships between the British and the Indians and men like Havelock, Jacob, Outram and the Lawrences felt more at home there than in England. The history of the British in India is not one of constant warfare and military dictatorship. It would have been impossible for a relative handful of men, administrators and soldiers, to police an area of approximately 800,000 square miles, inhabited by nearly 131 million natives. In reality, the relationship was a complex one, depending as it did on mutual trust and understanding. Wars there were, atrocities there were, but overall there was an abiding sense of harmony and in many ways the link between the two cultures was the Indian Army.

It had been recognized, however, for some time that this army needed to be reinforced and stiffened by the 'Queen's Regiments' which were more or less hired out to the Company even after the administrative split of 1833; it was for this reason that the 16th The Queen's Lancers had been posted in 1822. William Morris reached the regiment at Meerut on 23 March 1843. Meerut itself was an ancient city, almost halfway between the rivers Ganges and Jumna. It had all but collapsed until the British occupied it and built extensive cantonments and a church dedicated to St John, the oldest Christian building in Northern India.

In a rare moment of expansiveness Morris wrote to his father on 9 April:

> I arrived here on 23rd of last month, exactly eight months from the
> day I left England ... I am delighted with my Regiment. They are a
> splendid body of men and the best mounted in India ... The
> Officers too are a fine, handsome and agreeable set of fellows; in fact
> I can find no fault at all, unless from envy that every officer is a finer
> and better-looking fellow than myself. The Colonel [Charles
> Cureton] is an excellent Officer and although an old man, he is quite
> young when at the head of his men.

Morris's enthusiasm is infectious. Perhaps he felt at last he had found his niche,
after the insular childhood and the mediocre university career. How the
twenty-three-year-old Cornet was received by his fellow officers and men of
his troop, we do not know. Certainly he was green. He had no experience either
of the Army or India, but his horsemanship must have stood him in good stead.
Less certain is his fellow officers' response to his aptitude for study: 'I am
reading hard at the Cavalry movements; they are rather difficult to recollect
from being so numerous' and to his early ambition: 'I have some idea of going
to the Senior Department at Sandhurst when I have been a sufficient time in
the Army; it is an introduction to a good appointment.' Regimental officers of
the cavalry were not generally known for their education. Not even the later
tried and trusted ladder of the public school was all that common in this
period, as Morris's own case testifies. Details of the Mess expenses of the 16th,
which were rather heavy owing to 'the hospitality of the officers', are included
in the original of this letter but not in the memoir in which it has been quoted.[1]

The slur of the stupidity of cavalry officers has often been rather overstated
and stems from the fact that in the modern army, technicalities of weaponry are
so great that mere courage is by no means enough. In the days of lance and
sabre, it was appreciably easier, but still there were complex parade ground
formations and exercises to master, bugle calls to recognize, as well as sword drill
and horsemanship. In later years, officers like Winston Churchill, posted with
their regiments to India or elsewhere, underwent rigorous exercise in the riding
school along with the men, under the watchful eye of the Riding Master. It
seems unlikely that much of this was necessary for Morris, born to the saddle as
he was, although the military 'seat', squarely back on the horse's haunches and
with leg almost straight to facilitate lance and sword movements, was rather
different from the hunting seat to which he had become accustomed. Towards
the end of Morris's life, in the India of 1858, Evelyn Wood, then sharing
Morris's quarters, describes him euphorically as 'the champion swordsman of
the army'. Such descriptions are attributed to Louis Nolan as well, together
with 'best horseman in the army'. For officers, such phrases are meaningless.
Later in the century, to encourage proficiency of arms, there were competitions

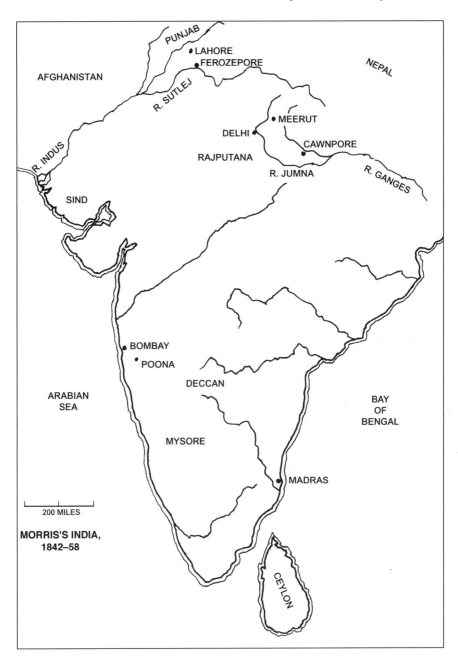

MORRIS'S INDIA,
1842–58

held and sleeve badges awarded for best swordsman in troop, squadron and
regiment, but never extra-regimentally and never for officers. Officers of
Lancer regiments did not carry the lance themselves, but relied on sword and
pistol. There were twenty or so sword positions, according to the 1796 Manual,
which remained in use until after the Crimea – nine guards (for defence), three
thrusts ('points'), the parry and seven cuts. Throughout the century arguments

raged over whether the best type of cavalry sword was a curved one for cutting or a straight, tapering blade for thrusting. The pattern William Morris would have bought in London and carried throughout the Sikh War was a compromise – the 1821 three-bar hilt – which could be used for both.

The field movements for cavalry – at which Morris was working so hard – were complicated. They were important because the daily drill was repeated under fire in battle conditions, and each man had instinctively to know his place and behave accordingly. This regimentation substituted for 'war games' and manoeuvres, which did not become commonplace until much later in the century. What Morris had to learn quickly, both on paper and on the ground, was this:

> There were twenty-one basic field movements with which the cavalryman was required to become conversant. The most important of these was the ability to ride across country, keeping in line and maintaining correct spacing. The operational unit was the squadron, divided into a right and a left troop. Each troop, not including the trumpeters and farriers, consisted in theory of twenty-four Other Ranks. The space between the front and rear ranks, into which these were divided, varied depending on whether the squadron (of which there were generally either two or three in a regiment) was in 'Order' (24 feet), 'Close Order' (8 feet) or marching in fours (4 feet). The normal interval between squadrons in line was 12 yards.
>
> There were numerous ways in which squadrons marched and manoeuvred, all of them designed to make advancing, retiring and changes of front speedily effective. Usually, the squadron leader [a major] and the two troop leaders [captains] rode in the front rank, while the three junior officers – the serrefiles – [Morris among them] rode (accompanied by the trumpeters and farriers) in rear of the rear rank. The squadron sergeant major generally rode in the centre of the front rank and the squadron marker behind and near the centre of the rear rank. When a regiment marched as a whole, it often did so in 'Close Column of Squadrons'. This entailed a massing of all the troopers [privates and NCOs] with their officers on the flanks, and all the trumpeters and farriers in the rear.[2]

Morris had about nine months in Meerut to cope with the rigours of life with the 16th. He does not record any sickness, though it was inevitable for Englishmen unused to the climate. When John Sylvester, the surgeon who was to join the 14th Light Dragoons and serve during the Mutiny, arrived in Bombay in 1854, he felt

> a more than usual lassitude. I felt no pain whatever and sank on my bed powerless; a deadly faintness and nausea ensued, followed by all

the symptoms of severe Asiatic cholera ... the terrible thirst and cramps in my limbs.[3]

Judging by the letter Morris wrote to his wife when he was ill with cholera at Varna, it is unlikely he had caught the disease before. He would have found sleeping in the hot, insect-noisy nights difficult. Private Tookey of the 14th Light Dragoons wrote of the hot months in 1848:

Unless a man gets lushy every night with arrack or the Company grog, which is strongly impregnated with opium, he cannot sleep a wink. With the officers [Tookey wrongly supposed] it is different, as they have a native to fan them during the night.[4]

A permanent station like Meerut, then the largest in Northern India, would host its balls and parties and the men and officers alike arranged horse races (Morris was to build a racecourse, complete with bridges, at Kirkee, the year before his death). Hunting for partridge, wild pig, black buck and tiger was also popular. But sword drill, cavalry exercises and steeplechases were all practice for the real thing. And in India, war came soon enough.

The political situation in India when William Morris arrived was critical. On the one hand, the province of Sind had recently been conquered by Sir Charles Napier and John Jacob. So impressive were these two and the officers and men under their command, that in five months (by June 1843) they had conquered an area the size of England using their initiative and local knowledge. Both traits were indispensable to a successful modern soldier; both were frowned on in the British Army. On the other hand an entire British Army, Lord Ellenborough's Army of the Indus, had been destroyed attempting a tactical retreat from Kabul. Only one man, Dr Brydon, staggered into Jellalabad alive. It was a salutary reminder that native troops ought never to be underestimated.

As so often happened in eighteenth- and nineteenth-century India, trouble occurred when a question of succession arose. In this case, Jankoji Rao Sindhia, the ruler of Gwalior, died in 1843 and the inevitable result was court intrigue and double-dealing in which the British resident at Gwalior and all British officers in the local units were forced to leave. This left an uncontrolled and potentially hostile force of 22,000 men and 300 guns on the frontier of British India. Lord Ellenborough, the newly appointed Governor General, placed what he called a 'camp of observation' in case of trouble. By their very presence, the British Army was inciting conflict and Ellenborough's phraseology fooled no one. He demanded that the Gwalior Army be reduced in size. This demand was ignored.

Morris and the men of the 16th were anxious for action. In a letter home, he wrote:

They have got a lot of prize money in Scinde. The 16th were applied
for to go, but Lord Ellenborough would not spare them and sent the
9th Native Cavalry instead ... there are rumours of more fighting; I
suppose we shall hear the event in a few days. Should things go
hardly with Sir Charles Napier they will send us up directly, so you
may suppose I do not wish them much good! The Governor General
does not know whether we go home next Winter or not, as Lord
Ellenborough talks of having another Army of Reserve assembled. I
have a shrewd suspicion that we shall form part of it.

The 16th were ordered south.

In August, a new Commander in Chief was appointed to India. He was
General Sir Hugh 'Paddy' Gough, a sixty-four-year-old veteran of the
Peninsula, famed for his courage and habit of wearing a white coat on the
battlefield – 'so that all should see me', as he said. He was the hero of Barossa
(1811) and recently arrived after a successful Chinese campaign. He was to lead
some 20,000 Queen's and Company troops, including the 16th Lancers, in what
has variously been called the Gwalior Campaign, the last Mahratta War and the
Forty-Eight Hour War, against a well-organized, well-disciplined force of at
least 18,000 men with 100 field guns, ably led by Bhagerat Rao Sindhia.

Gough split his command in two, leaving the left wing under Major General
Sir John Grey to advance on Punniar, while he took the right from Agra to join
up with Grey. Although it was known that the enemy had fortified Gwalior itself,
the exact location of the troops was uncertain. Lord Ellenborough accompanied
the army and had several ladies in his entourage, some riding elephants. Four
days after Christmas, Gough led his right wing into the field. This was not
essentially a cavalry action. It could be argued that Gough relied more on the
infantry because he had the instincts of an infantryman, but in addition to his
4,800 infantry (two Queen's and eight Company regiments) he had 30 guns and
1,340 sabres, divided into two brigades, flanking the rest. Morris and the 16th
Lancers formed the 3rd Cavalry Brigade, comprising in addition the Governor
General's Bodyguard, the 1st and 5th Bengal Light Cavalry and the 4th Bengal
Irregular Cavalry (Skinner's Horse), under the command of Lieutenant Colonel
Charles Cureton. Two troops of horse artillery accompanied them.

The Battle of Maharajpur is not one which is well documented and the part
played in it by the 16th Lancers is doubly obscure. No letters have survived
from Morris himself and his own description of the Gwalior Campaign, made
in a speech at Great Torrington, Devon, thirteen years later is, to say the least,
brief and unhelpful: 'In November 1843, after marching nine hundred miles,
from Kalafat or Meerhat, which all admit was a tolerably fair entrance for a
young soldier, I arrived at Punniar and was present with my regiment at the
engagement of Maharajpoor.' Hart's Army List for 1845 states: 'Captains
Bonham and Reynolds, Lieutenants Waugh and O'Conor, Cornets Orme,
Waller and Morris and Dr Currie were present in the action at Maharajpore

(Medal).' Having advanced on a broad front against the Mahratta batteries and the 3,000 infantry which defended the village of Maharajpur itself, Gough rolled on against the neighbouring village of Shirkapur, where he changed front to face a further 2,300 infantry and then to the high ground that skirted the River Asan, to the strongest fortified positions between Chonda and Dorpura. The Mahrattas looked upon their field places as sacred objects and most of the gunners died by their weapons, bayoneted to death.

The cavalry backed up the infantry assaults from time to time. Certainly the 4th Bengal Irregular Cavalry, the 4th Bengal Cavalry and Lieutenant Colonel Scott's 10th Cavalry captured guns and standards, harassing the enemy's right flank, but the possibility of outflanking the Mahrattas was scotched by the presence of a steep ravine which they were unable to cross. In personal correspondence, Gough blamed Major General Sir Joseph Thackwell, who commanded his cavalry, because he had not closed up the infantry's right flank, despite being so ordered. Thackwell in turn blamed Harry Smith, and thus the reality of the situation becomes lost in accusation. The only account to emerge from the ranks of the 16th is that of Corporal Cowtan, one of the new breed of literate and articulate men who were creeping into the Army in the 1840s:

> Our squadron formed the advance-guard of our Division, consequently our troop led the field.
>
> As soon as we arrived at good ground we formed line to the front under a heavy fire from the enemy's battery and galloped under it for about three miles to the right, but fortunately for us their guns were aimed for our lances, or half the regiment must have fallen. However, we managed to escape their shot very well, although we could hear them whistling like so much hail over our heads. Queer work, I can assure you.
>
> Well, we caught sight of the enemy's guns and charged them and just as we got within 50 yards of them we discovered a tremendous ravine between us and the guns, so that all we could do was retreat out of range of their fire. In this charge we lost two men and 21 horses killed; three horses and one man just in front of me fell. When we found we could not get at their guns we wanted to have a charge at their cavalry, but directly we advanced against them they turned tail and fled ...
>
> It was a tremendous hot day, the sun pouring down on us the whole of the time.[5]

It is likely that the Mahratta cavalry gave little fight because of the appearance of the Lancers. The lance had its detractors from the outset, since it was a cumbersome weapon to handle in the mêlée that usually followed a charge, but to young, inexperienced soldiers or running infantry, it was a formidable weapon to face. If Morris charged with the 16th, as seems at least likely, it would have been at the rear of his troop, as a serrefile. Judging by his later actions, he would have tied the sword knot around his wrist and busied himself keeping perfect pace, watching out for stragglers in the line and barking the order, along with the non-commissioned officers, to close up if horse or man went down. Although Maharajpur and Punniar between them cost Gough over a thousand men killed, wounded or missing, the 16th had come off lightly. Only Captain Pratt and Lieutenant Patterson are mentioned in Gough's flimsy despatches and William Morris had received his baptism of fire. Along with other units, the 16th were awarded a bronze star bearing the legend 'Maharajpoor' and the Scarlet Lancers themselves another battle honour. Perhaps Morris thought them both cheaply won.

His Aunt Catherine wrote to his father from Brighton on 9 March:

> My dear William,
>   Though I have written to you so recently yet I must send you and Jane our joyful congratulations on William's escape out of the terrible conflict that has occurred in India. We thank God in Heart and Soul for his safety ... As soon as we heard the news we purchased a Times newspaper ... as it contains some mention of the fortress and town of Gwalior.
>   William I trust is now sufficiently gratified in having been engaged in so brilliant and hard-fought an action and will I suppose in common with the rest of the officers be decorated with a bronze star. Do entreat him not again to try his valour in unequal combats with wild animals [tigers? wild pigs?]. Human life ought not thus to be risked and now that he has witnessed its lamentable destruction, I hope he will prize it at a higher rate.

Whether Lord Ellenborough saw the Gwalior campaign as a necessary preliminary to his duel with the Sikhs is uncertain. By 1846, the government of Lord Aberdeen was increasingly unhappy about his and his successor's further acquisition of territory.

Lieutenant General Sir Henry Hardinge, who succeeded Ellenborough in July 1844, was the former Governor's brother-in-law and another Peninsula veteran. His involvement as a soldier in the First Sikh War was to be much closer than Ellenborough's, caught up at Gwalior almost by accident. The Sikh War arose out of yet another Indian succession crisis, this time in the Punjab. The death of Ranjit Singh, the 'Lion of the Punjab', in 1839 threw open the palace doors at Lahore, the Sikh capital, to exactly the same sort of intrigue and jockeying for position that occurred at Gwalior and it paved the way for the most serious challenge the British Army had faced in India, against the most formidable opponents.

Chapter Five

Crossing the Sutlej

Sikhism is a religious cult found largely in the Punjab provinces in Northern India and most Sikhs were of Jat tribal stock. They wear the five Ks – *Kes*, or uncut hair wound into the turban; *Kacch*, short drawers; *Khara*, iron bangle; *Kripan*, sword; and *Khanga*, comb. In their turbans various sharp-edged quoits and missiles were carried in battle. Sikhs do not smoke tobacco, but they are not strict teetotallers and they reject all Hindu customs except reverence to the cow. The cult was founded by Nanak Singh in the early sixteenth century in an attempt to combine Hinduism and Islam into a single faith. Nanak stressed the non-sectarian virtues of benevolence, justice, honesty and loyalty and was succeeded as guru by nine leaders down to 1708. In the process two holy books, the *Adi Granth* and the *Daram Granth*, were compiled and the sacred city and temple of Amritsar built. The cult is not hereditary and a complex ceremony of ablution similar to Christian baptism initiated a man into membership of the elite warrior class. As the eighteenth century dawned, Sikh society became more militaristic and the warrior class, the Khalsa, the property of God, degenerated into a fanatical army.

Ranjit Singh, the greatest of the Sikh rulers, built up a large kingdom north of the River Sutlej and enhanced his dominions at the expense of the weak Afghan hill tribes and the preoccupied British (then engaged in earlier Mahratta wars). By remaining friendly with the British, signing various treaties and fêting British residents at Ludhiana, Ranjit Singh was able to make war unmolested on those Indians who stood in his way. Between 1806 and 1823 when Ranjit took Peshawar, he had extended his territory to an alarming extent, defeated Ghurkhas and Afghans under Shah Suja and obtained the Koh-i-Noor diamond. In keeping with many Englishmen of his day, William Morris was impressed by the legend of the man, still vibrant of course when he joined the 16th Lancers. Whether Morris knew that Ranjit had had his own mother murdered to gain control in the Punjab is not recorded!

H Lapel Griffin, writing in 1873, said: 'He was selfish, false and avaricious; grossly superstitious, shamelessly and openly drunken and debauched.' The

Victorians expected their statesmen to be made of purer stuff than that, but Ranjit had succeeded in welding together an entire society which was not hierarchical, in the sense that caste had disappeared, and which was not religiously split, because of the adherence to Sikhism itself. By British standards, Ranjit's government left much to be desired – he built no schools, no hospitals, no law courts. What law there was, was brutal. Hands were cut off for theft, yet outlawry and brigandage went unchecked. Perhaps his greatest weakness (and it was a common European failing too) was that he did not choose and groom a worthy successor for his regime.

The vacuum created by Ranjit's death in July 1839 brought uncertainty to a violent head. The Lion's cubs fought each other for power and the right to succeed. The Khalsa's two principal commanders, Tej Singh and Lal Singh, realized that their chances of power were limited with the army in existence. If the army crossed the River Sutlej, that would provoke the British into destroying it and leave the Cis-Sutlej Punjab to them. There were many in Lahore who would have preferred the occupation of a British Army to the banditry of their own. Between the imbecilic Kharak Singh and the 'bold but vicious' Nao Nihal Singh there was little to choose. It cannot have been chance that both Ranjit's claimants died on the same day and a wave of assassinations followed. As at Gwalior, the British under Lord Hardinge brought up their military units, to be poised at the border in case of trouble. As at Gwalior, the mere presence of these troops may have precipitated that trouble. The build-up of these troops had in fact been going on since 1838. There were three regiments and six guns dispersed between Sabatha and Ludhiana, about 2,500 men. Lord Auckland increased this number to 8,000, creating Ferozepur as a new camp. Ellenborough created three more camps – Ambala, Kasauli and Simla – about 14,000 men and 48 guns. Under Hardinge a conservative estimate brought the figure up to 32,000 men with 68 guns. The Khalsa crossed the Sutlej on 11 December 1845, a week before Morris's twenty-fifth birthday.

Eight months before the Sikh advance, William Morris was gazetted Lieutenant (14 May). No documentation has survived for this promotion except that Hart's Army List states that it took place without purchase and in many ways it was his least important move; he was still in position of serrefile for all tactical purposes. What it did mean, however, was that he was no longer the new boy. Five new cornets had been gazetted – Foster, Hodgson, Williams, Knight and Thackwell, and by the time of Aliwal, Morris is listed as the most junior of the lieutenants. There had been other movements. Cornet Orme was also a Lieutenant by 1846 as were Waller and Maycock. Lieutenant Waugh was promoted Captain (and was in fact Deputy Assistant Quartermaster General to Cureton who commanded the brigade), and a new man had arrived, Lieutenant Carew.

The crossing of the Sutlej by the Sikh Army may have caught Hardinge unawares. The very large Khalsa assembled near Ferozeshah, but did not attack the relatively weak garrison at nearby Ferozepore. Perhaps this was because of treachery or at least double-dealing on the part of Lal Singh, who seems to have been in constant touch with Captain Nicholson, the agent at Ferozepore and to have informed him of Sikh intentions. It is likely that forty years of courting British favour was a habit difficult to break. Equally likely is the fact that the Khalsa was relatively leaderless. Many of the rank and file appear to have had little faith in either Lal Singh or Tej Singh.

To meet the threat, Hardinge assembled the Army of the Sutlej, the usual combination of Queen's, Company and Irregular troops. Even in India, the European habit of marching with the kitchen sink was observed. The 16th carried a vast amount of baggage, including its regimental plate, much of which was to be captured by the enemy during the campaign. The marching out strength of the regiment was 28 officers, 501 non-commissioned officers and men, and 546 troop horses. The camp followers, however, swelled the column, creating a column of perhaps 10,000 men, women and children.

The Sikhs were over 800 miles away from Meerut and the pace of the column was appallingly slow – twelve miles a day at best. The rigours of moving, even in the Indian winter, took their toll. New drafts of men, some from England, some from other regiments, who had no experience of the march, keeled over in the blistering sun. The roads were narrow and badly made, and deteriorated still further as they neared the Punjab and were churned up by horses and pack animals. The horses had to be walked for part of the journey to rest their backs, but for the accompanying infantry, plodding through deep, white sand, there was no relief. Sunstroke took its toll, even with permission to drape cloths over the back of the head. Little other concession was made. The stiff leather stocks which kept the head upright continued to be worn as did the totally unsuitable serge jackets of scarlet.

Officers like Morris would have worn the short stable jacket and either the blue, gold-laced forage cap or the plain white lance cap without plume or battle honours. The rest of an officer's equipment was carried on camels. The official list, drawn up probably by Lieutenant Colonel McDowell, mentions a canvas bed, tent, blanket, a spare pair of breeches, a spare pair of shoes, half a dozen shirts, a spare flannel waistcoat, a pair of towels and soap. Many of the camels died of heat exhaustion, bad food and neglect. Desertion among the (civilian) camel drivers was endemic.

Morris had bought himself a young Arab horse at a racecourse before he left Meerut, and it carried him faithfully throughout the campaign ahead. Experience had shown, particularly in the 16th Lancers, that it was not wise to transport a regiment's horses direct to the theatre of war. India had the native, country-bred Kathiawari animals, 14 to 14 hands 2 inches high, fast and full of stamina. From 1794, the East India Company had established stud farms, and an Indian Remount service existed from 1819 to provide horses for the Company and Queen's regiments. Controversy raged throughout Morris's time in India as to the best horses available. Edwin Mole, Troop Sergeant Major of the 14th Hussars, writing in 1876, probably spoke for Morris: 'The Arab bred came nearer to perfection in symmetry, beauty, temper and performance than any horses I have ever seen and they were soon snapped up as chargers by our officers.'[1] The alternative was the larger, heavier Cape horse, about 15 hands. A pair of Cape stallions was presented by Lord Auckland, then Governor General, to Ranjit Singh in the 1830s. Ranjit's own Punjabi charger, the grey Kabutar (Pigeon), outlived his master and was inspected by visiting British officers in 1858 when thirty-five years old as a great pet of the Sikhs.

The Battle of Mudki had been fought on 18 December 1845 on a sandy plain between the little mud-brown village and deep jungle. The British troops converging there, from Ambala and Ludhiana were led by 'Paddy' Gough, and serving under him, as his second-in-command, was Lord Hardinge, the Governor General. They had been caught rather unprepared, exhausted after a harrowing series of forced marches similar to those the 16th were undergoing. Inexperienced soldiers perhaps expected a rabble, but in fact Ranjit Singh had trained the Khalsa on European lines, using Italian or French mercenaries like Avatabile to bring them up to parity with the British; and there may have been as many as fifty Europeans and even three Americans among the officers of the Sikh army. All words of command were spoken in French and the 'Sixes', as the British troops called them, were formidable artillerymen, rapid and accurate in fire. Many of these guns were superior to those Gough had with him.

The unimaginative Gough had bombarded the Sikh positions with his artillery and then attempted an encircling move with his cavalry. The brunt of this was borne by the 3rd Light Dragoons, whom the Sikhs colourfully christened 'The Devil's Children', but they were immortalized henceforth in the British Army as 'The Moodkee Wallahs'. In fact their charge had been broken by the thick thorn jungle and the choking, enveloping dust inevitable in such a manoeuvre. Gough's losses were high – 872 killed and wounded, including two Generals – Sale and McGaskill. Reynell Taylor, then a Lieutenant with the Governor General's bodyguard and later Morris's brother-in-law, was severely wounded at Mudki and was highly critical of parade ground tactics applied to real warfare and of Gough in particular: 'the Tipperary rush, though effective, is rather expensive in good material.'[2]

Expensive or not, justified or not, Gough did exactly the same thing at Ferozeshah three days later. Delayed until the arrival of Major General Littler's reinforcements from Ferozepore, Gough was prevented from going it alone by Hardinge and the attack did not begin until mid-afternoon on what was the shortest day of the year (21 December). The Sikhs, despite their hammering at Mudki, had slightly superior numbers and a heavy preponderance of artillery. Again, Gough and Littler adapted the full-frontal 'Tipperary tactics' and again the 3rd Light Dragoons were expected to negotiate tough country, including the Sikh tents with the accompanying problems of ropes and pegs, in order to silence gun batteries. Dusk had cut the day's action short, and the Sikhs kept up a bombardment throughout the night, adding to the bitter cold and thirst among the troops.

In the morning, the battle had virtually to restart, a dogged infantry struggle for possession of the trenches before Ferozeshah. There may have been a Sikh mutiny during the night, resulting in loss of men, guns and discipline. Tej Singh, either through indecision or treachery, did not commit a fresh army of 30,000. There was great confusion over this. The Assistant Adjutant General, Captain J R Lumley, gave the remarkable order for all British cavalry and horse artillery to march to Ferozepore. This order clearly made no sense at all and did not come from Gough or Hardinge. Lumley, probably dazed by shell shock, was allowed to retire shortly afterwards. It is just possible that this manoeuvre made Tej Singh's troops wary of a cunning outflanking move and withdraw rather than risk being surrounded.

As it was, Ferozeshah was a near thing. Hardinge said that another such victory would shake the Empire. British casualties were very high – 720 killed, 2,157 wounded, with a further 379 'missing' on the official list. The 3rd Light Dragoons were particularly hard hit, having lost nearly half their complement at Mudki and Ferozeshah. Anglesey quotes W K McGregor's claim that Hardinge during the battle would 'give half a lakh of rupees that H.M.'s 16th Lancers should arrive.'[3]

The fresh contingents Hardinge had been hoping for began to arrive on 6 January. By this time the Sikhs had recrossed the Sutlej at the ford nearest Sobraon and obtained reinforcements before returning. The main army fortified Sobraon itself while another force under Runjoor Singh crossed near Ludhiana, intending almost certainly to intercept the huge siege train moving towards Bassian, the largest military depot in the area. The train's slowness and the dust it raised made it an obvious and reasonably easy target, but perhaps Runjoor's troops might simply have intended to sack Ludhiana. Sir Harry Smith, with a mixed division of cavalry, infantry and horse artillery, was sent to stop them. Smith was one of those colourful characters who crop up at every level in the Victorian army. Now nearly sixty, he had served in the Peninsula with the Rifle Brigade and had rescued a fifteen-year-old girl, Juanita de los Dolores de Leon, from rape in the siege of Badajoz, probably the bloodiest encounter of the Peninsular War. She followed him as his wife on all his future campaigns and was thus on top of her elephant before Maharajpur.

The decision to send the 16th may have been an afterthought on Gough's part, as they were forced to cover the ground quickly to catch up with Smith. The cavalry were commanded once again, as they had been in the Gwalior campaign, by Colonel Charles Cureton. All the man's sons served in India, one of them as a cornet in the 16th, slightly senior to Morris. 'Charlie' Cureton senior had joined his regiment in 1819. He was a reckless youth and had embraced the 'cavalry spirit' to the extent that he was soon heavily in debt and decided to 'disappear'. He left his clothes in a bundle on the beach and the assumption was made that he had drowned rather than face the shame of a debt he could not pay. Disguised as a sailor, he went to London and enlisted under the name of Roberts in the 14th Light Dragoons, with whom he served throughout the campaign in the Peninsula. He was commissioned for gallantry in the field, reverted to his own name and exchanged back into the 16th. He was to die at Rumnuggar in the Second Sikh War, on 22 November 1848.

After an exhausting night march, the 16th, forming the advance guard of Smith's troops, came upon the Sikhs entrenched at the fort of Buddiwal, six miles west of Ludhiana. Smith could not attack, so he skirted the fort and pressed on towards Ludhiana. The six miles of flat sand took its toll, especially in the unseasonably hot weather and the infantry suffered terribly. Men of the 31st and 53rd Foot were hauled into the saddles or across the necks of exhausted horses, which now, with riders and equipment, were carrying 40 stone. McDowell, commanding the 16th, was forced to give the order for this charity to stop or his regiment would be useless for action. Nevertheless, the 16th went back time and time again to form front between the crawling infantry and the marauding Sikh horsemen – the ghorchurras – who began to threaten the slower baggage train in Smith's rear. In the skirmish that followed, Smith lost 200 men, mostly the sick and wounded who were carried in doolies or covered stretchers. All the personal belongings of the officers of the 16th were taken, but Morris does not record what was lost. Regimental histories of the 16th Lancers tell the extraordinary story of the silver gilt cup found in a pawnshop in York years later, engraved with the regimental crest.

The Sikhs certainly missed an opportunity at this point, for Smith's force, particularly his infantry, were in an appalling state, but they held off and this gave the troops time to recover in the safety of Ludhiana. The Khalsa moved from Buddiwal in the direction of Ludhiana and built a strongly fortified camp behind the villages of Bhundri and Aliwal. The strategic mistake which Runjur Singh had made is that his back was to the Sutlej. Any retreat would involve crossing water, almost certainly under fire.

On 27 January, at Buddiwal, Morris described the situation:

Forward Movements by this Point

1st, the troops will advance at daylight right point in 2 columns, the Cavalry advancing in such order as Brigadier Cureton may direct so as to cover the advance of the Infantry and Brigadier Cureton will be prepared to withdraw the Cavalry to the right to left as the enemy's position is approached.

The 16th Lancers and the 3rd Light cavalry advanced on the left of all with Turton's and Alexander's troops of Horse Artillery immediately on our right.

H.M. 53rd regiment detachments, 30th Regiment N.I. [Native Infantry] and the Shakawattee Brigade 3rd Columns.

H.M. 31st (24th and 47th N.I.) 1st Column.

Brigadier Godby's Brigade formed the 4th Column and moved on the right of the whole, except for the Shakawattee Horse and the 1st and 5th Cavalry and the [Governor General's] Bodyguard which was on the right of the whole.

The Artillery will in the first instance move in its usual place (viz.) – Two troops with the Cavalry, 9 pounders at the head of the 1st Division, the Howitzers will move on the left of the first Brigade, Lt. Col., Lancers and guns at the head of the 3rd Brigade and the two Shakawattee 9 pounders [with] their infantry – the two sixers [6 pounders] with the Shakawattee.

The Shakawattee were local troops raised in Bengal in 1835 to keep order in the territory near Jodhpur. As such they were units of Irregular Cavalry and Infantry, the latter becoming the 13th Bengal Native Infantry in due course. Morris omitted the 4th Bengal Irregular Cavalry which were with the 16th and the 3rd as the First Brigade under McDowell. The Second Brigade, composed entirely of Company and irregular troops were led by Brigadier Stedman. Smith's total strength is estimated at 12,000, of which about 3,000 were cavalry. There were eleven infantry regiments, including two battalions of Nasiri Ghurkhas, the first time the mountain men of Nepal had fought alongside the British. The Sikhs had perhaps 18–20,000 men and nearly 70 guns.

Smith's line formed up in perfect parade ground formation on an ideal flat plain, having marched six miles in a column as Morris outlines above. The 1st Cavalry Brigade under McDowell took post on the left and the 2nd under Stedman on the right of this line. The skirmishers of the 16th, specially equipped with carbines, moved forward on the sounding of the 'Advance'. It must have been a colourful sight – the scarlet of the British and Company infantry in the centre, the scarlet, blue and gold of the cavalry on the wings. In the distance, the blue and white turbans of the Sikh gunners must have become visible in the heat haze as the cannon opened up. Private Pearman of the 3rd Light Dragoons, now with the Horse Artillery, noted that the first Sikh shell whistled overhead at ten minutes to ten.

The Sikh line was about a mile long, like that of the British, with their cavalry on the flanks. This battle formation was a tried and tested one. Smith sent his infantry, the 31st Foot prominent, to take the village of Aliwal, in case the Sikhs should withdraw without giving battle. Runjoor Singh's left was exposed in the village, so he ordered his cavalry to close in to protect it. Stedman's cavalry on the British right charged the Sikh horse, who were driven back in the mêlée. If Smith could force this flank, he would drive a wedge between the Sikhs and the river and prevent escape by the fords, so he set up an infantry brigade to support the Company and Irregular cavalry. The Sikhs reformed on the other village of Bhundri, almost at right angles to the Sutlej, screened by their cavalry. It was during tactical movements such as these when the Europeans or European-trained Sikhs were changing front that they were most vulnerable. The cavalry were there to deter or repulse an assault made on the unformed line. Smith ordered up a squadron of the 3rd Bengal Native Cavalry, supported by the 4th Squadron the 16th Lancers under Captain Bere. It is clear that Morris was in Bere's squadron, for he wrote home the following day:

> We attacked the Sikhs ... and gave them an awful licking, with much less loss than I expected. After some very sharp firing for about an hour [in which the cavalry sat motionless and cursing while the shot whistled round them and the Horse Artillery of Alexander and Turton did some splendid retaliatory work] the 16th lancers charged in two wings ... [W]e went across an open plain and took the enemy's guns in spite of the thousands who guarded them. I was with the left squadron, which charged the extreme right of the enemy's position.

Most accounts mention wavering on the part of the 3rd Light Cavalry, but Pearman was impressed by the 16th: 'I took off my cap and hollered out ... such cutting and stabbing I never saw before or since.'[4] Bere rallied his men before they went too far and Morris takes up the tale:

> We attacked the only body of their cavalry that showed fight and sent them flying ... but we found we were surrounded by thousands of their Infantry, who formed square to prevent our getting back.

The Sikh cavalry were notably less impressive than their infantry and artillery. Perhaps it was the generally smaller horses and lack of weight which cowed them, although Louis Nolan, writing with the wisdom of men like Morris who had fought the Sikhs, believed this was an advantage in some ways for light cavalry, in that it gave them speed and manoeuvrability.

The infantry square was a European formation particularly favoured by the British for defence. With ranks kneeling and standing, officers and colours in the centre, the square was a parallelogram of death; shot, ball and bayonet combining to resist galloping horsemen. As a tactic on European battlefields it was rapidly to become obsolete, since high explosive shells lobbed into the centre could decimate an entire square. In the rather more outmoded weaponry of colonial warfare (the Sikhs used flintlock smooth bores called jezails), it could still be effective but it had to be steady and its rate of fire fast. The Sikh square was more an equilateral triangle. An anonymous Private in Bere's squadron wrote, 'They gave us a volley at forty yards ... then they threw away their muskets and taking their large shields, came at us sword in hand.'[5] Cowtan, who had fought at Maharajpur, recorded, 'As for myself, I went through cavalry and infantry squares repeatedly ... but my heart sickens at the recollection of what I witnessed that day ... After the first charge self-preservation was the grand thing and the love of life made me look sharp and their great muskets required all our vigilance.'[6] Morris wrote to his father: 'it would have done your eyes good to see how we dashed through them ... I first went at one of their standards, but it got away from me into a mass of the infantry.'

The near capture of the Sikh standard was exaggerated in years to come. In 1856 when Morris was presented with a ceremonial sword, at Great Torrington in Devon, the chairman of the day's events, Sir Trevor Wheler, Bt., mistakenly said that Morris *had* captured the standard. Morris was at pains to correct him:

> And here I must correct Sir Trevor Wheler with regard to the capture of the standard, as I did not take it on that occasion; he has been misinformed on the subject, but it was a very sharp affair and of the squadron to which I belonged, one officer was killed and two were wounded.

At Aliwal, he did what he was to repeat with nearly fatal consequences at Balaclava:

> I then attacked one of the officers [most of whom were wearing mail shirts over their robes] and sent my sword clean through him, but before I could disengage my sword, he hit me over the left eye, and gave me a slight wound, which I do not think will leave a scar.

Fyler's squadron now attacked more of the Sikh infantry, the stolid ranks which had held fast, then broken at Mudki, Ferozeshah and now Aliwal. The right of the 16th, under Major Rowland Smyth, were now ordered against a Sikh infantry battalion with 9 and 12 pounder guns in position. Since McDowell was commanding the 1st Cavalry Brigade, Smyth was officer commanding the 16th. James Lunt describes him as 'a remarkable Irishman and beau sabreur of beaux sabreurs'.[7] He was tall, well built, with a reputation for hard riding, hard drinking and hard fighting. He had killed a civilian named O'Grady in a duel in Phoenix Park in Dublin, was tried for manslaughter and served a year's imprisonment, for which his commanding officer had given him a year's leave!

'Now, Sixteenth,' Smyth shouted as his squadron trotted forward. 'I am going to give the word to charge. Three cheers for the Queen!'

Through the smoke the 16th smashed into another Sikh square, the popular Sergeant Harry Newsome shouting, 'Hullo, boys, here goes for death or a commission,' and was in the act of grabbing a standard as Morris had when, according to Sergeant Gould of C Troop, he 'fell from his horse pierced by nineteen bayonet wounds.' All the officers of C Troop were killed and Sir Harry Smith, riding past the 16th, shouted, 'Well done, Sixteenth. You have covered yourselves with glory,' and ordered them to join Bere's squadron, which had reformed. In went Bere's squadron again, against another square. Morris was bleeding profusely, but took part in this charge too before the whole tattered regiment, men reeling in their saddles, capless, faces blackened with sweat and smoke, rallied for a final charge.

The 16th with infantry, cavalry and horse artillery support drove the Sikhs back to the Sutlej, slashing, thrusting and bayoneting them as they advanced. At the river the scene was chaos, Runjoor Singh's army reduced to near rabble and wallowing about in the brown, reddening water. No quarter was given. At Mudki and Ferozeshah, European troops had noted that Sikhs whose lives were spared were quite likely to shoot or stab a victor in the back. The cry 'Remember Moodkee!' was to be heard time and again during both Sikh Wars.

Sikh losses were estimated at 3,000 killed, 67 field pieces captured and all their baggage, including vital grain stores in British hands. The official British losses were 589 officers and men killed, wounded and missing, but a high proportion of these – 245 – came from the cavalry. More than a quarter of that total came from the ranks of the 16th Lancers – eighty-eight killed and fifty-three wounded. Men like Harry Smith himself, who remembered the artillery of the Napoleonic campaigns, believed the Sikhs to be more deadly and certainly more tenacious because they held their guns sacred. Smith described Aliwal as 'a little sweeping second edition of Salamanca' and left the shattered ranks of the 16th with 'God bless you, my brave boys; I love you.'[8]

Morris underestimated the casualties:

> The squadron lost 40 men killed beside the wounded ... I do not yet know the loss on either side, but we are said to have taken 70 guns and have driven the enemy across the Sutlej ... [W]e had six Officers of the Regiment wounded and two killed.

It is a matter of Morris's upbringing rather than any feelings of callousness that he neglects to mention Other Ranks in his letters. Sir Harry Smith's official report of the 16th lists:

2 officers, 56 men and 77 horses killed.
6 officers, 77 men and 33 horses wounded.
1 man and 73 horses missing.[9]

Captain Pearson, a senior Captain in Smyth's squadron, wrote home on the same day:

> We have gained a glorious victory ... but I regret to say the 16th has suffered much, more so than in any battle of the Peninsula or Waterloo. Two officers killed, Williams and Swettenham; Major Smyth severely wounded, Captain Benn hit in the face, Captain Fyler dangerously wounded, Captain Pattel shot in the face, Morris slightly hit in the face.[10]

Pearson commanded the 16th while Smyth's wound healed. The Major was very lucky, for a Sikh bayonet had hit him below the waist, jabbing part of his jacket and sword belt into the wound and the bayonet had snapped. Like the hero he genuinely was, Smyth waited until all his men had been patched up before he was attended to. He was back in the saddle in six weeks and lived for another thirty years! Among the grisly tales of Aliwal's aftermath, the story was told of Corporal Mowbray, an expert lancer and swordsman, who lay surrounded by seven dead Sikhs, his lance and sword shattered. James Lunt recounts the horrific sight of a dead Lancer, still mounted, but horizontal on the ground, he and his horse having been killed simultaneously. In the Queen's Lancers Museum is a Sikh artilleryman's sword and written on the blade and scabbard is the following:

> This sword was taken from the hand of a dead Sikh Artillery Man who was found lying close to the body of Cornet George Bigoe Williams of the 16th Queen's Lancers by Lieutenant Arnold Knight, 16th Lancers, immediately after the Battle of Aliwal, 28th January 1846. It is suggested that the Sikh and Cornet Williams struggled together as their bodies lay side by side and at some distance from the rest.[11]

Morris wrote the next day:

> We took their camp standing as it was and as we had to lie on the ground all the night, I found some of their blankets very agreeable ... I suppose we shall cross the Sutlej in a few days. I am quite well, except my eye, which will be all right again in a day or two.

In the chill night air, the lance pennons of the 16th hung stiff with Sikh blood. In memory of Aliwal and the men who died there, the regiment has continued to crimp its lance pennons to the present day.

Morris was almost certainly hit by an Indian tulwar, a curved, light, very sharp sword. His wound was probably treated by Currie, the regimental surgeon, although in the hours after a battle like Aliwal, it was not always possible for a man to be patched up by his own regiment's medical staff. There is no record of it requiring stitches, but the head was peculiarly vulnerable in a cavalry charge.

Wounded or not, the men of the 16th had to march on. The Sikhs had withdrawn north of the Sutlej except at Sobraon. Gough's lumbering siege train had now arrived and the army of the Sutlej was reunited against an extremely strong position – the enemy with their backs to the river – defended by about 20,000 Sikhs with 70 guns, again commanded by Runjoor Singh. There were more Sikh troops on the far bank and Gough attacked with between 15,000 and 20,000 men at dawn on 10 February.

Morris himself is almost silent on the events of the Battle of Sobraon. Despite having promised to 'write by every mail while we are in the enemy's country'[12] only three letters have survived (and these are second-hand transcripts from Major General White-Thomson's *Memoir*). In the letter to his family dated 16 February, he makes only a passing reference to Sobraon.

As ever, Gough bombarded the Sikh positions with his artillery and as ever, sent his infantry in to take the trenches at bayonet point. Hardinge had become increasingly alarmed by Gough's 'Tipperary Tactics' but the fact was that the Sikhs were extremely stubborn fighters and Mudki, Ferozeshah, Buddiwal and Aliwal *had* all been victories. Sobraon was not a cavalry battle, and this accounts for Morris's slight reference to it. As part of Cureton's Brigade (together with the 3rd Bengal Native Cavalry and the 4th Bengal Irregular Cavalry), the 16th Lancers were posted some miles to the right as a feigned attempt to outflank the Sikhs by crossing the river. It was therefore the left wing, the 3rd Light Dragoons, the 4th and 5th Bengal Native Cavalry led by Sir Joseph Thackwell, who offered support for the hard-pressed infantry. Thackwell had lost an arm at Waterloo and personally led the 'Moodkee Wallahs' over the parapets and earthworks of the dry ravines which the Sikhs had fortified. By midday, the battle was over, the Sikhs floundering and drowning in the river as they were forced back over the Sutlej, as men thought, for ever. Again, Gough's infantry suffered heavy casualties – 320 killed and 2,063 wounded. The bridge of boats which the Sikhs had built was partially destroyed and the power of the Khalsa likewise damaged. Lord Hardinge was to describe Sobraon as 'one of the most daring [victories] ever achieved'.

The First Sikh War ended with Sobraon. Because the British did not annex the Punjab outright, but allowed the Sikh army, by the terms of the Treaty of Lahore on 9 March, to retain 20,000 infantry and 12,000 cavalry, trouble was always likely to recur. Perhaps the very presence of the brilliant Henry Lawrence as British resident exacerbated a delicate situation. He carried out Hardinge's resolve to westernize and modernize, offending Sikhs as similar moves elsewhere had offended Hindu and Moslem. Rumnuggar, in November 1848, where 'Charlie' Cureton was killed, and Chillianwalla in January 1849, where the cavalry seems to have panicked, were grim reminders of the narrow line between success and failure.

On 16 February, Morris wrote home:

> Here we are across the Sutlej, and in the Punjab. We crossed by a bridge of boats near Ferozepur on the 14th. I was on the regimental baggage guard [which must somehow have been replenished after Buddiwal] and you cannot fancy what work I had. We made a very short march, starting at 5 a.m., but not getting in till 3 p.m. It put me in mind of driving cattle through an English fair; only I had camels and elephants to drive instead of bullocks. Gholab Singh [the 'official' Maharajah] came in to the Governor-General yesterday and was received very coolly. He got off his elephant at some distance from the Durbar tent and the Governor-General did not rise to receive him. I hear all our terms were agreed to [these were ratified at Lahore on the 20th] so I fear we shall not have the pleasure of thrashing the Sikhs again this time. I did not think they would have allowed us to go to Lahore, but I suppose the heavy loss they sustained at the last battle [Sobraon] has created a panic among them ... Kuasoor [from which he wrote] is the name of an old Mohammetan town and must have been a very strong place but the people are in such dread of the Sikhs that the Muezzin calling them to evening prayer has not been heard for more than seventy years until last evening ... I hear there are a good many wild hog on the banks of the Ravee, and I am looking forward with much pleasure to a campaign against them now the thing is said to be over.[13]

A second letter to his mother followed from Lahore, the Sikh capital, on 28 February:

> We got here on the 20th. Everything is now settled [the terms of the Treaty of Lahore, 9 March, were that all territories south of the Sutlej became British; the Sikh government could not employ any foreigners without British consent; Kashmir became a puppet state under Gulab Singh and the British Resident at Lahore, Henry Lawrence, was to be protected by a small British garrison until the end of the year] ... I went through Lahore yesterday and never was in such a dirty place. I do not wonder that cholera killed such numbers last year; there is a stream of the blackest and most offensive fluid running through the narrowest street you can fancy ... I went to the unfinished tomb of Runjeet Singh and viewed it with great respect, for I look upon him as one of the greatest men the East has produced.[14]

The rest of Morris's letter tells his mother that he had applied via McDowell to Gough for leave and that he was looking forward to the prospect of a happy summer at home. This was standard practice, especially at the termination of a campaign, and it cannot have been long before the 16th were given orders to return to England. Morris sailed in May 1846. He had served in India for three years and two months. The regiment, with Morris still with them at this stage, marched with the 31st Foot from Lahore to Calcutta on 14 March. They travelled 293 miles in twenty-three days as the heat of the season increased. On 2 April they marched out of Meerut on foot, having handed over their horses. Morris probably sold his Arab in the same place he bought it – the Meerut racecourse. The 16th Lancers embarked on the troopship *Marion* on 12 August. They had served in India for twenty-four years.

Two problems remain unsolved concerning Morris's time with the 16th. The first is the story he told to Evelyn Wood in March 1858 while Wood shared his house in Kirkee:

> During the Panjab campaign a Sikh careering in front of the 16th Lancers challenged the regiment. Cornet Morris, a serrefile, galloped out and after an exciting encounter, killed his opponent.[15]

There is no contemporary account of this. If it did happen, and bearing in mind Morris's youth, exuberance and penchant for personal combat it is entirely likely, it would probably have been in the early stages of the Aliwal engagement when the 16th were raked with enemy fire or perhaps at Buddiwal in defence of the infantry or baggage. On the other hand, such an encounter was not likely to be approved by more senior officers as a set piece out of the pell-mell of the charge, for if Morris had been killed, the effect on the morale of the 16th might have been damaging. Wood was in low spirits at the time, suffering from neuralgia of the face, and such stories may have been embellished to cheer him up.

The second and more troublesome point concerning Morris's time with the regiment is that he somehow acquired the nickname 'Slacks'. It was an age of nicknames, especially in the Army. The other ranks referred to Lord Cardigan as 'Jim the Bear', and Frederick Shewell, Colonel of the 8th Hussars in the Crimea, was 'the Old Woman'. No doubt such sobriquets were developed by the other ranks so that gossip in the horse lines would not be understood by other officers and reprimands would not be handed out. I can find no contemporary reference to 'Slacks' at all. In his biography of Louis Nolan, Hubert Moyse-Bartlett wrote:

> This was Captain William Morris, of the 17th Lancers, known to his fellow officers as the 'Pocket Hercules' on account of his barrel-like 43 inch chest and stocky physique and to the troops as 'Slacks'.[16]

Moyse-Bartlett does not give his source, nor does he imply that it was a nickname acquired specifically in the 16th. Perhaps Morris wore his overalls looser than most on account of his Indian experience, where tight uniforms would have been uncomfortable in the heat. Perhaps – and again there is no evidence – he was more lenient with his men than some officers. One other possibility exists. It seems likely from his fragmented Cambridge correspondence that Morris followed the 'Fancy' around the prize rings at Newmarket. Eric Partridge, in the *Penguin Dictionary of Historical Slang*, gives this intriguing definition of 'slack': '2. A severe or knockdown punch: boxing; C19 ex. Jack Slack, a powerful hitter.' Jack Slack it is true, predates Morris by a long time. Slack was a Norwich butcher, known as 'the Knight of the Cleaver', and held the title of Champion of England for ten years (1750–60) before being beaten by 'the Nailer', Bill Stevens. After 1760, he backed, or managed, other fighters. Although the man is much earlier than Morris, the term 'slack' is not. Is it too fanciful to suppose that the men of the 16th called him 'Slacks' because of his interest in the Fancy and because of his powerful build?

Chapter Six
The Deaths

Morris went home by the shorter overland route through the Red Sea, then across the desert by camel and donkey train to Cairo or Alexandria and on through the Mediterranean and the Atlantic. It is possible that he travelled by steam packet, putting in to Aden for coal. Here he would have had the choice of an iron omnibus, a donkey or a horse. He would also have hired a servant and guide and hampers of food, together with 'mussocks', leather bags filled with water.

Morris returned to an England in ferment. The Corn Laws, the political symbol of the power of the landed interest – the 'field of corn' – which had dominated the rising millocracy of the 'field of coal', had gone; and with them, the torn government of Robert Peel. It is not too much of an oversimplification to see the rest of the century in terms of the progressive order of industrialism against the more entrenched paternalism of the *ancien régime*.

Since 1844, increasingly alarming reports from Ireland over the state of the staple potato crop added fuel to the Corn Law fire. The Irish were starving in their tens of thousands because they could not afford seed corn – this anyway was the repealers' argument – and faced with such a prospect in England, of having to go over on a massive scale to potato production, Peel forced the repeal through. It was a sensible, humanitarian and progressive measure, though it did little for Ireland and there was a negligible effect at first on the price of bread in England. It cost Peel his career.

For the rest of Morris's life, the British government was to be largely a series of flabby, uncoordinated coalitions, responsible in large measure for the chaos of the Crimean War in the 1850s. What Morris's views were on the Corn Laws, on Peel or indeed on any political matter, remains a brick wall. Unlike many of his contemporaries who allowed themselves free rein in personal letters and diaries to family and friends, attacking people and institutions, Morris's later letters are either irrelevant to such themes or are guarded and circumspect.

His father had died the previous year and presumably by this time the columnar grave with its vaults and railings had been erected in Hatherleigh churchyard. It reads 'William Cholmley Morris of Fishleigh. Born Aug 11th 1793, Died Aug 21st 1845.' He had just celebrated his fifty-second birthday. In due course, Jane his wife and other members of the Morris family would be interred there. The 1840s witnessed something of a high water mark in funerals. It was an age of pomp and circumstance, when small fortunes were spent on black trimmings, hearses and horses, ostrich plumes, weepers, mutes and miles of crape. London funerals, of course, tended to be the most lavish, but no doubt the Morrises of Fishleigh followed the trend.

Morris did not spend long at Fishleigh. Fulford Williams, writing in 1964, and White-Thomson, in 1902, both paint a picture of a man who longed to be with his family on his beloved Hatherleigh Moor, but in fact there is little actual evidence of this. As the eldest son, Morris would inherit Fishleigh in due course, but as his mother, one brother and sisters were still living there, it would probably remain a family home for some time to come. Those brothers nearest to him in age were in South Africa and he himself was on half pay.

The institution of half pay was a means of saving money by the government. The pay of an officer was not lavish and, in any case, the capital outlay for uniform, chargers and mess bills was bound to outweigh it. Once the Sutlej campaign was over and the 16th Lancers recalled, the various allowances that Morris would have received – field allowances for the transportation of baggage, forage allowances for his horses and so on – would have ceased. Without the files of Cox and Co., whose papers for the 16th Lancers no longer exist, and any information concerning the income from the Fishleigh Estates, it is not possible to gauge Morris's financial status and how much of a financial blow half pay was. He clearly enjoyed army life, but there seemed little prospect of advancement in the 16th.

Perhaps for this reason, Morris toyed with an exchange into a (cheaper) infantry regiment, as Charles Cureton's letter, written from Simla, India on 10 September, makes clear:

> My dear Morris,
>   I readily comply with your desire for a testimonial of my opinion of you whilst under my command in the 16th lancers.
>   I have no hesitation in declaring that I have rarely met with a more promising Cavalry Officer than yourself. Your habits, temper and acquirements eminently qualify you for it. Your knowledge of, and attachment to, horses, your superiority in, and fondness for, riding and all manly exercises, your quickness of eye as to country and your ability and willingness to undergo fatigue and privation, early attracted my attention. I had full opportunity to observe them as well in cantonments as during the campaigns in Gwalior and on the Sutlej, and it is upon them that I have formed the opinion I have given above.

I should much regret for the good of the Service as well as upon your own account, that you should quit the mounted branch of the Service. Your conduct as a gentleman whilst under my command was unexceptionable, and is best shown by the universal esteem and regard of your brother officers, as well as that of your sincere friend,

Charles R. Cureton, Colonel,

Late in Command 16th Lancers.

Cureton had watched Morris grow from the greenest of subalterns to an experienced and seasoned campaigner – something of a rarity in the early Victorian army. Armed with this and whatever his next purchase price was, Morris exchanged into the 17th Lancers. The commission is not dated until 18 April 1848.

What did such an exchange mean and why did Morris choose the 17th Lancers? They were then the most junior of the cavalry regiments, stationed at the time in Dublin and a smaller establishment than the 16th. There is no correspondence regarding the exchange. Perhaps Cureton's eulogy quoted above had persuaded Morris to stay with the cavalry and perhaps, too, he felt more at home in a Lancer regiment. There may have been more personal considerations. Augustus Saltren Willett, then a Captain in the 17th, was a Devon man and it is likely that Morris knew him before he joined the regiment. Undoubtedly an overriding reason for Morris to join the 17th was simply that there was a vacancy and accordingly he took ship for Ireland.

As in 1842 there was considerable expense involved in equipping himself with uniform and other essentials. Whether he took a charger with him from Devon or bought one in what was, after all, the best horse country in Britain, we do not know. The regimental tailors were Messrs Rogers and Co. of 57 Jermyn Street, London. Unfortunately, their records from that period have long since vanished, so we are unaware of the exact cost of items. Because each regiment was unique in the way of facings and appointments, there is very little that Morris could transfer direct from the 16th to the 17th Lancers.

Fulford Williams pictures 'Slacks' as a popular new arrival, 'with his tanned face, his medals and his tales of valour'. That assumption depends on the mettle of Morris's fellow officers of the 17th; how experienced they were, how professional and in what sense they regarded such experience. The attitude of Lord Cardigan, Colonel of the 11th Hussars, towards 'Indian Officers' was well known and bordered on contempt. He cannot have been alone in his view.

Morris's new regiment had been raised in the same year as his old one – 'Annus Mirabilis', 1759. Its founder was Colonel John Hale, an able and energetic infantry officer who had been a confidant of General Wolfe, news of whose death – and his victory at Quebec – Hale had brought back from Canada. The first years of the regiment's existence are confusing. Two troops, both given the number 17, were raised by the ineffectual Lord Aberdour and were later disbanded. Hale's regiment, originally given the number 18, took up the defunct number. The Death's Head and the motto 'Or Glory' chosen by Hale have long been associated with the death of Wolfe, and the badge of course led to the late nineteenth-century nickname of the regiment, 'The Death or Glory Boys'.

Hale obtained his men from the Home Counties and the Midlands and in seventeen days had six full troops based at Coventry. This association with the city was long-lived. Many of the privates of Morris's troop in 1851 enlisted from there.

The first action seen by the regiment was in the thirteen colonies, soon to become States, in the American Revolution. The 17th were posted to Boston, where they remained for eight months, low on food and morale, before being evacuated to the relative safety of Halifax. There was no lack of heroism during the war, the 17th working alongside the 16th in the Monmouth campaign of 1778, before being assigned to the British Legion under Banastre Tarleton.

On their return to home service in 1783, the 17th were issued with the new Light Dragoon uniform and twelve years later were posted to San Domingo in an attempt to halt the colonial ambitions of revolutionary France. Yellow fever proved their major opponent. The muster roll for late 1796 shows 80 deaths from a total of 130.

Home service intervened until 1806 when the 17th, this time without horses, were posted to South America. It was a weird campaign, singularly out of joint with the times, when Napoleon dictated the pace and direction of an almost purely European war, and the regiment was back in England by January 1808. Within six weeks they were to sail for India. The various campaigns of the 17th in the subcontinent are complex. Battle and climate combined to kill off hundreds of men during their fourteen-year period of duty. Returning via St Helena in 1823, the regiment learned of its conversion to Lancers.

The 17th Light Dragoons (Lancers) received lance drill at the barracks at Chatham. By this time the nucleus of experienced men had dwindled because of the heavy toll of sickness after India and 250 new recruits tried to master the Pimlico Divisions of the lance. Carbines were removed from service and not until 1842 did non-commissioned officers receive pistols. Accoutred in this way, the regiment was commanded from 1826 by George Bingham, later Earl of Lucan, who modified the uniforms of his men and spent a fortune buying excellent horses for the 17th. Money was no object to men like Lucan, who obtained the lieutenant colonelcy for £25,000. Like his brother-in-law, Lord Cardigan, Lucan was a martinet. As commanding officer of the 17th, he shouted, bullied and punished and generally made himself detested by officers and men alike.

In 1830, in keeping with William IV's edict, 'Bingham's Dandies' adopted the scarlet jacket and also lost the moustaches they had been forced to grow in 1823.

An incident in 1843, recounted in most regimental histories of the 17th, did nothing for the regiment's reputation. While stationed in Birmingham, a troop on morning exercises approached a railway bridge. Much to the amusement of passers-by, the arrival of a train terrified the horses and the result was panic and chaos, leading to some nasty injuries. In some ways it was a prophetic 'victory' – the iron horse over the flesh – but if there was a lesson, it was lost on the cavalry spirit of the 17th, which was not to disappear until well into the twentieth century. In that year of 1843, George, Duke of Cambridge, a cousin of Victoria, became Colonel of the 17th. Their official title from then was the 17th (Duke of Cambridge's Own).

The Casual and Squad Drill Book, a leather-bound volume among the Morris papers, details members of his troop and gives us a fascinating, unpublished vignette of life in a cavalry regiment in the middle of the nineteenth century. The book itself, intended as a manual for officers, was written by M D C St Quintin, Lieutenant Colonel Commanding, and printed by William Frazer, Army printer, at 37 Arran-Quay, Dublin, and is dated April 1851.

The average weight carried by a troop horse in complete marching order is specified in the book as set out below:

	st	lb	oz
Average of Men	10	10	0
Dress cap	0	2	0
Dress jacket with Epaulettes, Girdle and Lines	0	4	2
Pouch belt (10 rounds of Ammunition)	0	2	11
Sword and belts	0	5	8
Lance	0	4	0
Pistol	0	3	4
Valise packed according to Regimental Regulations, with corn sack and nose bag	1	6	7
Cloak	0	8	8
Saddle, bridle, Collar and Chain, Horse Log, Curry Comb and Brush, Blacking, Oil Tin and Picker	2	7	8
Shabracque and Sheepskin	0	7	8
Horse Blanket	0	8	0
Total average weight of the Lancer in Complete Marching Order	17	13	8

Length of Lance: 9 feet; Length of Sling: 1 foot 3 inches; Breadth of Tying: $2^1/_2$ inches.

The method of packing the valise comes next. In the near-end were the 'necessaries' – drawers, shirt, socks, towels, shoe-brushes, hair-comb and brush, clothes brush and hold-all. In the off-end, overalls, vest, another shirt and a spare pair of socks. For so much to fit in so small a space required practice and a meticulous following of orders. The implication is that *all* lancers carried a pistol, whereas many reference works imply that only sergeants and above were issued with them, and the spare holster contained horse log, curry comb and brush.

In the barracks a similarly exacting method of layout of kit was demanded:

	Head of Bed-Stead	
	Valice on top of Bed	
LEFT SIDE	CENTRE	RIGHT SIDE
1 Flannel Jacket	Girdle	1 Shirt
1 Pr Cotton Drawers	Holdall Complete	1 do.
1 Pair socks	(inc. small book)	1 Towel
1 Pair do.	Tin of Blacking	1 do.
1 Gauntlet	Hair Comb and Brush	1 Pair Gloves
1 do.		

Button Stick
2 Pairs Straps
2 Sponges
1 Boot and Spur, Surcingle folded; 1 Boot and Spur between the boots
Horse Brush and Curry Comb
Oil Tin, Hoof Pick and Brush Bag

NOTE: Shirts and Flannels to be neatly folded, with the mark uppermost; Brushes with the mark up; Gauntlet with Gloves uppermost.

The prices of these necessaries are listed next and the Bounty – £5. 15s. 6d. plus £1. 2s. for cavalry equipment, making a total of £6. 17s. 6d. for the recruit on joining. The recruit therefore began his life with the 17th with a bounty of £9 eroded to 16s. 5d.!

Perhaps it says something about the British cavalry at this time that only on page 11, *after* all this regimentation to do with kit and its layout, are instructions for grooming listed. The order ran that when the horse had been out, its feet were to be picked and washed. It was then brushed, beginning with the neck, shoulder, chest and forelegs, then body, belly, quarter and hind legs, near side first, then offside. Damp hay was then rubbed over the animal in the same order of succession. Once in its stall, the horse's mane and tail were to be sponged and brushed, as well as the nostrils, ending with 'Collar up' when dock and tail were attended to. There are special instructions for different seasons, for example, the coating season, spring and autumn, when the brush was only used on legs, mane and tail.

Officers of troops and especially captains of troops (as Morris became by 1851) were expected to be totally familiar with the current state of the troop, the heights and ages of men and horses, the rate of daily pay, the number on furlough or in hospital, the marital status of the men, any sleeping out of barracks or in custody, either in the guard room or with the civilian authorities and much more. All this was to be learned and St Quintin expected answers to any such questions without reference to the Squad Book. The total number of men listed is in fact sixty-six, although the number in response to the Abstract of Answers is sixty-five. There were ten sergeants, three corporals, two trumpeters and forty-nine privates. The daily rate of pay for regimental sergeant major was 3s. 7d.; for troop sergeant major, 3s. 1d.; for sergeant, 2s. 3d.; for corporal, 1s. 8½d.; for privates, 1s. 4d.; and for boys under fifteen, 10d. This rate included beer money to all except the boys. Although comparisons are difficult, a farm labourer in 1851 might expect to earn about the same as a private, but of course his wages varied with the season and even the weather and he was subject to the lottery of the Mop or Hiring Fair. Labouring men in great demand such as navvies (though perhaps already past their heyday) might command as much as a troop sergeant major.

When Morris compiled the Squad Book, there were two men sick in hospital and they were stopped 10d. a day from their pay.

A number of men were employed on the staff of a regiment in a variety of capacities: Sergeant Thomas Hughes was in the Pay Office; Sergeant John Eccleshall in the hospital; Sergeant James in the Orderly Room; Sergeant Gough was the schoolmaster; Sergeant James Tuffin was Armourer (and incidentally was reduced to private in 1855); and Sergeant James Scarfe was a saddler. Private Aston worked as a tailor and Privates Burnes, Duff, Flowers and Palethorpe were servants (batmen) to various officers, one of them presumably to Morris himself.

No one was on escort duty or furlough or recruiting drives when Morris compiled the Squad Book. Neither were they in custody for offences, either regimental or civilian. Six men were receiving good conduct pay at 1d. per day, three at 2d. and one at 3d. It was the beginning of the psychology in the British Army of rewarding good behaviour rather than simply relying on the deterrent of the lash to ensure discipline. No one was sleeping out of barracks, and the 68th Clause of the Mutiny Act is inserted in the book by St Quintin to remind troop officers of billeting arrangements when the regiment was on the march.

Of the troop horses, eighteen were geldings and twenty-six mares, thirteen of them English and thirty-one Irish. The 'official' range of ages available for animals in the 17th was from three years to fifteen. Their height range was 15 to 16 hands and their daily rations amounted to 12 pounds of hay, 8 of straw and 10 of oats.

I make no apology for quoting extensively from Morris's Squad Book in that it gives the closest view of the men with whom he worked and a fascinating insight into the sort of men who became soldiers in the mid-nineteenth century. It is worth pointing out that various details set out in the Squad Book either confirm or contradict the monumental *Honour the Light Brigade*, representing twenty years of research by Canon Lummis, still the most detailed survey of the 'Six Hundred'. Clearly, Lummis did not have access to the Morris Papers and the evidence presented here for the first time will I hope be valued by aficionados of the Light Brigade.

Regimental Sergeant Major John Chadwick Number 451, was thirty-four years old, 5 feet 10 inches tall and weighed 11 stone 4 pounds. He had served for fifteen and a half years, enlisting at Manchester in July 1835. A former clerk, he was married and rode horse Number 37. By the time of the Crimean War, Chadwick had been elevated to Cornet (27 February 1852) and, typical of intelligent men from the ranks, had the post of Adjutant.

Number 493 Troop Sergeant Major Abraham Ranson seems to have been particularly close to Morris. He is referred to specifically in at least two of Morris's letters and headed the list of affidavits produced to back Morris's claim to the Victoria Cross in 1856. He was thirty-two at the time of the Squad Book, 5 feet 10 inches tall, weighed 13 stone and had served for fourteen and a half years. A former tailor and married, he had enlisted in November 1836 at Bury St Edmunds. After the Charge of the Light Brigade, his career took a downward turn. He was reduced to sergeant on 10 November 1854 and to private on 4 December 1854. The citation for his Sardinian War Medal reads, 'Was present at the battles of the Alma, where he distinguished himself; Balaklava, where he again distinguished himself by engaging and cutting down a Russian officer; and Inkerman; Siege of Sebastopol. Was never absent from the regiment.' He died less than a year after Morris, on 11 June 1859, at Gwalior.

Sergeant Major Thomas Hughes was forty-two, the oldest man in the troop. He had enlisted in March 1832 at Ballincolig, Ireland, was 5 feet 10 inches, weighed 11 stone 2 pounds and was married. He was born at Carrick-on-Suir, County Donegal, and had been a clerk prior to his enlistment. His wife Anne shared the lot of the barrackroom with the other army wives and children. He had been tried once by general court martial, but there is no space in the Squad Book for any details of proceedings.

Trumpet Major Henry Joy had enlisted in London in May 1833, as a bandboy. He was thirty-five years old, 5 feet 9 inches in height, weighed 10 stone 13, was married and is formerly listed by Morris as a musician. He had been appointed Trumpet Major in September 1847 and was in charge of the band at Wellington's funeral on 12 November 1852. At Balaclava, Joy was Orderly Trumpeter to Lucan and sounded the Charge of the Heavy Brigade on his bugle. He subsequently rode that charge and had two horses shot from under him. Later, despite a wound, he carried a flag of truce into the Russian lines and appeared before General Liprandi.

Sergeant Gough, the schoolmaster, listed by Morris as a factor (travelling salesman) prior to enlistment, was thirty-nine, 5 feet 9 inches tall and weighed 12 stone 10 pounds. He had served for seventeen and a quarter years and was married with two children, a boy and a girl. Like Joy, he had received one general court martial.

Sergeant James Tuffin, Number 806, had enlisted in March 1846 at Brighton. He was only twenty-three (very young for a sergeant) and an armourer by trade, which probably accounts for his rapid promotion, to fill a need within the troop. Like Morris, he was 5 feet 7, weighed 11 stone 4 pounds and was married with one son. He had faced a general court martial.

Sergeant James Scarfe was thirty-five. He had enlisted at Ipswich in September 1836, stood 5 feet 8$\frac{1}{2}$ inches, weighed 12 stone 3 pounds and was married with three children, two boys and a girl. His former occupation was that of saddler, tailor-made for the cavalry. Badly wounded in the Charge of the Light Brigade, he was among those visited by Queen Victoria at the Brompton Barracks, London, on 3 March 1855. He was unhorsed in the Charge and escaped by grabbing a Cossack mount, but he had ten sword wounds to his body, including head, neck, thigh and both hands as well as impaired sight.

Sergeant John Eccleshall was twenty-five. He had enlisted at Birmingham in December 1843, was Morris's height, weighed 11 stone and was single. He had been a clerk prior to enlistment.

Sergeant James had enlisted in Dublin in May 1849, at twenty-two the youngest of the sergeants. He stood 5 feet 8 inches, weighed 10 stone 2 pounds and was single. He is also one of the very few to have 'none' listed under trade prior to enlistment.

It is very telling that others in this category also came from famine-haunted Ireland. Number 556 Sergeant Edward Talbot, who was to be decapitated in the Charge, was thirty-two when the Squad Book was compiled and had enlisted at Coventry in April 1838. He was 5 feet 9$\frac{3}{4}$, 11 stone 5 pounds, single and a buttonmaker before enlistment.

Sergeant William Jekyll had been a clerk, enlisting in London in January 1842. He was twenty-nine, weighed 11 stone 4, stood 5 feet 9$\frac{1}{4}$ inches tall and was single. He rode horse Number 5.

Corporal Allen was thirty-one, had joined the regiment in June 1836 from Ipswich, stood 5 feet 11$\frac{1}{2}$ inches, weighed 13 stone 4 pounds, was single and had been a clerk in civilian life.

Number 961 Corporal William Wallace Graham, like the other Irishmen, had claimed no trade prior to enlistment in June 1848 at Dublin. He was twenty (young for a corporal), stood 5 feet 8 inches, weighed 11 stone 1 and was single. He was eventually to reach the rank of captain before retiring on a pension in 1878.

Corporal William Purviss had been broken to private by the time he rode the Charge. He had enlisted in August 1846 at Armagh, was single, and, very unusually in rural Ireland at that time, had the job of factory guider prior to enlistment. He was twenty-three when the Squad Book was drawn up, stood 5 feet 8$^1/_2$ inches and weighed 10 stone 13. He was wounded in the Charge, but lived to become Sergeant Major and Drill Instructor to the Walsall Troop of the Staffordshire Yeomanry between 1870 and 1888.

Last of the corporals is Joseph Reilly, who despite Irish ancestry had enlisted in Coventry in May 1846. He was a Private again by the time of the Charge, was twenty-one in 1851, stood 5 feet 7, weighed 11 stone 4 and is listed rather grandiosely as a veterinary surgeon. He had received one district court martial.

Trumpeter Charles Kidby was, at 5 feet 6$^3/_4$ inches, the smallest man in Morris's troop. A musician prior to enlistment at Brighton in 1845, he was an Irishman born in Ballincolig, weighed 9 stone 2 and was single. He died in a regimental hospital in June 1855, only six days after his arrival in the Crimea.

Last of all is the decidedly enigmatic 'Jones', no rank or serial number. It is likely he is Trumpeter Thomas Jones, listed as Private Number 743. Morris says he rode horse Number 45, was a farrier prior to enlistment in about 1842 and he died on his way to India in January 1859.

It would be tedious to recount the rest of the troop in such detail, but some deserve note. There was George Broom, thirty-three, who had enlisted from Ipswich in 1836. He appears to have been one of the 17th's rogues, having been tried twice by regimental court martial and listed as single with one son! He was to be killed in the Charge at Balaclava. Thomas Davis was twenty-six, a brass toolmaker prior to enlistment. He wrote letters to his mother from the Crimea, which have survived, and in the Charge his haversack was blown from his side by a shell fragment. He died at sea in September 1858 on his way home from India. George Dunn, the Irishman listed as butcher prior to enlistment, who had joined at Dublin in 1838, holds the record of courts martial for the troop – one district and four regimental.

George Flowers, who was thirty-four, had enlisted at Coventry. He was born in Beccles, Suffolk, and was an iron founder before enlistment. His wife Elizabeth accompanied the regiment to the Crimea, where her husband, who had two good conduct badges, was killed in the Charge. Samuel Hunscott, Number 944, was a servant prior to joining the 17th in January 1848. He was one of those who signed affidavits regarding Morris's actions in the Charge and so must have ridden it himself. He died at Jhansi, India, on 22 October 1859.

James Ikin Nunnerly, enlisting at Dundalk in July 1846, was a draper in civilian life. He was twenty-three, 6 feet tall and weighed 12 stone 4 pounds. By the year after Morris compiled his Squad Book, Nunnerly was promoted Corporal and in this capacity attended Wellington's funeral. He was discharged as sergeant in 1857 and retired as Sergeant Major of the Lancashire Hussars in 1881, opening a draper's shop in Moor Street, Ormskirk.

John Vahey, the colourful butcher of the 17th who rode the Charge in his bloody apron, was a labourer prior to enlistment in March 1838 at Wigan. He was thirty-one in 1851 (the same age as Morris), 5 feet $9^1/_2$ inches tall, 12 stone 7 pounds in weight and was married. By the time the regiment reached India to quell the Mutiny, Vahey had acquired a reputation as a drinker and earned extra money by digging graves. He died of cholera on the march to Secunderbad on 8 March 1860 and was buried in one of his own graves.

Of the troop horses, three were grey (one was that of Henry Joy, the Trumpet Major, a typical colour for buglers' horses), one black, the others bay, chestnut or brown. Virtually all were bought locally in Ireland. The largest was Thomas Dunn's grey, at 16 hands $1^1/_2$ inches; the smallest at 15 hands were Wragg's chestnut and Ratcliff's bay. The animals' ages on joining ranged from two years to four.

Although it is always dangerous to make generalizations from so small a statistical field, Morris's troop does furnish the historian with interesting data. The average age on enlistment was eighteen. The average age of the men in 1851 was twenty-seven, but there were six men in the troop over thirty-five and the two eldest were both forty-two. The average height of the men was 5 feet $8^1/_4$ inches, only half an inch taller than the *pocket* Hercules, and their average weight 10 stone 13 pounds, giving the lie to the undernourished, vitamin-deficient figures which many historians have assumed existed in the Army at this time. Admittedly, the cavalry were more selective then the infantry in the bearing and appearance of their recruits. Louis Nolan, in his books on cavalry which were to make their appearance soon afterwards, advocated that the height of the true light cavalryman ought to be no more than 5 feet 4 inches. The tallest man in the troop was 6 feet and $^1/_2$ an inch, the shortest 5 feet $6^3/_4$ quarter inches (this was Private Kidby, who was also the lightest at 9 stone 2 pounds, and who had enlisted earlier than anybody, as a trumpeter at the age of thirteen). Seventeen of the troop were married – these tended to be the older men and the non-commissioned officers – and forty-seven were single. Not much faith can be placed in the last statistic. Morris's entry on Broom as being single with one son underlines the fact that marriage among the rank and file was not a necessary institution and that army women often felt more loyalty to a particular regiment than to a particular man.

Occupations prior to enlistment provide a fascinating spotlight on the social scene of the 1830s and 1840s, when most of the enlistment took place. As might be expected, labourers form the bulk (twelve) but next come the rather unexpected clerks (seven), again pointing the difference between the general educational standards of the cavalry and the infantry. Six of Morris's troop had been servants, three butchers and three – all of them Irish – unemployed. Other than that, the range is quite astonishing – armourer, bleacher, bootmaker, brass tool maker, brickmaker, buttonmaker, draper, engine fitter, engraver, factor, factory guider, farmer, farrier, file cutter, fishmonger, gardener, iron founder, miller, musician, painter, saddler, shoemaker, shopman, slater, stonemason, tailor, warehouseman and weaver. Many of the trades listed above are clear evidence that it was by no means only country bumpkins who took the Queen's shilling at county fairs, but men of some education and skill. It must be remembered that the period of enlistment under consideration coincided with economic depression – the Hungry Forties – which had seen increasing unemployment since the mid-1830s; and simply because a man claimed a skill or trade does not mean he was actually employed at the time of enlistment – and if he was, we know nothing about his financial state.

An interesting snippet from the Morris Papers has a bearing on the facts and figures gleaned from his troop. From the Royal Barracks, Dublin, on 8 March 1848, Regimental Sergeant Major Thomas Taylor wrote: 'I certify that I measured Mr Morris this morning and found him a trifle above five feet seven and three quarter inches.' I am unaware of the tradition of measuring *officers* as opposed to men within a regiment, but the fact that it was done, coupled with Evelyn Wood's later reference to Morris's 43-inch chest and his colossal strength, may well have given rise to the nickname the 'Pocket Hercules' among the officers of the 17th.

Ireland when Morris and the 17th were stationed there was a land seething with discontent and hatred of the English. The Irish Question was very much in the forefront of people's minds as 1846 and 1847 saw the height of the 'Great Hunger' in which hundreds of thousands of Irish men, women and children died of starvation in their mud hovels or were forced by abject poverty to flee to England or America. The appalling stories which reached the press and parliament were disbelieved by some. The more informed, like Lord Palmerston, who was an atypical absentee landlord, knew them to be true and he personally paid the passage for many of his tenants to begin a new life in the United States.

A new nationalism had arisen, particularly the Young Ireland movement, led by the MP William Smith O'Brien. Like everyone else who formed the Irish bloc in the Commons, Smith reported with indignation the revolting spectacle in Limerick of people eating potatoes the English would not have fed to their pigs. The Young Ireland leaders in the end turned out to be more theorists and pamphleteers than anything else. O'Brien himself did not want armed rebellion but his followers became carried away by the events on the Continent in 1848 – the Year of Revolutions.

'Then up with the barricades and invoke the God of battles,' wrote Meagher, another Young Irelander.[1] Their newspaper, *The United Irishman*, gave instructions in urban guerrilla warfare in Dublin, where the 17th Lancers were stationed. Windowpots, furniture, logs and pokers were to be thrown from buildings onto troops below. Broken glass was to be scattered in the streets to foil the cavalry. Soldiers were to be lured into alleyways, where boiling water and grease as well as home-made grenades could be hurled at them.

On 15 March, O'Brien spoke at a rally in the Music Hall in Abbey Street, Dublin, calling for the creation of an armed national guard and reminding those who cared to listen that one-third of the British Army was composed of Irishmen. Taking his tub-thumping seriously, the authorities had sent 10,000 troops onto the Dublin streets by the summer, the 17th among them. Two warships hovered off the coast in case of a spread of rebellion. In the event, O'Brien's rebellion was a damp squib. He himself was tried for sedition in May and acquitted by a Quaker judge. Of the revolutionary clubs which the movement tried to establish throughout Ireland it is probable that no more than eighty existed, totally uncoordinated. By July, O'Brien's vaunted 50,000 men, if they ever existed, had been reduced to fifty and he wept 'silent tears of shame and despair'.

It is only with hindsight that O'Brien's rebellion can be dismissed so easily. The sheer numbers of troops involved in Dublin, Cork and elsewhere indicated that the government was taking it all very seriously. They suffered from the age-old problem of governments – not being able to keep their ears sufficiently to the ground and therefore tending to over-react. The cavalry in particular were on constant standby, ready to ride to the sound of guns. 'Aiding the Civil Power' was the least pleasant of the cavalry's duties and it must have been made worse by the number of Irishmen in the 17th; some, in Morris's troop, from the very towns which O'Brien claimed were most loyal to him.

It was with relief all round that the 17th came home in 1850 to attend the first manoeuvres at the newly established camp at Chobham Ridges in Surrey. It was an irony that for many these all-important wargames came too late.

Chapter Seven

The Staff College and Amelia

The first letter that Morris wrote to his father on his arrival in India spoke of his intention to join the Senior Department at Sandhurst, as he saw it as a means 'to a good appointment'. It is doubtful whether in 1843 many officers shared his view and it is this more than anything else that separated Morris from most of his contemporaries – the ardent professional from the casual amateurs. Sandhurst's reputation left much to be desired and so was shunned by the majority. Such things were all right for the 'inferior' types who entered the Artillery or Engineers, and the 'Shop' at Woolwich trained them accordingly, but it would not do for true gentlemen. As long as this attitude prevailed, Sandhurst's reputation was not likely to improve.

There was no shortage of military academies in France and other European states, but in England there was no substitute for the real thing, so young men who wanted such a career joined their regiment. Arthur Wellesley, the future Duke of Wellington, for instance, was forced to go to a French Academy at Angers because of the absence of such an institution in this country. Even there, it must be admitted, Wellesley received a gentleman's education, rather than an officer's.

It was undoubtedly the pressures of war against Revolutionary France which prompted Lieutenant Colonel John Gaspard Le Marchant of the 7th Light Dragoons to contemplate a school for the training of cavalry and infantry officers. Le Marchant was a native of Jersey and very like Morris in the sense of his fierce professionalism. Like Morris he joined the 16th Light Dragoons as Cornet and in 1795 wrote a report for their Lordships at the Horse Guards entitled *Rules and Regulations for the Sword Exercise of the Cavalry*, which was adopted the same year and became the official manual; it was still in vogue fifty years later in the Crimea. The manual was subsequently criticized as being too constricting, and survivors of the Light Brigade in October 1854 complained that the Russians were not following the precise cuts outlined in it! But the average soldier of Le Marchant's day was poorly educated, if at all, and probably illiterate. The whole of military science dictated that parade ground formations and battlefield manoeuvres could only be performed by rote and continual mindless practice.

A Royal Warrant recognizing the Royal Military College was provided on 24 June 1801, although it had been in existence at High Wycombe for nearly two years. A second Warrant of January 1802 stated the aims of the Senior Department:

> To instruct commissioned officers who have served a specified number of years with their regiments, in the scientific parts of their profession, in view of enabling them the better to discharge their duties when acting in command of their regiments and qualifying them for employment in the Quartermaster-General's and Adjutant-General's departments.[1]

The whole institution, Junior and Senior Departments, moved to the village of Sandhurst in Berkshire in 1821, when new regulations were devised which still pertained in Morris's time.

When William Morris entered the Senior Department in January 1849, the place was bleak and barren, with a few small hamlets in the vicinity of the college. For Morris, after Cambridge and his service with the 16th in India and the 17th in Ireland, this must have represented 'slumming', because the Senior Department had no Mess. The proximity of London and the Army and Navy Club (which Morris had joined in 1842) with its heady social life made up for this in part and some officers were frequently absent as a result. Those who stayed on site were expected, a little unreasonably perhaps, to muck in like the Juniors, who were after all schoolboys. No official games were played but naturally hunting was popular. A Mr Garth became Master of Sir John Cope's pack in 1850 and rabbits and snipe were plentiful on the open heathland.

The Senior Department by the time Morris joined it was really only an appendage of the Junior Department. The establishment was made up of fifteen officers, each of whom had to be over twenty-one years of age and to have served either for three years abroad or four years at home. Written testimonials for entry had to be submitted to the Governor of the College, the septuagenarian Lieutenant General George Scovell, and the names of hopefuls were selected, the average time taken between application and admission being two and a half years. There were no entrance examinations before February 1858 and the course lasted for two years with a six-month reduction for those who had passed through the Junior Department. Morris technically completed it in a year and ten months, the certificate awarded on 9 November 1850.

The annual subscription was 30 guineas, along with £2 to be paid on admission as a donation to the college library. Quarters, such as they were, were provided free, whether in the Terrace or York Town. Soldier servants were allowed to accompany their masters, though because of lack of space this was discouraged. We must assume that these quarters were rather inferior to Morris's staircase at Cambridge. A forage allowance for one charger was provided for field sketching to those who had made sufficient progress. Other than cash and the testimonials referred to above, the only entrance requirements were that officers had to have mastered the elements of plane geometry and to have a thorough acquaintance with common arithmetic.

The working hours in the Halls of Study or in the field were from 10 a.m. to 3 p.m. but most of the work was done privately in quarters. The syllabus was reminiscent of Morris's Cambridge course. In the first six months (there were examinations half-yearly) he studied the first six books of Euclid. What was different from Cambridge was the additional study of permanent fortifications and the work of Vauban, the foremost military engineer in the early modern period. His designs and practical constructions could be found all over Europe in the eighteenth and nineteenth centuries. He pioneered the ricochet shot and the ring bayonet, and left a vast body of literature for succeeding generations to digest.

The second six months was given over to the rest of Euclid, practical geometry on the ground, plane trigonometry and mensuration. Field and permanent fortifications continued and a sketch had to be produced under the fortifications professor. In the third half-yearly period field fortifications were completed, algebra and spherical trigonometry were explored, and private, squad and trail sketches took place. In the final six months, conic sections and practical astronomy were studied, as well as the attack and defence of fortresses and the final sketch. Between early March and May and again between September and November prior to the vacations, Morris received practical instruction in the tracing and throwing up of field works and mining and sapping. Any officer who failed in the examinations was returned to his regiment.

Virtually the whole of this instruction was provided by another septuagenarian, Professor John Narrien, FRS FRAS. He had been at Sandhurst for thirty-two years by the time Morris arrived, officially designated Professor of Mathematics, Fortification and Astronomy in 1824. He was popular and respected – 'that highly talented and beloved mathematician', 'one of the best, the most amiable, the most talented and scientific of men', 'a man who unites extraordinary ability with uncommon uprightness of character'. Though a civilian himself, he mastered the complexities of fortification, had an observatory built for astronomy, and designed Fort Narrien, which was constructed later behind the college buildings by the Royal Engineers.

Morris's certificate, signed by Scovell, Taylor, the Lieutenant Governor, and Colonels Wetherall and Prosser, is glowing and indicates that he had achieved something out of the ordinary, although the ordinary was not of a particularly high standard. The certificate after 1836 was modified by three classes. Morris had clearly grown up since his prankish student escapades shinning over the cloister wall at St John's. Sadly, many of his contemporaries had not. A commission in the 1850s commented upon: 'Absence and irregular attendances, frivolous and childish conduct when present at lectures; and inattention to the drawing required by regulation.'[2] It was the old story of men who had seen action – or at least active service – finding it difficult to adjust to being once again on the 'other side of the desk'.

> At a half-yearly examination held this day [9 November 1850] Lieutenant W. Morris, 17th Lancers, a student at the Senior Department ... appeared before the Board; and having passed an Examination in the several branches of study appointed for Officers of the Senior Department, to the satisfaction of the Board: and it having been stated by the Governor, that his general conduct at the college, as well as his application to study, has been such as to merit approbation; the Board judge him to be deserving of this their certificate and recommendation to the favourable notice of His Grace the Commander in Chief.

Wellington's title has been inked in by hand, as has the following:

> And Lieutenant Morris having not only acquitted himself with the greatest credit in this examination in the prescribed course of studies, but having also extended his acquirements beyond its limits into the highest branches of mathematical science, the Board desire, by recording this fact, in a special addition to their certificate, to mark their sense of his superior merits and talents.

Impressive as this is, it must be asked how useful a first-class certificate with additional honours was in 1850. It is likely that when Morris obtained his Staff appointment in the spring of 1854, he did so on the strength of his Indian experience and not because of the acquisition of a piece of paper. Such was the low prestige of the Senior Department in the eyes of most officers, including very probably Wellington himself, that it may even have been regarded as a handicap. Of 216 officers who held Military College Certificates between 1836 and 1854, only 20 ever obtained staff posts. In 1852, only seven officers on the Staff had passed through the Senior Department. Hart's Army Lists outline the reason for this – the age and conservatism of senior officers. Collectively suspicious of both reform and education, they rallied under Wellington and sat out the 'long peace'. In the early 1850s, thirteen generals still on the active service list had over seventy years' experience and their average age was eighty-eight – only seven were under fifty-eight.

Genuine concern could be levelled at the Senior Department in that the syllabus was ludicrously narrow, hidebound by mathematical studies. In fact, the Staff roles which Morris was to fill, those of Assistant Quartermaster General and Assistant Adjutant General, bore no relationship at all to what he had learned at Sandhurst.

Part of the problem was that the role of Staff Officer was curiously ill-defined. Indeed, the importance of a staff of trained officers whose job it was to plan campaigns and prepare for any eventuality was lost on the military amateurs of the Army in the mid-century. Once again it smacked of professionalism and once again it was taboo. It is significant that the Prussian General Staff dates from 1813; the British from 1904. As part of the welter of criticisms levelled against the Army over the conduct of the Crimean campaign, Sidney Herbert lashed the Senior Department in the House on 5 June 1856:

> The Senior Department ... has languished because, during peace, you have not taken officers from it for the Staff ... There has been no proper staff employment and there having been no great necessity for good Staff Officers the Senior Department at Sandhurst has lost its prizes and with them, its efficiency.[3]

In William Morris, the British Army had another John Le Marchant, another ardent professional. On leaving Sandhurst he ought to have been given an immediate staff appointment and given a job to do which suited his talents and experience; to help the Army shake off the cobwebs of thirty-five years of idleness and laurel-resting. Instead, because the Army was run by crusty geriatrics who mistrusted education, who mistrusted 'Indian' officers and who mistrusted youth, all he could do was to return to the 17th Lancers, where his talents were confined to one troop and the endless parade ground rituals.

*****

Amelia Taylor, the girl who became Mrs William Morris in April 1852, is a shadowy figure. This is partly due to the vagaries of historical chance – the random survival of photographs, letters, keepsakes. It also reflects the status of women, particularly officers' wives, in this period. They were not Dora Copperfield-like simps. Many of them were tough, independent and brave. Not only the obvious examples of Victorian womanhood like Florence Nightingale and Fanny Duberly, both of whom Morris was to meet in the Crimea, but the more anonymous ladies who perished with their children in their quarters at Cawnpore, were women of such mettle. But with the notable exception of the few like the extraordinary Creole adventuress, Mary Seacole, who put her experiences into print, they were also quiet, respectful, taught all their lives to know their place, hold their tongues (at least in public) and to be adornments to their menfolk.

Amelia's father was Major General Thomas William Taylor, who was Lieutenant Governor of Sandhurst in Morris's time and although there is no tangible proof, it is possible that he exerted quite an influence on Morris in a variety of ways. Born in 1782 at Coombe Royal, Devon, Taylor was the grandson of another Thomas, who had run the estate at Denbury and who with Sir Thomas Carew, the owner of the Haccombe estate nearby, dominated as gentry the south of the county. Across Dartmoor lay the Fishleigh and Inwardleigh Estates soon to be acquired by the Morrises. It is possible that those families – the county set – knew each other, but no credence can be lent to Peter Carew's claim in *Combat and Carnival* that Morris and Amelia were childhood sweethearts, as Taylor wrote to another old friend, Trevor Wheler, to ask if he thought Morris was suitable material for a son–in–law.

By 1830, Taylor was a veteran of Waterloo and superintendent of the Cavalry Riding Establishment at St John's Wood, where his most famous son, Reynell, was born. He hated this post and became Inspector of Yeomanry at a crucial time, for such units were on permanent standby to 'aid the Civil Power' at the time of the Reform Bill agitation. Taylor was made Groom of the Bedchamber in 1833 by his friend the Duke of Clarence, now William IV, and remained a confidant of the king until the latter's death in 1837, when he obtained a full colonelcy and was appointed Lieutenant Governor at Sandhurst under George Scovell. In Victoria's Coronation Honours List, Taylor was made Companion of the Order of the Bath.

How instrumental Taylor was in Morris's life we cannot now say, but as Lieutenant Governor he was in a position to exert some influence not only over Morris's decision to join the Senior Department but perhaps behind the scenes in getting him in. This in no way denigrates Morris or belittles his own achievements. Independent sources like Narrien were clearly impressed by him. But it was still an age of influence and patronage. Taylor himself had risen on those terms and he presumably saw no reason to stint any help he could give to ambitious young men coming after him. By 1845, he was a Major General and a powerful man. In one respect, however, Morris had beaten him to it – Taylor became Colonel of the 17th Lancers in 1852, by which time Morris had been with the regiment for five years.

Something of the magic of Amelia's Devon childhood is hinted at in Chapter 1, from the biography of her big brother Reynell by Gambier Parry. The sisters adored their brother and girls like Amelia had been taught to be subservient to men, be it their fathers, brothers or future husbands. They had also been instilled with the idea that to die an old maid, on the shelf, was somehow a symptom of failure in their entire education, in themselves.

Taylor's eldest daughter, Ann, had married the boorish but wealthy Sir Walter Carew, now himself master of Haccombe. His second daughter, Harriet, had likewise married a local squire, William Fortescue of Fallapit, who in that county of huntsmen kept a pack of hounds and shot pheasant. His third daughter, Georgina, married Lord Willoughby de Broke, later Earl of Warwick. It was left to Amelia Mary Margaret, the fourth daughter, to marry the suitor who was to become most famous, Morris himself. By coincidence, Amelia's little sister, Eliza, was to marry another survivor of the Light Brigade, Robert Portal of the 4th Light Dragoons, in 1856.

In what may have been a whirlwind romance, Morris and Amelia were married on 13 April 1852. It is likely that the couple had known each other for some time, but the form of their courtship is utterly unknown. There are no references to Amelia in the Morris Papers before the wedding and he does not seem to have corresponded with her.

The Annual Register for 1852 reads:

> 13th April, At Sandhurst, Berks, William Morris Capt. in HM 17th Lancers, and of Fishleigh House, Devon, to Amelia Mary, fourth daughter of Major General Taylor, CB.

The venue was the parish church of St Michael at Sandhurst in the County of Berkshire, but the officiating vicar was Henry Taylor, the Rector of South Pool, Devon, some twenty miles from Ogwell. He was Amelia's uncle, and also present was her elder brother, Fitz, who was Rector of East and West Ogwell. Morris, who is described as a bachelor of full age, was a Captain in the 17th Lancers, residing at the time of his marriage with his regiment at Canterbury. His father is listed, though dead some seven years, as William Cholmley Morris, Esq. Amelia Mary Margaret Taylor, spinster, also of full age, resided at Sandhurst, and Thos. William Taylor, her father, is described as Lieutenant Governor Royal Military College. The witnesses were W T Carew (Walter, Ann's husband), Ann Carew (Amelia's elder sister), Fitzwilliam J Taylor, H Taylor, the vicar, and an A Taylor, who must be Arthur, Amelia's second eldest brother and a Captain in the Royal Artillery. A E Hardinge, Captain in the Coldstream Guards, was 'the bridegroom's man' and he and Robert J Barnard were the other witnesses. The local schoolchildren turned out in new clothes for the occasion, lining the road to the little church, waving flags and throwing flowers. Reynell, the darling of the family, was not present but returned home from India, after twelve years' service, on 9 July. All those members of the family then in England went to meet him and it is likely that Mr and Mrs Morris joined this group, as well as the other social events of the season – the Ascot Races in June, the great camp and review at Chobham (brainchild of Prince Albert), when, according to Eliza Taylor, 'Uncle Willy forgot to ask the vicar to say Grace before lunch in the tent of the 17th and so asked him to do it at the end!'

Where the Morrises spent their honeymoon has gone unrecorded. Morris was now a Captain, having purchased the rank in April 1851, and would have had to spend more time with his troop. Time, however, was short. Ominous rumblings throughout 1852 and 1853 heralded another turn in the Eastern Question which haunted Europe throughout the century and was not to be answered finally until the Armageddon of the Great War, a war which neither Major General Taylor nor Captain Morris would have understood.

The Taylor clan met for a splendid Christmas at Haccombe in 1853 and the Morrises were with them, but early in the New Year the old man caught a severe cold, and died on 8 January of inflammation of the lungs, his favourite son Reynell, his 'Benjamin', by his bedside. He was buried on the 17th of that month in the little churchyard at Denbury and did not see the war clouds gathering.

Chapter Eight

The Crimea

The Crimea is a peninsula of the Ukraine with an area of 23,312 square miles. It juts defiantly into the Black Sea and is joined to the Russian mainland by the narrow isthmus of Perekop. The south of the region where the Crimean War was largely fought is hilly and fertile and was in the nineteenth century the playground of the Tsar and the Boyars. Formerly under Turkish rule, then independent, the Crimea had been annexed to Russia in 1783 and became the focus of attention for the world in the middle of the 1850s. These were years of intense Russophobia in Britain, despite the fact that the average Englishman probably knew no more than he had seen of Russia in the Great Exhibition, which opened its doors on 1 May 1851. Behind the opulence and exoticism lay the notion of unspeakable barbarism and cruelty; a nation that still subjected its people to serfdom was unthinkable in Britain.

The more informed Englishman was also aware that Russia, like a foraging octopus, had been encroaching on the Eastern principalities for years, threatening not only British trade in the Mediterranean, but also the vital land link across Egypt to the Red Sea and British India. Since Tsar Alexander I's Holy Alliance of Russia, Austria and Prussia had emerged from the Congress System of the 1820s, Russia had represented a powerful and dangerous force, pledged to perpetuating the Imperial powers by crushing militarily any liberal or nationalist movement anywhere within an increasingly wide circle.

The problem for Britain lay in the fact that to the south of the vast, greedy Russian Empire stood a rapidly disintegrating Ottoman Empire, once all-powerful and the foremost military force in the East, now governed by an ineffectual sultan, a corrupt and inefficient government – the 'Sublime Porte' – attempting to police a sprawling empire riddled with racial, political and religious divisions. In the *Punch* cartoons, Russia was portrayed as a bear intent on sweeping aside 'poor little Turkey', the 'sick man of Europe' with a swipe of his paw. It was this very weakness and the problems it engendered that created the prolonged 'Eastern Question', but the causes of the Crimean War date most obviously from 1850 and had a religious pretext at least – the protection of the holy places in the Turkish empire. As Kinglake describes it in his monumental work on the Crimean War:

> Stated in bare terms the question whether, of the purpose of passing through the building into their grotto, the Latin monks should have the key of the chief door of the Church of Bethlehem and also one of the keys of each of the two doors of the Sacred Manger, and whether they should be at liberty to place in the sanctuary of the nativity a silver star adorned with the arms of France.[1]

Stated in terms as bare as these the immediate causes of the war seem fatuous; causes of wars often are. In essence, it is *people* who cause wars and the rulers of both Russia and France in their personalities exacerbated a delicate situation. On the one hand, Tsar Nicholas I, an idealist and dreamer, used the mystic concept of the Holy Alliance to give him a right to protect the Christian subjects of the Moslem Ottoman empire. On the other, the newly enthroned Napoleon III, who as Louis Napoleon had staged a coup in 1850, was hot-headed and insecure and desperate to recreate 'La Gloire' of the first Napoleon by being seen as a champion of liberal Western Europe and if at all possible to avenge the defeat of his uncle by the Russians in 1812. By a quirk of history, both the Greek Orthodox Church, championed by Nicholas, and the Catholic Church, championed by Napoleon, had the right to protect the Christian shrines and Christian subjects within the Turkish Empire. By December 1852 rioting had broken out and Orthodox priests were killed.

A duel of wits followed, in which Prince Menshikov, the Russian General who was to assume command in the Crimea, argued not only with the Porte but with the foremost British authority on Turkish affairs, Lord Stratford de Redcliffe, the British Ambassador at Constantinople. A French fleet was already on its way to the East and the Russians gave Turkey an ultimatum and eight days to accept it. Despite the fact that the four major European powers – Britain, France, Austria and Prussia – supported Turkey, failures in diplomacy led to war. France and Britain came to a separate understanding and a combined fleet sailed up the narrow straits of the Dardanelles. With a large Russian army crossing the Danube and marching south through the Caucasus, the Sultan felt he had no choice but to declare war on Russia on 5 October 1853.

In fact, diplomacy continued long after the declaration of war between Russia and Turkey, creating in, A J P Taylor's phrase, 'the war that would not boil', and at any point before the disembarkation of the British army on Crimean soil, the whole venture could have been called off. In the meantime, war was fought on the Danube, in Asia Minor and in the Baltic.

Morris had been given the post of Deputy Assistant Quartermaster General in March 1854 while still serving with the 17th at Hounslow and Hampton

Court. A handwritten letter from the Horse Guards dated 21 March confirms it:

> Sir,
>
> I am directed by the General Commanding in Chief to acquaint you that Her Majesty has been graciously pleased to appoint you to serve upon the Staff of the Army proceeding to the East under the command of General the Right Honourable Lord Raglan GCB, Commander of the Forces, with a view to your being employed either as Deputy Assistant Adjutant General or Deputy Assistant Quartermaster General [DAQMG].

The vacillation concerning Morris's exact appointment on the part of their Lordships at the Horse Guards is indicative of the amateurish way in which the whole campaign was conceived. 'The finest army ever to leave our shores' did so in April to July 1854 not sure where they were going and whether they would fight or not when they got there. British troops had not been committed to a land engagement on European soil since Waterloo, thirty-nine years earlier, and the lack of expertise showed from the outset. The indecision of Morris's post also outlines the blurred and confused nature of staff work in the 1850s. In his

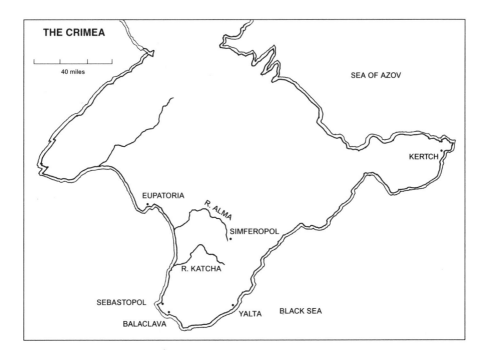

heart, Morris must have known that he had been selected for his Indian experience and not his Sandhurst qualifications. And the vacillation has also created the myth among recent writers that Morris was on Raglan's staff. Technically, as DAQMG, he was on Airey's.

The Quartermaster General at the outset was in fact Lord de Ros, but he was invalided home almost immediately from the camp at Varna on the Black Sea and was replaced by one of the youngest of the Crimean Generals, fifty-one-year-old Sir Richard Airey. The role of Quartermaster General was to supervise the embarkation, disembarkation and encamping of the army, a monumental task in itself, in which de Ros's and Airey's departments were to co-operate closely under Lord Lucan, commanding the Cavalry Division, and with General Estcourt of the Commissariat, who handled pay and supplies. The extraordinary muddle which pertained here, to an army encumbered with civilian contractors and on totally alien soil (among the Generals, only Lucan had seen the Russian army in action), was a recipe for disaster.

Amelia Morris, in a biographical memoir of her husband written some years after his death, states that he was sent on special duty 'to see if it were practical sending in troops via France to Turkey' – and certainly this was the original intention, to march the British army across France and to embark from Marseilles or Toulon. In the event, the sight of British troops, formerly deadly enemies, on French soil was thought too provocative for Anglophobic French peasants and the project was shelved.

Morris sailed in April, though from where and in which ship is not recorded. It is possible that he sailed with his regiment, which embarked between 18 and 25 April from Portsmouth in five ships. If this was the case, he was probably on board the Headquarters ship, the *Eveline*, with Lieutenant Colonel Lawrenson. The cavalry, some 3,000 men and horses in all, sailed in a motley collection of troopships. Some, like the Pacific & Orient's 3,438-ton *Himalaya*, were new screw steamers and could do the journey from Queenstown to the Black Sea in sixteen days, which included a stop-off at Malta. Others were sailing vessels and correspondingly slower. One which left on 20 May did not arrive until 14 July! The horses were winched on board at Portsmouth and elsewhere, Morris's Old Treasurer among them. The horses were head-to-head in their stalls and could not lie down. Some of them were injured in the storms and squalls on the way and had to be destroyed. The 17th lost twenty-six horses in all.

Fanny Duberly, wife of the Paymaster of the 8th Hussars, was horrified by the horses' condition, adding to her reputation as someone indifferent to the suffering of people. The men bathed the animals' noses with vinegar and water and tried in vain to make them eat. Their own diet, recorded Sergeant Mitchell of the 13th Light Dragoons, comprised salt pork, salt beef, gin and barrels of peas dated 1828! It was all pretty inedible. Inevitably, officers fared better – Colonel Hodge of the 4th Dragoon Guards had fresh bread and meat every day.

After the appalling storms in the notorious Bay of Biscay, and the fire in which the Inniskilling Dragoons lost their colonel, eighteen other ranks and all their horses, morale began to improve. The band of the 17th Lancers played on deck. Steamers had to tow becalmed sailing vessels stranded off Constantinople and some officers went ashore in what was after all the magic city of the Golden Horn. It was frankly disappointing. Robert Portal of the 4th Light Dragoons could compare it 'to no Irish village for filth'. And so the Light Brigade came to Devna.

The 17th Lancers and the 8th Hussars were the first to arrive, and Morris was faced with the immediate problem of disembarkation. The troopships could not get sufficiently near the shore and in the end the incredibly difficult task was accomplished by lowering the horses into rowing boats. The *Shooting Star*, carrying Captain Henry and Fanny Duberly, arrived in this chaos on 1 June. Fanny, with the irrepressible glee of a schoolgirl on her first outing, described Varna, to which the bulk of the army was now marching, as a 'small but clean-looking town' and must have been relieved after her husband's description of Constantinople: 'The dilapidation!' she wrote, of the interior of the barracks at Kulaki, 'The dirt! the rats! the fleas!! These last are really so terrible that several officers have been fairly routed by them,' and this contrasted vividly with the sights of astonishing beauty the Duberlys had seen on their voyage: 'the glory of the sunset ... the still water [of the Aegean] reflecting every beautiful colour like a lake of mother of pearl.' Neither were Morris's problems confined to disembarkation. At the height of the summer, the Turkish plain was excruciatingly hot. 'A broiling day,' wrote Fanny Duberly on 2 June. 'There is no tree or shelter of any sort near our encampment, which is finely situated on a large plain fronting the lake ... The horses are wild with heat and flies and they scream and kick all day and night.'[2] The infantry were bivouacked on mounds, the graves of Russian soldiers who fell in the Turkish campaign of 1828–9. Throughout early June, cavalry units continued to arrive, including Lord Cardigan and his staff.

James Brudenell, the 7th Earl of Cardigan, was to lead the Light Brigade, which put him automatically under the command of his brother-in-law Lucan, who attempted to control both brigades which made up the Cavalry Division. Stupid, autocratic and overbearing, Cardigan has been called the English Murat,[3] an insult to one of the truly great leaders of cavalry. Having refused permission for light cavalry patrols out from Varna to carry their cloaks – he considered them 'effeminate' – he led the infamous and pointless 'sore back reconnaissance' at the end of June, which was designed to estimate the size and proximity of the Russian army, but which in fact resulted in the deaths of five horses and made another seventy-five unfit for further service.

Cardigan's lack of experience was of course the nub of the Crimean problem. The 'long peace' had stultified the Army; the only officers with experience were the 'Indians' whom Cardigan despised. Such men were invariably junior in rank and carried little weight with the Cardigans and Lucans of this world. Ironically, of course, William Morris, the DAQMG, was just such an 'Indian' officer and had he been consulted on the matter of a reconnaissance would probably have advised against it. If neither Lords Raglan nor Lucan could keep Cardigan in his place, what chance did Captain Morris have?

The food was beginning to deteriorate. On 30 June, Fanny Duberly wrote, 'We can get little else but stale eggs, tough chickens and sour milk,' and news of barbarism was trickling through from Silistria, where the Turks and Russians were already engaged:

> I hear the Turks are hardly to be restrained from mutilating their dead foes. If they can do so unseen, they will cut off three or four heads and string them together through the lips and cheeks, carry them over their shoulders, like a rope of onions.

Mrs Duberly's editor, when her *Journal* was published, denied this: 'Such a practice is utterly abhorrent to the Turks themselves, who know how to combine the highest degree of bravery with the most chivalrous humanity.'[4]

Unknown to Fanny Duberly or William Morris, Lord Aberdeen, the vacillating and pacifist Prime Minister, had taken the grudging decision at Pembroke Lodge in Richmond Park to commit Raglan's army to the Crimea. It was to be a limited offensive – to give the Russian bear a bloody nose by taking the naval base of Sebastopol. There was to be no rash Napoleonic invasion of mainland Russia. The whole thing could probably be over and done with very quickly. And most of the talking on that sultry night at Pembroke Lodge had been done by Palmerston – the 'terrible Milord' – who joined most Englishmen in their Russophobia and chauvinistic pride. For many of Raglan's army, the news came too late. On Sunday, 22 July, Fanny Duberly wrote, 'The cholera is come amongst us!'[5] At home, when news of the disease broke, *Punch* went into print:

> Death was busy in the daytime, was busy through the dark;
> They that lay down hale and healthy, by the dawn were stiff and stark,
> And France and England in dismay looked on and could not save;
> And glory brought no laurels to deck the soldiers' grave.[6]

At that stage, the disease was not in the cavalry at all, but in the Light (Infantry) Division and in the camp of the French nearby. Outbreaks of the disease had appeared in England the previous year and carried off thousands in the urban settlements, where the risk of infection was greatest. The micro-organism responsible for it was not discovered until 1883, but it was found widely in India and the East and it is very likely that Morris had seen it before. The usual carriers were infected milk and water and in the confines of any camp where both were drunk and the huge, heavy flies of summer spread it too, an outbreak was probably inevitable. The usual incubation period was between two and five days and the symptoms were severe abdominal pain and diarrhoea, followed by rapid weight loss, cramps in hands and feet, restlessness, and collapse of circulatory and renal systems.

On 4 August, Captain Levinge of the Royal Horse Artillery died as a result of an overdose of laudanum taken in an attempt to ward off incipient cholera. By 10 August, Major Willett of the 17th Lancers was ill in the village of Jeni-Bazaar, where he had been moved for peace and quiet. A fire at Varna on the next day did not help matters and the 5th Dragoon Guards, one of the regiments of the Heavy Brigade, was very seriously hit by the disease. Fanny Duberly's servant, Mrs Blaydes, died of it on Sunday, 20 August.

One letter exists which touches on the nature of Morris's work at Varna. It is signed by Raglan and dated 2 August. It refers to the arrival of the Scots Greys, the last of the cavalry regiments to reach the area, and orders Morris to take the steamer *Albatross* to the Bosphorus to deliver a letter to Admiral Boxer (in command of the Naval Division in the Black Sea area) and Viscount Stratford de Redcliffe. Raglan wanted the Greys to be lodged in the barracks at Kulaki, but for that he needed permission from his allies of the Porte. Should the Kulaki barracks not be available, Morris was to place the Greys at Scutari, where there was also a barracks.

At the end of the month, the cavalry began to decamp. Mrs Duberly, though ill, had got round the surprisingly sentimental Cardigan, her husband's commanding officer, and he had given her permission to sail for the Crimea. She did so under Lucan's nose on 1 September. As DAQMG, Morris would have been one of the last men to leave Varna, for his duties necessitated his staying until all the cavalry had gone. In the event, he was to stay longer. Robert Portal wrote to his mother from Varna on 22 August:

> Poor Morris has been very ill indeed with diarrhoea almost amounting to cholera. Last night the doctor had all but given him up. This morning I saw him and could not have supposed that a strong fellow like him would have been so reduced in two days; he looked really more like a dead man than a living one. He is a little better and now there is some hope of his rallying.[7]

The next day, he wrote again:

> I write particularly to ask you to write *immediately* to Mrs Diggle to beg her to break to poor Mrs Morris the news of the very bad state of her husband's health. I have already told you ... how ill he was yesterday and the day before; and I have just heard that he is no

better and if things do not take a turn for the better immediately nothing can save him. He expressed a wish yesterday for soda water and I went immediately to a ship in the bay to get him some. I gave it to him myself late last night and he was most grateful for it. I then thought he was better. I asked him if he wanted anything done for him and he said 'Nothing'. I do not think he has written to his wife of his state, so it would be a great kindness to prepare her for what I fear must be the result. To-day they would not let me see him at all. He has been vomiting everything they give him; now they are giving him champagne. It is a sad thing.

The Light Brigade landed near Calamita Bay in heavy surf, after a crossing of 300 miles which had taken twelve days. Eleven horses were drowned at the shore. Miles away and weeks later, *Punch* was buoyed up by it all:

And still they land – along the strand close forming as they come,
Close girt for strife; ne'er a scream of fife; ne'er a roll of throbbing
    drum.
On shore or height no foe in sight! Behind his walls he cowers.
Now forward – France and England – and Sebastopol is ours![8]

Mrs Duberly went ashore on Monday, 18 September, to find well-furnished houses complete with pianofortes, pictures and books. More ominously, however, the Cossacks watched and waited at a safe distance 'like a flying cloud'.[9]

Back at Varna on 4 September, Morris wrote to Amelia:

My dearest,
    I have been very ill since I wrote last [this letter has not survived] as I know you have heard from several kind friends. Elliot and Portal have been most kind and attentive to me – the whole Army is on Board-ship except the Heavy Cavalry Brigade which waits here the return of the Steamers, after they have landed the 1st Dragoons – I cannot describe to you the feeling of being left behind, but 'tis the hand of Providence and I have nothing to say – all the Doctors say that I shall be sure to get over this now – Dr Mitchell [presumably a Staff Surgeon] who attended me most assiduously went on board yesterday with Ld Lucan and I am now trying to be removed to a house in Varna, if I can get one, where I shall stay some time, till I see what is likely to be done with me. I am wretchedly weak and my memory is almost gone but they say will return with strength.
    Give my best love to my dear Mother, tell her I often thought of her when nearly at the worst – and with love to all.

William.

Pray for me, Dearest.

– and there was a PS:

I go into Varna tomorrow I believe, you can hardly fancy how weak I am, I cannot stand without holding by something, but I am getting stronger every day. I will let you know myself what is to become of me but *don't think* of coming out till you hear from me that I wish it, as I may be sent home straight from Varna.

We see Morris here at his lowest ebb. Not even in his letters to Amelia after the Charge does he sound so low and sorry for himself. It rankled that the troops had gone without him. A powerful man like him felt utterly frustrated at his sudden physical weakness. And the thought of being sent home without even setting foot in the Crimea was mortifying. His reference to Amelia's coming out – which she was to do in December – is not so strange. Among the men, the wife of one in six was allowed to go with the Army and lots were drawn for the privilege. The fact that Mrs Duberly followed her husband everywhere is indicative of the attitude taken by most people at the time, despite token censure from the High Command. Fanny Duberly remarked early in October of the surprise among the French to see a lady in their lines, but they had *cantinières*, girls employed to provide food and sustenance for the regiments and cannot have been as surprised as all that.

The British Army which landed unopposed in the Crimea and which found the local Tartars more friendly than the Bulgarians at Varna, was led by the seventy-year-old Arthur Fitzroy Somerset, Lord Raglan. On Wellington's staff at Waterloo, Somerset had had his right arm badly mangled by shot and it was amputated on the field that night without anaesthetic. The story is well attested that when the orderly carried away the limb, Somerset called out to him, 'There's a ring my wife gave me on the finger. Can I have it back, please?' Courage was something that Raglan possessed in great measure, but he lacked virtually everything else. From 1827 until the Duke's death in 1852, he had held a desk job as Wellington's Military Secretary. Since 1852, he had been Master General of the Ordnance. The largest formation he had personally commanded in the field was 200 men. He was quiet, refined, a skilful diplomat and had a vast amount of second-hand experience fed to him by Wellington. Whether we follow the kind views of Christopher Hibbert in *The Destruction of Lord Raglan* or the barbed ferocity of Norman Dixon in his book on military incompetence, the wisdom of appointing a geriatric cripple to a field command can at the very least be doubted. Dixon says of his aloofness and gentlemanly courtesy, 'this idiosyncrasy often rendered his role upon the battlefield rather less effective than that of a regimental mascot.'[10]

The first of the five infantry divisions was commanded by the Duke of Cambridge, who at Morris's age of thirty-four was by far the youngest general in the Crimea. He owed his appointment entirely to his birth. He was a cousin to the Queen, a grandson of George III and had served for sixteen years, mostly on the Staff. The Second Division was commanded by Sir George de Lacy Evans, at sixty-six one of the best of the British generals, with forty-seven years' service, including the Peninsula, India, America (the War of 1812) and the Spanish Carlist Wars of the 1830s. The Third Division was led by Sir Richard England, aged sixty-one and known, like Colonel Shewell of the 8th Hussars, as 'the Old Woman'. The Fourth Division was led by Sir George Cathcart, aged fifty-nine, whose service had been spent in the Cape (South Africa) and Napoleonic Europe. He was to command the Army in the event of Raglan's death. Sir George Brown commanded the Fifth (Light) Division. At sixty-six he had served in the Peninsula, more recently as Adjutant General, and was universally detested as a martinet. One of the oldest generals at seventy-one was Sir John Burgoyne, the Chief Engineer, who had served in Egypt, in the Peninsula and at Waterloo.

The cavalry division was led by Lord Lucan, unpopular, a disciplinarian, an Irish absentee landlord. He was sixty-four and had seen service uniquely with the Russian army against the Turks in 1828–9. Below him were James Scarlett, fifty-five, who commanded the Heavy Brigade. Popular and friendly, he had no experience of war at all. Neither had Lord Cardigan, fifty-seven, who led the Light Brigade. His army career had begun as a Cornet in the 8th Hussars in 1824 and using his immense wealth he bought rapid promotion – a lieutenancy in January 1825 and a lieutenant colonelcy by December 1830. In March 1832 he took command of the 15th Hussars, having paid a vast sum for it, well over regulation price. As a commanding officer, Cardigan was a tyrant, though the men liked him well enough, calling him 'Jim the Bear'. He paid them out of his own pocket to stand at street corners and salute him as he passed by them. Removed from his post as Lieutenant Colonel of the 15th after a prolonged row with Captain Augustus Wathen of his regiment, Cardigan moved rapidly to the 4th Light Dragoons and to their intense relief on to the 11th in the same year. While in command of the 11th (made Hussars and 'Prince Albert's Own' in 1840), Cardigan became involved in countless scandals. His officers flattened a cornfield in Canterbury and when the owner complained Cardigan offered to fight a duel with him. Two officers named Reynolds (no relation) fell foul of Cardigan's temper and hauteur, one of them being arrested for presuming to bring a black bottle of common porter into the Mess. Another former officer named Harvey Tuckett criticized Cardigan in the press and the two men fought a duel on 12 September 1840. Tuckett was wounded and Cardigan tried by the House of Lords where he was acquitted in 1841. In 1843 he outraged Victorian sensibilities by having a soldier flogged on Palm Sunday. Since then things had been quite quiet, but Cardigan, who sailed to the Crimea in his yacht the *Dryad*, was not the right man for the job in this campaign.

The French army was to emerge from the Crimea with a far higher reputation than the British. Enemies of centuries do not make quick and steadfast allies and most of the supposedly joint offensives of the war were in fact each army going it alone, the British, at least in the early stages, bearing the brunt of the damage. It was commanded by the fifty-three-year-old Marshal St Arnaud, who had led the military operations which had brought Napoleon III to power in his coup of 1851. Like Raglan, he had been at the War Office for years, but unlike him, he was ill, dying in fact from stomach cancer. Under him commanding the four infantry divisions were Generals Canrobert, Bosquet, Prince Napoleon Bonaparte (nephew of Napoleon I) and Forey. Their average age was forty-three and they were all, except Prince Napoleon, men of considerable experience. They suffered as the Russians did, but the British did not, from interference from their Commander in Chief. Both the Tsar and Napoleon III saw themselves as military men (in the case of Napoleon, even desperately trying to *look* like his famous uncle) and continually interfered with their generals. All the French divisional commanders were closely connected with Napoleon III and his seizure of power and thus owed him far more than their British counterparts owed to Lord Aberdeen or the Queen. With rampant chauvinism, British officers' letters home refer to the drunkenness and lack of discipline in the French army, apparent even in the sloppy but far more practical *confort* of French uniforms – wide baggy pantaloons, low loose collars and light headgear – and disguise the fact that the French army was higher in morale and superior in professionalism to the British.

The Turkish army were known to be heroic in the face of a vastly superior Russian force in various actions along the Danube and their colourful fezzes and jackets had a romantic appeal for people like Mrs Duberly. They played only a small part in the siege of Sebastopol but were not impressive. British troops spoke of their untrustworthiness, their cowardice and their lack of discipline. The whole army became tainted by the behaviour of the Bashi-bazouks, irregular horsemen somewhat akin to the Russian Cossacks, who were little better than 'bandits on horseback'.

The Russian army, that great unknown quantity to everyone except Lucan, was essentially a conscripted one. Its officers were either from the various cadet schools and unlike other European armies, had titles but no land or court status; or they were non-commissioned officers in effect elevated from the ranks. These 'Junkers', as they were called, had to pass a written examination to the officer class, in marked contrast to the British system, but it was not particularly rigorous. Many of these officers were thus wholly reliant on their meagre pay and in common with the British Army, tactical training and initiative was wholly confined to the rigours of the parade ground, made worse by the fatuous goose-step and the barbarity of the 'tooth pick', a rifle butt in the jaw of soldiers who failed to march properly. The ordinary soldier in the Russian army – 'Ivan Ivanovitch' – was usually a serf, almost always a peasant and as such was used to a life of grinding poverty and brutality found only in parts of Ireland at the height of the famine. Discipline was harsh. Diet was frequently buckwheat porridge, cabbage soup and rye bread. The common soldier was steadfast and courageous with what G A Embleton calls 'an immense fatalistic capacity for dumb suffering'.[11] Conditions in the Russian army, with its huge cavalry division (the largest in the world at sixty regiments), were the worst of all, largely because of incompetence and indifference from the Tsar down.

While Mrs Duberly stayed on board ship because Henry was sharing a tent with three men, and while Cardigan's Light Cavalry clashed with Cossacks at the Bulganek river and the whole army except the cavalry gave the Russian bear a bloody nose on the heights above the Alma on 20 September, William Morris recovered in his house at Varna. Water would have been boiled for him and he would have done well to stay away from fruit and uncooked food. Still far from well and thin from endless vomiting, he sailed for the Crimea on or about 12 October to find the Army encamped above the village of Balaclava, some seven miles from the deep water harbour which Fanny Duberly found so picturesque and which by the time Morris got there was jammed tight with immovable ships and the rotting corpses of horses. The ships contained supplies vital to the Light Brigade, which, because of lack of planning and foresight, they would now be without all winter.

Robert Portal says that Morris had been in the Crimea only a fortnight before the Battle of Balaclava, but it would have been less than that. Rather curiously, the 'potted' biography handwritten apparently by Amelia Morris says that her husband took command of the 17th five days earlier, that is, 20 October. Other accounts, including Morris's own letters, talk in terms of the 24th, the day before the battle.

The reason for his taking command rather than staying with Airey's staff is that the two senior officers of the 17th – Lawrenson and Willett – were variously unavailable. Lawrenson had been on board ship in Balaclava harbour since 21 September and was granted leave of absence on 23 October. He was to return in the summer of 1855 to command first the Heavy Brigade, then the Cavalry Division. Major Willett had assumed command of the 17th in his absence, but he died of a combination of cholera and exposure on 22 October.

Morris had probably less than a day to decide where he was most needed – or where his loyalties lay. He chose the 17th and did not have time to order up his regimental uniform from the transports in the harbour.

Chapter Nine

'Damn Those Heavies'

Morris's decision to command the 17th on 25 October was almost a fatal one. In common with many other members of the Light Brigade, he must still have been weak from cholera. The Battle of Balaclava and particularly the Light Brigade's Charge which constituted its final phase, has tended to dominate the entire Crimean War. In terms of achievement, in terms even of the losses involved, it should scarcely merit a mention, although the latest book on the subject tries to change our perception of this.[1] In terms of sheer stupidity on the part of the British Army, its personnel and the system which bred them, the Charge has rightly gone down in history.

William Howard Russell, *The Times*'s war correspondent with the Army in the East, takes up the story:

> At half past seven o'clock on the morning of the 25th, an orderly came galloping into the headquarters camp with the news that at dawn a strong corps of Russian horse, supported by guns and battalions of infantry, had marched into the valley and had nearly dispossessed the Turks of the Redoubt No. 1 (that on Canrobert's Hill, which was furthest from our lines) and had opened fire on the Redoubts Nos 2, 3 and 4.[2]

These redoubts were the second of the two lines of defence which had been (all too hastily) thrown up around Balaclava. They were built on a ridge, called the Causeway by the British, which had the Worontzoff (Vorontovsky) Road running just below it. The Causeway separated the valleys into North (Chernaia Rechka) and South (Balaclava). The first redoubt to be attacked, Number 1, stood somewhat isolated from the rest, about 2,000 yards north-west of a village called Komary. Redoubts 2 and 3 were about 500 yards apart and Number 4 was again isolated. Two other redoubts, 5 and 6, were still under construction. Each redoubt was a rectangular post of earthworks and timber manned by about 250 Turkish troops, British artillery (12 pounders) and a

British artillery non-commissioned officer. The Russians found these no real obstacle, especially when Lord Lucan, who had been in the redoubts, was forced to withdraw his Heavy Cavalry, in Russell's phrase, 'owing to the superior weight of the enemy's metal', leaving the unreliable Turks to hold out alone. The Russian plan was to take the redoubts and then attack the cavalry 'occupying the fortified positions adjacent to Kadikoi and Balaklava'.[3]

The Russian advance was co-ordinated by Lieutenant General P P Liprandi, Commander of the 12th Infantry Division, which had recently arrived from Bessarabia by forced marches. Under him, brigades of infantry, cavalry and artillery were led by Major Generals K P Semiakin and F G Levutsky. While this advance took place in what seemed a concerted attempt to dislodge the British from Balaclava, a column of some 5,000 troops under Major General Zhaboritsky was to take the Fedioukine Heights to the north of the North Valley and to prevent any involvement by General Bosquet's Frenchmen. Liprandi himself cheered the men on and Levutsky's guns began an initial bombardment of the redoubts at six o'clock.

This attack was not unexpected. The Turks and the British had been warned of it days earlier, but the Crimea was crawling with spies and Raglan distrusted them as liars and thieves. Consequently nobody was ready for the bombardment when it started and the Turks in the redoubts seem to have collapsed in panic very quickly. The area around the redoubts had not been cleared of scrub and the advancing Russian infantry had plenty of cover. By half past seven the Russian flag flew over the first redoubt. Liprandi claimed the allies lost all three guns and 170 dead, which indicates that resistance here was the most stubborn offered. The garrisons of Numbers 2 and 3 redoubts fled towards Balaclava Harbour, shouting 'Ship! Ship!', and that of Number 4 deserted their posts before a further Russian attack could be launched. According to Russell, writing with his tongue firmly in his cheek: 'The Turks fired a few rounds at them [the Russians] … then bolted with an agility quite at variance with the commonplace notions of Oriental deportment on the battlefield.'[4]

Today's politically correct historians have praised the Turks in the redoubts, but there is little question that only the first displayed real courage. Raglan's Headquarters staff had been forced into action at the first sight of the huge grey mass of Russians. The Duke of Cambridge's 1st Infantry Division and Sir George Cathcart's 4th Division advanced at the galloper's orders and Bosquet's 3rd Division was similarly ordered up by Canrobert. The 1st Division used the Worontzoff Road, but the 4th was late starting because they had been up all night in the trenches and were cold, exhausted and hungry. Two French Infantry Brigades, one under Vinoi, the other under Espinasse, were now moving in addition to Bosquet's troops, as well as two cavalry regiments of the Chasseurs d'Afrique, under General Allonville. The sheer time taken to mobilize this number of men meant that by the collapse of the last redoubt only a relative handful stood between the Russians and the sea.

What this meant in essence was that the 93rd Foot were the real backbone of the defence for the time being, as the Turks had already proved their unreliability and their two battalions broke at the sight of the Russian advance. This was composed of four squadrons of the Ingermanlandsky Hussars under General Ryzhov, the Cossacks on the wings fanning out to form an enveloping pincer movement. General Colin Campbell's 93rd were lying down in part perhaps to surprise the enemy, who could not see them because of the ground, and in part to escape the Russian fire. Campbell was a remarkable soldier. Born in 1792, the son of a carpenter from Glasgow, he had served with distinction in the Peninsula and was a Lieutenant Colonel by 1832. On 14 October 1854, by now a Major General, he was placed in command of the defences of Balaclava, where he commanded the Highland Brigade under the Duke of Cambridge. Carrying a 1796 pattern cavalry sword in all his campaigns, he went home to Scotland in 1855 and was Commander in Chief India in the suppression of the Mutiny, becoming a Field Marshal in 1862, the year before his death.

At a signal from Campbell, the Highlanders stood up and marched in close company formation with bayonets fixed. The British artillery now opened up on the Russian Hussars and they wavered. The men of the 93rd, according to some accounts, advanced and fired. According to others, they stood like rocks, two lines deep, and poured volleys of murderous fire into the Hussars. 'With breathless suspense,' wrote Russell,

> every one awaited the bursting of the wave upon the line of Gaelic rock; but 'ere they came within the hundred and fifty yards, another deadly volley flashed from the levelled rifle and carried terror among the Russians ... men scarcely had a moment to think of this fact, that the 93rd never altered their formation to receive that tide of horsemen. 'No,' said Sir Colin Campbell, 'I did not think it worth while to form them even four deep!' The ordinary British line, two deep, was quite sufficient to repel the attack of these Muscovite cavaliers.[5]

In fact, the action of the Russian cavalry seems to have been lethargic all day. True, they were advancing unsupported against infantry and artillery, but their numbers were vastly superior. Probably to cover and excuse the failure of his cavalry, Liprandi wrote on 26 October to Menshikov, the Commander in Chief, that he had believed the stand of the 93rd and the advance of Scarlett's Heavy Brigade to be a single concerted move and had therefore ordered the cavalry to break off so as not to be outflanked. It seems much more likely that the withering fire of the 93rd – 'the thin red streak'[6] as Russell called them – had given them a bloody nose and they pulled back to the safety of Liprandi's infantry divisions.

Raglan ordered the Heavy Brigade to support the 93rd and in negotiating the vineyard and nearby orchards, they caught sight of the flashing lance tips of the Russian uhlans and changed front.

Lieutenant Colonel Edward Cooper Hodge, commanding the Dragoon Guards, described in a few lines what was to become known as the Charge of the Heavy Brigade:

> A large body of cavalry came into the plain and were charged by the Greys and the Inniskillings. We were in reserve and I brought forward our left and charged these cavalry in flank. The Greys were a little in confusion and retiring when our charge settled the business. We completely routed the hussars and Cossacks and drove them back.[7]

The fact that these bodies of horsemen had met at all was rather a matter of chance. Raglan on the Sapouné Heights could see all the forces on the plain and valleys below him and his first order to Lucan, commanding the cavalry, had been to ride west to support the infantry of the 1st and 4th Divisions. His second order had been to support the Turks and Campbell. In doing so, the open column of the Heavies, the 5th Dragoon Guards ahead, followed by the Greys and Inniskillings and the 4th in reserve, met about 2,000 Russian cavalry: 'evidently corps d'élite,' Russell thought, 'their light blue jackets embroidered with silver lace ... A forest of lances glistened in their rear and several squadrons of grey-coated dragoons.'[8] Among the Heavies, it was probably Scarlett's Aide-de-Camp (ADC), Lieutenant Alexander Elliot, who had nursed Morris at Varna, who saw the Russian cavalry first.

The short-sighted Scarlett took Elliot's word for it and decided to charge, but such a manoeuvre was complicated by the vineyard and its wall, not to mention the remains of the Light Brigade camp, and it took a little time for the men to get their dressings right. Ryzhov, whose cavalry, according to Russell, advanced at a canter, then slowed to a trot and finally nearly halted (totally the *wrong* way to execute an effective cavalry attack), wrote:

> I ordered Voinilovich's Kiersky [regiment] to take the left so that they should engage the English red guard dragoons and, because of their extended line, I was obliged to use both hussar regiments together side by side, without any reserve. It was surprising how the enemy, *superior to us in numbers* allowed us to come up the hill and deploy at our leisure.[9]

The rest of the passage, like the assertion of superiority of numbers (the Heavy Brigade could not have mustered more than 300 sabres), veers violently from the truth of what actually happened. While the Russians had halted to make their line conform to that of the British and for the Cossacks to form 'wings', Scarlett put his spurs to his horse and, with Elliot in hot pursuit, charged.

'The trumpets rang out again,' wrote Russell,

and the Greys and Enniskilleners went right at the centre of the Russian cavalry … The shock was but for a moment. There was a clash of steel and a light play of sword-blades in the air, and then the Greys and the redcoats disappeared in the midst of the shaken and quivering columns.[10]

The Scots Greys differed from the other Heavy regiments in two respects. First, they rode grey horses – 'ces terribles chevaux grises', as Napoleon had called them at Waterloo – whereas grey horses in other regiments were reserved for the trumpeters so that they were easily recognized. Second, they wore tall bearskin caps, reinforced with leather, which cannot have given as much protection as the brass helmets of the other regiments. As Scarlett and his tiny staff vanished from view, successive squadrons of the Heavy Brigade crashed into the milling Russian cavalry. Lieutenant Temple Godman of the 5th Dragoon Guards was among them:

> The enemy seemed quite astonished and drew into a walk and then to a halt; as soon as they met, all I saw was swords in the air in every direction, the pistols going off, and everyone hacking away right and left. In a moment, the Greys were surrounded and hemmed completely in; there they were fighting back to back in the middle, the great bearskin caps high above the enemy.
>
> This was the work of a moment; as soon as we saw it, the 5th advanced and in they charged, yelling and shouting as hard as they could split, the row was tremendous, and for about five minutes neither would give way, and their column was so deep we could not cut through.[11]

Watching the Charge from the Sapouné Heights was General Richard Dacres, who wrote to Hodge's mother: 'The 4th came up at a very slow trot, till close to, when they charged them in the flank at a gallop and sent them to the right about. It was well and nobly done and Edward showed himself every inch a soldier by the way he did it and got much commendation for the same.'[12] Major Forrest, Hodge's second-in-command, commented on the difficulty of the ground: 'first thro' a vineyard, and over two fences, bank and ditch, then thro' the Camp of the 17th and we were scarcely formed when we attacked.'[13] 'At length they turned,' wrote Godman to his father the next day, 'and well they might, and the whole ran as hard as they could pelt back up the hill, our men after them all broken up, and cutting them down right and left.'[14]

The Royal Dragoons, in reserve, seem to have joined their colleagues in the mêlée and even one member of the Light Brigade, Private William Hope of the 11th Hussars, rode with the Greys. Hope was a Welshman with a history of petit mal. He was in the guard tent on the morning of 25 October on a charge of being asleep on duty. Seeing the cavalry forming up, he assumed it was a general advance by both brigades, grabbed a troop horse of the Greys and subsequently rode *both* charges. He lived to tell the tale. According to Lucan, the whole charge had lasted eight minutes. Major Thornhill, who rode the charge, said: 'It was just like a mêlée coming out of a crowded theatre, jostling horse against horse, violent language, hacking and pushing, till suddenly the Russians gave way.'[15]

Complaints were made against the swords the Heavies were using. Lieutenant Colonel Griffiths of the Greys ranted, 'When our men made a thrust with the sword, they all bent and would not go into a man's body,' but he had been making similar noises since at least July of that year, when the Greys had been stationed in Manchester. 'Some men', Griffiths went on, 'lost their lives entirely for the unserviceable state of their arms. They were quite good enough for Home Service but quite unfit for active service.'[16] Evelyn Wood, then with the Navy in Balaclava Harbour, spoke to Naval surgeons who attended the wounded:

> and they described to us that evening the effect of some of the sword cuts inflicted by our Heavy dragoons on the heads of the Russians as appalling; in some cases the head-dress and skull being divided down to the chin. The edge of the sword was used, for the greatcoats worn by the Russians were difficult to pierce with the point.'[17]

It seems likely that some units among the Heavies were equipped with the new 1853 pattern three-bar hilt; others still carried the 1821 pattern; the blade, length and weight of the weapons were essentially the same. The inefficiency of swords was felt (quite literally) by both sides. Temple Godman wrote to his father: 'I got a bruise under my right wrist, which makes my hand stiff, and I cannot write quite so well. It was a sword cut which went through my coat, but not the thick woollen jersey I had on.'[18]

Some hundreds of yards from the scene of the Heavies' charge sat the Light Brigade, Cardigan motionless at their head. Mrs Woodham-Smith takes up the story:

> In the 17th Lancers there was one of those 'Indian' officers whom the cavalry generals and their Commander-in-Chief united in despising ... Captain Morris at thirty-four had taken part in three campaigns and charged with cavalry in four battles, including the famous battle of Aliwal ... he had passed with great distinction through the Senior Department of the Royal Military College at Sandhurst. Short, stocky, immensely powerful, nicknamed 'the Pocket Hercules', Captain Morris was a popular regimental character.[19]

The only known photograph of Morris, probably taken at home, either in 1848 or in 1855.

Anonymous painting of Morris, probably painted before he left the 16th Lancers in 1847.

The church of St Michael's, Sandhurst, where Morris married Amelia Taylor in April 1852.

The various awards, medals and decorations which Morris acquired during his service in India and the Crimea. The clasp for Balaclava is the only one he received, because he was absent through illness at the Alma and had gone home wounded before Inkerman.

Lord Raglan's headquarters at Khutor-Karagatch, drawn by William Simpson. Morris must have known this building well.

ord Cardigan, the 'man of the Serpentine', a
debound martinet who nevertheless, in
orris's phrase, 'led like a gentleman'.

Captain Louis Nolan, Morris's impetuous friend
whose actions at Balaclava may have destroyed
the Light Cavalry.

ord Lucan, Morris's ultimate superior, who
ommanded the cavalry division in the Crimea
nd failed to get Morris the Victoria Cross.

Lord Raglan. The Commander in Chief was
possibly too courteous and certainly too old for
a field command.

A panoramic view of the Charge, as recorded by William Simpson. Morris is the central horseman of the three riding ahead of the nearest squadron in the front line.

The climax of the Charge, as portrayed by Christopher Clark. Cardigan, on Ronald, has reached the guns. Morris would have been close behind him, but off to the right of the painting.

The aftermath of the Charge: 'All that was left of them, Left of six hundred', by Caton Woodville. 'It was a mad brained trick,' Cardigan said, 'but it was no fault of mine'

The sword presented to William Morris at Great Torrington, Devon, in 1856. The weapon is of the Mameluke type with steel scabbard, ivory hilt and acorn sword knot. The inscription reads: 'To Major William Morris, from his friends and neighbours, in the North of Devon, to replace his sword, lost when he was severely wounded, in command of the 17th Lancers, at the glorious Charge of the Light Cavalry, at Balaklava, October 25th 1854.'

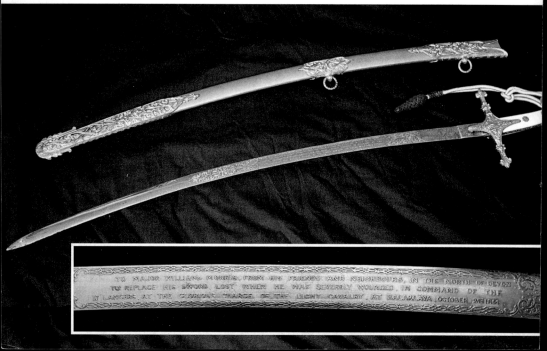

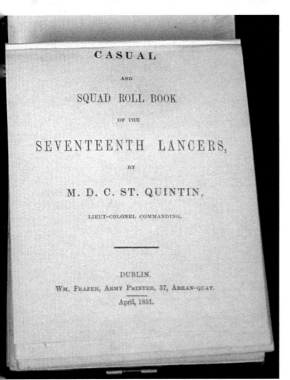

CASUAL
AND
SQUAD ROLL BOOK
OF THE
SEVENTEENTH LANCERS,
BY
M. D. C. ST. QUINTIN,
LIEUT-COLONEL COMMANDING.

DUBLIN.
WM. FRAZER, ARMY PRINTER, 37, ARRAN-QUAY.
April, 1851.

The Casual and Squad Roll Book of Captain Morris, 17th Lancers, containing fascinating details of the men in his troop.

Pages from the Squad Book, showing details of some of the men who rode behind Morris in the Charge of the Light Brigade.

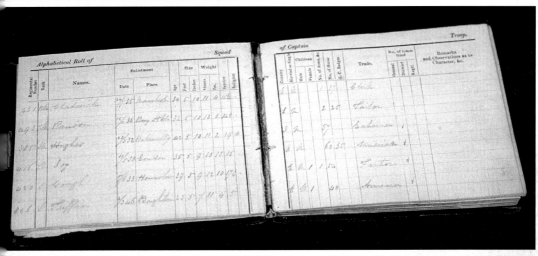

The monument erected in 1860 in memory of William Morris stands high over Hatherleigh Moor, North Devon.

The bas-relief of Morris being carried semi-conscious from the 'Valley of Death' by surgeon James Mouat and men of the 17th Lancers.

BALAKLAVA

In his otherwise excellent book on the Charge of the Light Brigade, Mark Adkin assumes that Morris was 'a complete stranger to his men', presumably because of his absence on staff appointment. As we have seen, as a Troop Captain, Morris knew many of the men riding behind him that day very well and they him. He had only been away from the regiment for five months. Kinglake wrote, more than a century before:

> Whilst Lord Cardigan sat in his saddle expressing, under cavalry forms of speech, his envy of the heavy Dragoons ['Damn those Heavies'] and adhering to that hapless construction of Lord Lucan's orders which condemned him, as he thought, to a state of neutrality, he had at his side an Officer, comparatively young, and with only the rank of captain, who still was well able to give him that guidance which, by reason of his want of experience in war, he grievously, though unconsciously, needed. Captain Morris ... was a man richly gifted with the natural qualities which tend to make a leader of cavalry, but strengthened also by intellectual cultivation well applied to the business of arms and clothed, above all, with that priceless experience which soldiers acquire in war ... After having first armed himself with a portion at least of the education which Cambridge bestows, he had served with glory in India ... When opportunities of gaining warlike experience were no longer open to him, he returned to the labour of military study, and carried away from Sandhurst ample evidences of his proficiency in higher departments of military learning ... *Captain Morris was one of those who might have been wisely entrusted with an extended command of Cavalry.* Few could be more competent to point out to Lord Cardigan the error he was committing.[20]

As angry as anyone at the Light Brigade's inactivity, Morris rode over to Cardigan and asked his Brigadier to take the Brigade in support of the Heavies. In fact he had already given orders to John Brown, his field trumpeter, to sound the trot, supposing perhaps that that was what Cardigan was about to order himself. Cardigan wheeled his horse towards Morris and in the gruff, barking voice for which he was known shouted, 'What are you doing, Captain Morris? Front your regiment!'

'Look there, my lord,' said Morris, pointing with his sword at the Russian cavalry flank now exposed by the impact of the Heavy charge.

'Remain where you are, sir,' Cardigan replied, 'until you get my orders!'

With the Russians retreating in disorder, Morris tried again. 'My lord, are we not going to charge the flying enemy?'

'No,' Cardigan replied. 'We have orders to remain here.'

'Do, my lord, allow me to charge them with the Lancers. See my lord, they are in disorder!'[21]

Donald Thomas, in his biography of Cardigan, *Charge! Hurrah! Hurrah!*, goes on:

> For some time the argument grew warm between Cardigan, tall and splendid in his Hussar uniform, and the stocky figure of Morris in a blue frock coat and a forage cap with gold-edged peak. Then even the troopers sitting on their horses some distance away from the two men heard Cardigan's hoarse, sharp words.
> 'No, no, sir!'[22]

According to Private Wightman of the 17th, one of those survivors of the Light Brigade who afterwards told of their experiences, Cardigan also said again, 'We must not stir from here,' and Morris, furious almost to the point of insubordination, roared to fellow officers nearby, 'Gentlemen, you are witnesses of my request.' He pulled his horse back, slapping his leg with his sword, saying, 'My God, my God, what a chance we are losing.'[23]

Donald Thomas quotes Morris's Adjutant, Robert White, as saying to him, 'If I were in command of the regiment, I would attack by myself and stand a court martial. There is a C.B. staring you in the face as you cannot fail.'[24] But the moment was lost. As Kinglake says:

> The man of the Sutlej entreating that the Brigade might advance to the rescue, but rebuffed and over-ruled by the higher authority of the man from the banks of the Serpentine, who sits erect in his saddle and is fitfully damning the Heavies instead of taking part in their fight – these might seem to be creatures of the brain evoked, perhaps, for some drama of the grossly humorous sort, but because of the sheer truth their place is historic.[25]

Various modern writers – and even old soldiers like Evelyn Wood – have tried to excuse Cardigan for not having taken Morris's advice. Cardigan himself, later to be accused somewhat fatuously of not having led the Light Brigade to the guns (the subject of the famous Calthorpe lawsuit of 1863), denied that Morris had ever made the suggestion. Cardigan wrote later:

> I entirely deny that Captain Morris ever pointed out to me my opportunity of charging the enemy, or said anything to me of the kind; and it is quite untrue that I said I was placed in that particular spot, and should not move without orders, or anything to that effect. I further deny that Captain Morris ever begged me to be allowed to charge with his regiment alone, or that he ever gave me any advice, or uttered one word to me upon the subject of attacking the enemy. I remember upon one occasion during the engagement, after the

Light Brigade had been ordered [by Lucan] to join the Heavy Brigade in the valley, Captain Morris broke away from the column with his regiment without orders [presumably the incident referred to above] upon which I asked him, sharply, why he did so and desired him to fall again into column. That was all that occurred on the day in question, between myself and Captain Morris.[26]

Kinglake, in a footnote, quotes a letter written by Morris to the War Office:

Having read a letter from Major Calthorpe [a fellow staff officer] in which he throws between Lord Cardigan and myself the settlement of the question as to whether I asked Lord Cardigan on the 25th October, 1854, to attack the Russian Cavalry in flank at the time they were engaged with the Heavy Brigade, and which Lord Cardigan most positively denies, I wish to declare most positively that I did ask Lord Cardigan to attack the enemy at the time and in the manner above mentioned.[27]

Evelyn Wood, who, as we have seen, later joined the 17th and shared quarters with Morris in India, thought it 'out of character for Cardigan to be guilty of "wilful misstatements"'.[28] Perhaps mutual misunderstanding between the cavalry officers is the explanation. Mrs Woodham-Smith, a little more tongue in cheek, perhaps, says that Cardigan's 'recollection was at fault'. It did not help matters that Lucan had sent his son, Lord Bingham, acting as ADC and had later reinforced to Cardigan himself, exactly what Morris had been urging: 'My instructions to you are to attack anything and everything that shall come within reach of you.'[29]

Louis Nolan had written in his excellent, ground-breaking book on cavalry tactics:

The tactics of cavalry are not capable of being reduced to rule … With the cavalry officer almost everything depends on the clearness of his coup d'oeil and the ferocity with which he seizes the happy moment of action.[30]

Mrs Woodham-Smith gets it right: 'Smartly as Lord Cardigan could handle a brigade of cavalry on a field day, these were qualities he did not even remotely possess.'[31]

And Cardigan's tragedy, even more a tragedy for the Light Brigade and the British war effort, was that he knew perfectly well he did not possess them. A more honest man than Cardigan would never have accepted a field command in the first place. But the same could be said of all the High Command in the Crimea. At very least, Cardigan should have had the humility and the intellect to take sound advice when it mattered. Sadly, Cardigan had neither intellect nor humility. He could therefore only follow the rule book, the rigid code of lack of initiative which characterized the stupid officer, promoted through a system wholly reliant on money and influence. And when criticized for this, he simply lied his way out. Kinglake, in the fifth volume of his monumental *Invasion of the Crimea*, sums up the situation:

> If the plan of defence [of Balaclava] were to rest at all on our cavalry, there was cogent need of an effort to neutralize in some measure the vice of Lord Hardinge's peace-service appointments, and to make arrangement for giving more or less of initiative power in the field to men such as Morris, who [was] practised in war, and knew by [his] own experience what it was to lead squadrons in battle. No such effort was made.[32]

The question remains, and it must be one of conjecture, what Morris hoped to achieve by going to the full support of the Heavy Brigade. Lord George Paget, in command of the 4th Light Dragoons that day, was to say in his *Light Cavalry Journal* that the ground over which Morris intended to charge was broken and difficult and there was always the chance of a Russian attack from another direction which would have caught the Light Brigade in the flank, although Paget was not that close to this ground and agrees that 'Captain Morris and others' thought the tactic sound. No such attack, of course, took place. Neither was it ever threatened. And George Paget, for all he was the son of the redoubtable 'One Leg' of Waterloo fame, was as inexperienced as his Brigadier at Balaclava. It seems at least likely that the whole of the Russian cavalry could have been driven off and badly mauled, if not totally destroyed, by a concerted effort of both brigades.

Recalled by the government to account for his conduct at Balaclava, but denied the right of court martial as no charge was ever brought against him, Lucan made a speech to the House of Lords in March 1855. Concerning the lack of support by the Light Brigade at this stage of the battle, Lucan said:

> I know it has been imputed to me that I did not pursue the routed enemy with my light cavalry as I should have done. To this I will not allow myself to say any more than that they had been placed in a position by Lord Raglan [his third order of the morning] that they were altogether out of my reach and that to me they were unavailable.[33]

In the appendix to the speech is written:

> So disappointed was Lord Lucan at not having the support of the Light Cavalry Brigade that he sent by the first Staff Officer that became disposable to desire that Lord Cardigan would always

remember that when he (Lord Lucan) was attacking in front, it was his (Lord Cardigan's) duty to support him in a flank attack.[34]

In the light of this, Captain White's urging of Morris to defy Cardigan – 'there is a CB staring you in the face as you cannot fail' – makes some sense. But it was this very flexibility which was not tolerated, especially in officers as junior as Morris. Can we really believe, even with the commonsense statements expressed by Lucan above, that he would have come to Morris's aid in the event of a court martial and probable disgrace? As Kinglake says: 'By the will of our military authorities at home, the man versed in war was placed under the man versed in quarrels. Lord Cardigan had been charged to command; Captain Morris to obey.'[35]

As it was, the chance, as Morris said, had been lost, and during a lull in the battle the Heavy Brigade licked its wounds. The casualties were not that heavy. There were an estimated ten killed and ninety-eight wounded, although some of this occurred later as the tired Heavies tried to help their comrades in the Lights. Temple Godman told his father that the 5th had two fatalities, with the likelihood of a third, nine wounded and fourteen injured horses. Russell wrote:

> Lord Raglan at once despatched Lieutenant Curzon, Aide-de-Camp, to convey his congratulations to Brigadier-General Scarlett and to say 'Well done!' The gallant old officer's face beamed with pleasure when he received the message. 'I beg to thank his lordship very sincerely' was his reply.[36]

When Morris wrote to his wife on 4 November from the troopship *Australia* 'lying in the Bosphorus', he mentioned a number of men of the Heavy Brigade who had been killed or wounded. First was 'Alex Elliot, a good deal cut about the face'. Alexander James Hardy Elliot (1825–1900) is one of the few referred to by his abbreviated Christian name and he must have been a personal friend. Kinglake puts Elliot on a par with Morris as one who had 'earned fame in honest war'. He had served with distinction in India in the Bengal Light Cavalry, but ill-health had forced him to leave the subcontinent and he purchased a lieutenancy in the 5th Dragoon Guards in 1850. On 25 October, Elliot was ADC to Scarlett and as such rode immediately behind him when the Brigadier galloped hell for leather into the enemy cavalry. He was wearing his cocked hat, the full dress requirement for a staff officer and this would have given his head virtually no protection. Ironically, he asked permission of Scarlett to be allowed to wear the more comfortable staff forage cap (as Morris did) but the Brigadier had refused – 'Damn the order! My staff shall be properly dressed!' His chinstrap was loose and he stuffed a large silk handkerchief into the cap to secure it. It is possible that the Russians believed that he and not Scarlett was the senior officer by virtue of the cocked hat and they seem to have made a beeline for him. As Morris was to do, Elliot skewered a Russian officer with such force that the sword penetrated nearly to the hilt. Slashing around him with his extra-long blade, he was 'doing great work ... till his hat was knocked off and he got three cuts – one bad one, right into the bone at the back of the head, one on his forehead and his nose nearly cut off – but he has got it stuck on and it has grown up quite a good job.' Only the thickness of the handkerchief appears to have saved his life. Elliot went home in the spring, along with Scarlett, and despite talk of his exchanging into the Foot Guards, he was promoted Major in the 5th in August 1855. Temple Godman was delighted: 'He is the only staff officer I know who *deserved* promotion and he certainly did much more than many of the C.B.s.'[37] Elliot obtained his Companionship of the Bath in the same gazette as Morris. He was to the Heavy Brigade what Morris was to the Light – the most experienced man his blinkered brigadier had.

The second Heavy to whom Morris refers is Darby Griffiths, the Colonel of the Greys, who complained so bitterly about the inadequacy of his men's swords. As Morris's principal duty at Varna had been the disembarkation and embarkation of troops, he would have worked closely with Griffiths. He was probably the first casualty of the Heavy Charge, having his bearskin taken off and his head grazed by a carbine shot. His horse swerved, but he galloped on. He was clearly an outspoken man, as his letter of complaint to the War Office indicates, and in November he was complaining loudly to Lucan about the inadequate shelters for his regiment. Forrest, of the 4th Dragoon Guards, did not like him (but Forrest seems to have disliked most officers, especially if they were senior to him): 'I do not think Griffiths is the man to show [Lucan] up. He is a bombastic fellow himself and is said occasionally to talk very wide of the mark and to imagine that he did a great deal more than was ever accomplished by him.'[38] He was also famed among the Heavy Brigade for his hospitality. Colonel Hodge, of the 4th Dragoon Guards, mentions a 'swell affair' in February 1855, when Griffiths gave a breakfast to the Colonel of the 1st Zouaves. On 30 March, Hodge dined with him – 'a soufflé made to perfection and some good mutton' – although he had to admit Griffiths's chef was inferior to Scarlett's. Cornet Fisher of the 4th was impressed, however. Griffiths 'brought the Mess Cook out with him as his private servant and has lived in great style.'[39]

Morris next mentions Cornet Prendergast of the Greys, riding a huge horse that placed him above his Russian adversaries in the Charge. He was taken first to Balaclava and then to Scutari, almost certainly in the same transport as Morris and the wounded survivors of the Light Brigade.

Next of the Heavies is Captain the Honourable Gray Neville, whose horse, tangled in the ropes and pegs of the Light Brigade camp, went down. Godman, in the same regiment (5th Dragoon Guards) explains what happened:

> and poor Neville was a *bad* rider and too weak to use his sword well, was soon dismounted and had it not been for one of our men who stood over him, Private Abbott, he must have been killed. He was

wounded in the head and three places in his back and they fear that his liver is injured, in which case he cannot recover.[40]

He lost his brother in the Guards at Inkerman in the first week of November and Godman ends the story on 22 November:

> You will be sorry to hear poor Neville died of his wounds on November 11th at Scutari. [He had been there five days.] I suppose the lung was touched. I think he must have heard of the death of his brother in the Guards ... he was very fond of him and this must have taken much hold of poor Neville's mind, a sad thing for his family, two killed in one week.[41]

Lieutenant Frederick Swinfen of the 5th Dragoon Guards was run through the hand and according to Godman 'had a lance wound in the chest, very slight'. By 7 December he had recovered but was very ill at Scutari. He was going home and laid up sick at Malta by 2 January. 'I don't think Swinfen will come out again,' wrote Godman. 'I daresay he would sell out if he could.'[42]

Also wounded was Captain Elmsall of the 1st Dragoon Guards, William de Cardonnel Elmsall, who had obtained his cornetcy in July 1842 and had remained with the same regiment throughout, buying his troop in September 1849.

Next, Morris refers to Lieutenant Colonel John Yorke of the 1st Royal Dragoons. Yorke led the regiment in the Charge and was disabled for life with a shattered leg.

Last among the Heavies, Morris lists Captain W R N Campbell of the 5th Dragoon Guards. His horse had gone down with Neville's in the early stages of the Charge and this may have exacerbated an earlier wound. On 22 November, Godman wrote that he was 'laid up for a month with a bad leg (an old affair) in a little tent' and that he was toying with exchanging to half pay. Like the lovesick Paget of the 4th Light Dragoons, Campbell was engaged and his spirits were low. By early December he had gone ill to Scutari and on 29 December Godman wrote:

> Poor Campbell, who died a few days ago at Scutari – he owes his death entirely to the disgraceful mismanagement of our medical department. They would not let him go away till he was so ill he was nearly insensible and in this state sometimes wet through in his bed, as the water comes through in our tents. He died of dysentery; a very sad thing indeed, a man who had already gained three Indian medals and several clasps and had been all through this campaign to die like a dog through neglect. He was a very clever and agreeable man ... we shall miss him much, because he was so cheery ... all through the cholera and bad times.[43]

It could almost be an obituary for Morris himself three and a half years later.

Chapter Ten

'A Smart Little Affair'

Back at Balaclava, there was more to come. There was a lull, to the extent that some men thought the action was over for that day. Raglan attempted to recover the redoubts with Cathcart's 4th Division, but there was delay and confusion, not least because of the time taken by the 'galloper' (an ADC named Captain Ewart of the 93rd Foot) to reach Cathcart and lead the Division by the necessary route. The 1st Division under Cambridge was also moving nearer, but Raglan was anxious to hit Liprandi's force before they withdrew out of reach. Only the cavalry was near enough to act and Raglan clearly believed they could hold the Russians until the infantry arrived to support them. He sent orders to that effect to Lucan: 'The cavalry to advance and take advantage of every opportunity to recover the Heights. They will be supported by infantry which has been ordered to advance on two fronts.'[1]

Accordingly, the Light Brigade moved up into position alongside the reforming Heavies, with d'Allonville's Chasseurs to the rear. The Light Brigade had been standing to since before dawn. Most of them had not eaten, although in the hour that now passed before further orders arrived, some of the officers munched hard-boiled eggs. Paget, with the 4th, allowed his men to dismount and light their pipes and cigars. In the inactivity, which made the plumed hats around Raglan's position seethe with annoyance, the Russians decided to evacuate the redoubts, perhaps because they found them untenable. They roped up the British guns and began to haul them away, although some authorities doubt that this actually happened. It was very well known to Raglan that Wellington had never lost a gun and this perhaps more than their practical loss irked him. It was nearly eleven o'clock and the Commander in Chief dictated a fourth and final order to Lucan, which Airey duly copied down in pencil, resting the paper on his sabretache:

Lord Raglan wishes the Cavalry to advance rapidly to the front – follow the Enemy and try to prevent the Enemy carrying away the

guns. Troop Horse Artillery may accompany. French cavalry is on
your left. Immediate.

    Airey.[2]

This message, the original of which has survived, was to have been carried by
Captain Calthorpe, Raglan's ADC, but Raglan ordered Nolan, on Airey's staff,
to take it. The reason is not clear, but Raglan wanted speed and Nolan's
horsemanship was well known. Nolan, riding a troop horse of the 13th Light
Dragoons, took the fastest way down the scarp slope. In Kinglake's words,
'straight, swift and intent – descending, as it were, on a sure prey – he swooped
angering down into the plain where Lord Lucan and his squadrons were
posted.'[3] Nolan was a familiar sight to the Brigade. Though a staff officer, he
had not had time before being sent ahead on remount duty to Turkey to obtain
a new uniform. Consequently, he wore his full dress jacket and pelisse of the
15th Hussars. He rode through the Brigade, between the front lines of the 13th
Light Dragoons and the 17th Lancers.

    All witnesses agree to the conversation that followed. Nolan called to
Morris, 'Where is Lord Lucan?'

    'There,' said Morris. 'On the right front [near the Heavies]. What is it to be,
Nolan? Are we going to charge?'

    Nolan shouted over his shoulder, 'You will see. You will see.'[4]

    The Aide gave Lucan Raglan's order. It was of course incomprehensible.
The view from the valley floor, where the Light Brigade waited, was totally
different from Raglan's on the heights. Lucan could not see the redoubts or the
guns being towed away. The message was very vague. There was no sign of
Horse Artillery, and the French cavalry, the Chasseurs d'Afrique, were moving
up, it seemed, independently of the Lights. Lucan looked blank. Nolan was
furious. Most modern writers regard the combination of his excitable Italian-
Irish temperament and his enthusiasm for cavalry as the key to what happened.
The job of a 'galloper' was to explain a written order if there was any confusion
about it. According to Calthorpe, both Raglan and Airey had spent some time
lecturing Nolan on this. It was probably Nolan who had christened Lucan
'Lord Look-On' after the cavalry's inaction in the war thus far (the earlier
events of this day excluded), and for a staff officer, especially, he was extremely
outspoken. Lucan pointed out that the order did not make much sense and
Nolan promptly reminded him that the order said 'Immediate'. 'Lord Raglan's
orders were that the cavalry should attack immediately,' he said.

    'Attack, sir?' snapped Lucan. 'Attack what? What guns, sir?'

    Nolan flung his arm behind him, almost certainly without looking where he
was pointing, and said, 'There, my lord, is your enemy! There are your guns!'[5]

    As John Harris says, 'For a hundred years and more, historians have been
trying to decide what Nolan meant.' Was he, as Kinglake and Harris assert,
genuinely mistaken about Raglan's intention? Was he really, in Mark Adkin's

phrase, one of the 'four horsemen of calamity'?[6] Bearing in mind Nolan's obvious intelligence and experience, this would seem unlikely. Was he, as others have suggested, deliberately misleading Lucan into a headlong charge in his belief in the superiority of British cavalry and their ability to ride over anything? Tantalizingly, the last paragraph of Nolan's book, *Cavalry: Its History and Tactics*, says:

> For our purpose let it suffice that we have shown to our cavalry that it [the ability of cavalry to break infantry and other dangerous feats] *can* be done and we leave it to them to remove all doubt on the subject so soon as they shall have an opportunity.[7]

Did that opportunity present itself at Balaclava? Ironically, the one man who may have been able to tell us, William Morris, his friend and confidant, said nothing on the matter for the rest of his life.

Witnesses differ as to how explosive this exchange was between Nolan and Lucan. Harris, who believes with some justification that Lucan was a better soldier than history has given him credit for, says that he kept his temper in check and rode over to Cardigan with Raglan's order. Mrs Woodham-Smith, whose book *The Reason Why* so expertly opened up a fascinating field for a whole generation, bases her book on the false premise that it was the dislike between these brothers-in-law that led to the disaster which followed. Certainly, their conduct was not likely to make for a smooth campaign, but on the morning of 25 October, they behaved impeccably towards each other. And Cardigan's reply to Raglan's order proves he was not quite the fool some writers have made him out to be: 'Certainly, sir, but allow me to point out to you that the Russians have a battery in the valley to our front and batteries and riflemen on both sides.'

'I know it,' Lucan told him. 'But Lord Raglan will have it.' And he spoke what was to be an epitaph for an entire antiquated system of command as well as for many brave men when he added, 'We have no choice but to obey.'[8]

Another altercation followed, this time between Cardigan and Nolan, although no one later testified as to exactly what was said. Cardigan snapped: 'By God! If I come through this alive, I'll have you court martialled for speaking to me in that manner!'[9]

Nolan rode over to Morris and asked his permission to ride with the 17th, which was duly granted. In their sabretaches, the two men carried letters: Nolan carried Morris's to Amelia; Morris carried Nolan's to his mother. Whichever of them survived was to deliver the letter he carried, bringing news of the death of the other. Nolan took up position, between the two squadrons of the 17th, to Morris's right, a little behind him. It is surely inconceivable that in the minutes that followed while Lucan insisted the 11th Hussars pull back (much to Cardigan's annoyance) to form a more compact unit, Nolan should not have discussed with Morris what was about to happen. Mrs Woodham-Smith seems of the opinion that Morris believed the attack was to be delivered on the battery of guns in position at the end of the North Valley, but I am unaware of any evidence for this. Mark Adkin too believes that this was Nolan's intention.

The story of the Charge of the Light Brigade has been told and retold countless times – most simply and heroically perhaps, by Tennyson, the Poet Laureate:

> Flash'd all their sabres bare,
> Flash'd as they turned in air
> Sabring the gunners there,
> Charging an army, while
>   All the world wonder'd.

Cardigan dined out on it for the rest of his life. The poem had been prompted by Russell's account in *The Times*:

> At ten minutes past eleven, our Light cavalry Brigade advanced …
> They swept proudly past, glittering in the morning sun in all the
> pride and splendour of war. We could scarcely believe the evidence
> of our senses. Surely that handful of men were not going to charge
> an army in position?[10]

The watchers, with Raglan and Russell on the Heights, remembered the stillness, except for the jingle of bits and the creak of leather. At that distance, in the autumn haze, the Light Brigade seemed to creep forward. Because the story is so well known, the narrative here concentrates on Morris and his regiment, except where essential explanation is necessary. Someone heard Cardigan say, 'Here goes the last of the Brudenells' as he walked his chestnut, Ronald, to the front of the Brigade. 'The Brigade will advance. First squadron of the 17th Lancers direct.' Donald Thomas states that Cardigan gave the order to the trumpeter of the 17th (John Brown, Morris's field trumpeter) to sound the advance. This is unlikely because Cardigan had his own trumpeter, Whitton, who rode behind him with the Brigade staff officers, Lieutenant Colonel Mayow and Lieutenant Maxse and Cornet Wombwell, his ADC. Most survivors of the Charge affirm that no trumpet call was sounded, although the 'Balaclava Bugle' carried by William Brittain of the 17th is now in The Queen's Royal Lancers Museum at Belvoir Castle.

Behind Cardigan's group, moving at a walk as though on a parade ground, rode the 13th Light Dragoons, commanded, because of sickness, by Captain John Oldham, who had recently been put under arrest by Lucan for a minor disobedience of orders. He was to die in the next few minutes, last seen, wounded and bleeding, with a pistol in one hand and a sword in the other. His body was never found. The 13th wore their shakos cased with oilskin covers, their swords carried 'at the slope' on their shoulders, watching their dressing and the wide sandy valley ahead.

This was not the Valley of Death photographed by Roger Fenton in the spring of 1855, but a shallow valley formed by a cluster of hills to the north and a low ridge to the south. It was about one and a half miles – almost exactly Tennyson's 'half a league' – from the Brigade's starting point to the guns, and the valley about a mile wide. The Brigade was deployed over about one-fifth of its width, according to John MacDonald in *Great Battlefields of the World*, and for the first 400 yards the enemy had time to fire nine rounds of solid shot or shrapnel. Between 600 and 200 yards away, either two rounds of solid shot or three of canister could be fired. For the last 200 yards only two rounds of canister could be fired before impact. About 70 per cent of the Russian shot seems to have been round shot. All of it was deadly. On the left of the 13th, Morris in his undress staff uniform led the 17th, still with their lances erect at this stage, the troop officers slightly ahead, riding behind Nolan. Behind them, at an interval of several yards rode Lieutenant Colonel John Douglas and the men of Cardigan's old regiment, the 11th Hussars, magnificent in their laced jackets and crimson overalls. Harris describes him as 'tall, handsome, a friend of Paget's and for a long time the long-suffering second-in-command to Cardigan'.[11] He came through the day unscathed. Then came the 4th Light Dragoons led by the love-sick George Paget, dressed, not unlike Morris, in his undress frock coat and forage cap, resolutely determined to give Cardigan the 'full support' the man had asked for and to keep his cigar alight. Lastly, the 8th Hussars (their pelisses had been sunk with a ship in Balaclava Harbour) led by Lieutenant Colonel Frederick Shewell, 'the Old Woman', renowned as a prude, who had kicked a man out of the Brigade moments before for smoking when he had been told not to. His charger and that of Cornet Clement Heneage, who rode behind him, were the only two to escape unhurt in the entire Light Brigade.

Exactly how many men rode in the ranks of the 17th that morning will probably never be known, still less in the entire Brigade. Tennyson's 'noble six hundred' was accepted for a long time and the consensus now seems to have settled on 673, the figure listed by George Paget in his *Crimean Journal*. Lord Anglesey veers towards the lists 'carefully compiled from Regimental records and verified as far as possible by the statements of some of the survivors' compiled by Colonel F A Whinyates for his book *From Corunna to Sevastopol*, which gives a total of 661, including Cardigan, Mayow and Maxse. This figure may well not include Nolan, however, so perhaps Whinyates's real total is 662. In what is an exhaustive piece of original research and a labour of love, Canon William Lummis, former Chaplain to the 11th Hussars, compiled over twenty years a comprehensive list of those who rode in the Charge and other members of the Light Brigade. Terry Brighton, the Brigade's most recent historian, lists 666 as the likely figure. As we shall see, they are all wrong.

Riding behind Morris were his Troop Captains, Morgan, Webb, White and Winter. They held the same rank as he, but lacked his seniority within the regiment and most definitely his experience. Morgan, son of the 1st Baron Tredegar, was twenty-three years old, riding a charger called Sir Briggs. He had been educated at Eton and obtained a cornetcy in the 17th in July 1849. He had been a Captain for eighteen months and had a younger brother, Fred, serving in the Crimea with the infantry. A painting by Richard Buckner of around 1853 shows a handsome man with large eyes and a magnificent set of Piccadilly weepers. Webb, born near Barnard Castle, was about twenty-two, gazetted Cornet in December 1848. Like Morris and many others of the Light Brigade, he had contracted cholera at Varna in September and was probably not that well on the morning of the Charge. White (later the same White-Thomson who wrote the memoir of Morris delivered as a lecture by his wife in 1902, shortly before his death) was twenty-seven. An Irishman from County Meath, he had been educated at Rugby and Trinity College, Dublin and purchased his cornetcy in October 1847. White commanded E Troop and led the second squadron in the Charge. For a time in the year before the Crimea he was ADC to the Lord Lieutenant of Ireland.

Morris's lieutenants rode serrefile with their troops, riding behind the lines to keep formation tight. William Gordon, whom John Harris describes as 'modest and painstaking', was twenty-four and had succeeded his father as 6th Baronet at the age of thirteen. He was educated at Cheltenham College and bought his cornetcy in June 1850.

Lummis says that John Hartopp *may* have ridden in the Charge, but it is safe to assume from Morris's letter to Amelia on 4 November that he did, despite, Lummis assures us, his receiving no medal clasp for Balaclava. He is one of several men to whom the official record has been unkind. He is not listed at all in Terry Brighton's appendices on the Light Brigade strength that day. Hartopp was twenty-five, the son of Sir William Hartopp, 3rd Baronet, and had purchased his commission in September 1851.

John Thomson is a rather shadowy figure whose photograph is in the National Army Museum, a rather plain young man, the brother of Captain White and born at Hatherleigh. He obtained his cornetcy in the 17th in April 1850 and it seems at least likely that Morris being in the regiment played a part in this.

John Chadwick was Morris's Adjutant. Lummis gives no information on him before his purchase of a cornetcy in February 1852, but Morris's squad book tells us that Chadwick had risen from the ranks.

Archibald Clevland (also spelled Cleveland), to whom Morris referred in his speech at Great Torrington two years later, was the nephew of Major Willett of the regiment and was on the point of selling out to claim the fortune he had inherited when the war broke out. He was twenty-one and was born at Tapeley Park, North Devon, the son of an officer and Waterloo veteran. Educated with Winter at Rugby, he had first joined the 7th Dragoon Guards in November 1852 but exchanged into the 17th in April of the following year.

Last among the officers came Cornet George Wombwell, although he rode at Balaclava in front of the 17th, a little behind Cardigan, by virtue of being the brigadier's ADC. He was twenty-two, the son of Sir George Wombwell, 3rd Baronet, and had been educated at Eton. He obtained his cornetcy in September 1852.

The pace in the valley quickened. The Light Brigade were not the smart unit they had been on embarkation. The entire Brigade was not much stronger than a single regiment at home. Their uniforms were stained and scruffy, their horses shaggy and hang-dog in appearance. The instinct of pace, the noise of the Brigade moving, the pressure of knee against knee quickened the spirit of horse and rider alike. Without further commands, swords came up to the vertical. The lances still pointed skyward. As they moved forward, the Piedmontese 'observers', Major Grovone and Lieutenant Landriani, joined the line, probably with the 13th or 17th, although who gave them permission is uncertain. Jack Vahey, the butcher of the 17th, joined his regiment late, riding a troop horse of the Heavies. He had buckled a heavy dragoon's sword on over his bloody apron and rode in his shirt sleeves, smeared with blood.

As the riflemen on the crests began to take up positions and the astonished Russian gunners looked to their weapons, Nolan broke away from Morris, spurring his horse forward. Why he did this has never been decided for certain and it never will be now. Morris seems to have believed that Nolan, the cavalry enthusiast, was carried away with the exhilaration of the charge: 'That won't do, Nolan. We've a long way to go and must be steady.'

Cardigan believed Nolan was attempting to force the pace and ride ahead of the Brigade. He had already clashed with the impetuous Nolan minutes before and was furious at his behaviour now. He crossed from left to right, waving his sword and shouting. Later, some witnesses thought he was shouting 'Come on.' Others believed that it was 'Threes right', which would have turned the Brigade if the order had been followed. Kinglake assumed that Nolan had realized the fatal mistake and was trying desperately to do something about it. The first shell from the Russian artillery hit him, killing him instantly. Cornet Wombwell of the 17th describes it: 'Nolan's sword dropped to the ground but his arm remained high in the air. The muscles of his thighs still gripped the saddle but his body contorted and bent as though in a spasm.'[12] Private Wightman wrote, 'The weird shriek and the awful face as rider and horse disappeared haunt me now to this day, the first horror of that ride of horrors.'[13] Wightman believed that it was the impact of the shell which tore Nolan's chest open that caused his horse to swerve to the right. Cardigan did not know Nolan had been hit, as he never turned his head, but likened his scream to that of a woman and determined to have him court-martialled when the action was over. Morris must have seen Nolan go down, but he never put his immediate reactions to paper. The Brigade swept on and over him, at the trot now, but swords were wavering. The crash of gunfire burst among the ranks, horses swerving and colliding, officers and non-commissioned officers barking at the men to look to the dressing and keep tight. The Russians cannot have believed their luck, but they were hard at work now, struggling with the guns to hit the Brigade with everything they could. Cardigan was impeccable. Wearing his gold-braided pelisse closed rather than slung like the rest of the 11th, he remained in Wightman's phrase, 'steady as a church', turning his head slightly only when the 17th began to crowd him – 'Steady, Captain Morris. Steady the 17th Lancers.' But there was steadiness and steadiness. Cardigan's orders were not born of wisdom and experience but the drill book and the parade ground. He was also acutely vain and no mere Captain of Lancers, however experienced, was going to dictate the pace and direction of *his* Brigade.

The shell fire worsened: 'It thinned us like a sickle through grass,' Maxse wrote later,[14] and the ranks closed in to the centre as gaps appeared. Morris and White moved forward again, this time forcing Cardigan to shout, 'Stay, sir! How dare you attempt to ride before your commanding officer.' He held his sword across White's chest. Rifle fire from the hills on each side began to take its toll. The pace quickened at this point to a gallop and the dressing became ragged. The lance tips of the 17th came down, and with 'hell opened up on us', as Wightman said, the first two lines rode hard for the guns, Captain White driving his spurs home. The 13th jostled with his squadron in the centre – 'Don't let those bastards of the 17th get in front!' White's squadron countered with 'Come on, Deaths, come on!' Morris's sword arm extended to the 'Right Engage' position. Immediately behind him his ranks were being decimated. Trumpeter 926 John Brown was hit in the leg, Captain Webb's shin was smashed and Cornet Clevland's horse was hit. Private John Lees, riding on Wightman's right, went down with the inexplicable words 'Domino, chum.' 'He was a good old soldier,' said Wightman. 'He had served long in India,' and he remembered Lees's grey mare 'trading on and tearing out her entrails as she galloped.'[15]

Sergeant Edward Talbot, in Morris's troop in 1851, had his head blown off by round shot, but the headless corpse remained upright in the saddle. Private Thomas Dudley, riding near him, shouted to his right-hand man, 'Did you notice what a bloody hole that shell has made?' Corporal Marsh, typical of the surprisingly God-fearing soldier of his day, rounded on his comrade, 'Hold your foul-mouthed tongue, swearing like a blackguard when you may be knocked into eternity next minute.' The artillery had found their range now and a long way behind Morris, the Heavies, ordered by Lucan to support the Lights, pulled back because they were being hit. It was Lucan's decision and probably the right one: 'They have sacrificed the Light Brigade; they shall not have the Heavy if I can help it.' Scarlett's Brigade sat their horses and watched the last line of the 8th Hussars vanish into the smoke.

Wightman was hit in the right leg and his horse was bleeding from neck wounds. Marsh told him to fall out, but the pace and fury of the Brigade made that impossible. The 11th and the 4th were gaining ground somewhere behind them and the shattered first line of the 17th and the 13th followed Cardigan as he jerked Ronald back on course after a shell burst and he leapt the guns. Behind them, George Paget, still smoking his cigar and only just now remembering to draw his sword, yelled 'View Halloo!' and drove home his spurs. The Russian gunners had had their chance and now they were at the mercy of galloping, plunging horses, probing lances and slashing swords, but in the mêlée and the smoke, a massive bloc of grey-coated cavalry emerged, moving forward at a trot.

These were by no means as steady as some writers on the Charge have believed. General Ryzhov first sent the light-armed Cossacks against the British Cavalry, but they wheeled away rather than face the desperate Light Brigade with their blood up, and began hacking at their own troops to forge a way out. The Kievsky and Ingermanlandsky were thrown back on each other like a concertina with the impact of the Charge, which, although broken to an extent by having to negotiate the guns, was still devastating. The Lights slashed and hacked at the Russian cavalry, driving them back towards the river and their own transport lines. An officer called Kozhukhov, with the 12th Artillery Brigade, saw the Charge in all its horror and glory and reckoned the British Brigade outnumbered by about five to one.

In the chaos behind the guns, Cardigan found himself surrounded by Cossacks who jabbed at him with their lances, more in curiosity than with murderous intent. In one of those bizarre coincidences of the war, he recognized their officer, Prince Radziwill, whom he had met in London before the war. The Prince may have intended that his men take Cardigan prisoner, but in the event, the officers saluted each other with their swords and Cardigan, who seems to have been genuinely dazed by the noise and action, wheeled his charger and rode back through the smoke looking for his Brigade. He found some and began attempting to reform them. The Shakespearean actor Private Frederick Melrose of the 17th fell before the guns, aptly bellowing out the line from *Henry V*, 'What man here would ask another man from England?'[16] Sergeant John Berryman's horse refused to jump the obstacle and Berryman dismounted to find the animal's leg broken. Captain Webb, in agony with his shattered leg, rode up and asked Berryman what he should do. Berryman urged the delirious officer to stay with his horse and grabbed a riderless mount for himself, but the animal was hit by rifle fire as he mounted and Berryman rolled with it.

Morris had galloped wide of the guns, lashing Old Treasurer with his spurs. Terry Brighton believes that he had missed the guns altogether in the confusion and smoke and it is true the battery was not an easy target to find, but Morris had charged artillery before and it seems at least likely that he had deliberately ridden to the left in order to outflank the guns and give the Charge more impact. It also got him away from the petulant behaviour of Cardigan, who though Morris was to admit later had led the Brigade well, now had no idea what to do. Wightman, who seems to have ridden in White's right-hand squadron and was cut off from the others, nearly trampled the wounded Lieutenant Maxse and was wheeling round trying to rally a group. He eventually joined Corporal Morley, who had lost his horse early on and been forced to catch another. They had no officer left to lead them and Morley compared the last seconds before the guns as 'riding into the mouth of a volcano'. Troop Sergeant Major Denis O'Hara succeeded in organizing a handful and Morris had about twenty men with him. He reined in, giving his men time to draw their swords or steady their lances as circumstances dictated, and, turning in the saddle, yelled, 'Now, remember what I have told you, men, and keep together.' Morris's little knot of horsemen sliced through the stationary Russian cavalry and they broke in disorder, but they then met an enormous force of Hussars and Cossacks who were still holding their ground. Morris lunged at their commander and drove his sword, exactly as his friend Elliot had done with the Heavies, through the man's body to the hilt. Two things counted against him at this critical moment. First was his own strength. The second was the entirely sensible precaution he had taken of tying the gold acorn sword knot around his wrist so as not to lose the sword. The Russian officer crumpled and slipped from the saddle and Morris had no choice but to go with him. As his men swept past and Morris was desperately trying to extricate himself, he was caught above the ear by a sabre and knocked unconscious by a sword cut through his forage cap and skull. Kinglake has the most detailed description of the wound: 'Morris received a sabre cut on the left side of the head which carried away a large piece of bone above the ear and a deep, clean cut passing down through the acorn of his forage cap, which penetrated both plates of the skull.' Morris said later: 'I don't know how I came to use the point of my sword, but it is the last time I ever do.'[17] He can only have been 'out' for a few seconds and when he came to, his sword was free and he was on foot. A group of Cossacks had circled round him and he now received a third head wound through the temple. Troop Sergeant Major Abraham Ranson remembered:

> Then I saw an act of heroism; [Captain] Morris was on foot, his head streaming with blood, engaging five or six Cossacks. I made the remark to Corporal Taylor near me that poor Captain Morris, I was afraid, was taken prisoner, there was so much odds against him.

Kinglake takes up the story:

Morris sought to defend himself by the almost ceaseless 'moulinet' or circling whirl of his sword and from time to time he found means to deliver some sabre cuts upon the thighs of his Cossack assailants. Soon, however, he was pierced in the temple by a lance-point, which splintered up a piece of bone and forced it under the scalp. This wound gave him great pain and ... he believed that his life must be nearly at its end.[18]

His face a mask of blood, weak and in agony, he expected to die, and reversing his sword gave it up to a Russian officer whose arrival probably saved his life. Two other officers of the 17th, Cornets Chadwick and Wombwell were likewise fighting for their lives and in the mêlée, Morris and Wombwell collided. Since the Russian to whom he had surrendered had vanished in the smoke, probably harassed by the 4th Light Dragoons and the 8th Hussars, who must have reached the guns by this time, Morris no longer felt obliged to stay where he was. He shouted to Wombwell to catch a horse, which the ADC duly did. 'It is interesting to observe that in spite of his own dreadful condition, Morris still had a word of timely counsel that he could give a brother officer.'[19] Wombwell was probably referring to Morris when he wrote, 'and looking round to see what my friends who had charge of me were about, and there they were in a great state but did not dare follow me (as if they had done so they would have run up against our troops).'[20]

Morris eventually grabbed a horse, but his head was bleeding profusely and he must have had difficulty in seeing. He clung to the saddle, being dragged defenceless along the ground until he lost his grip and collapsed. The ever solicitous Bob Portal, galloping past with the 4th Lights, probably saw him at this point and concluded that Morris had been shot. As the shattered remnants of the Light Brigade fought their way out as best they could, Morris regained consciousness again. A Cossack was riding up to him; his watch and sword had already gone, but his undress coat, sabretache and scabbard had a value to a scavenging soldier and Morris forced himself to run to grab a second riderless horse. He hauled himself up into the saddle this time and began to ride, but the crossfire in the valley on the way back was nearly as murderous as it had been on the way there, although by this time, the Chasseurs d'Afrique had silenced a number of Russian guns on the Heights and his new troop horse went down, pinning Morris beneath it. He passed out again.

It was Sergeant Major George Loy Smith of the 11th Hussars who saw him next. 'This is warm work, sir,' Smith called out to him. Morris had recovered yet again and was staggering on foot up the valley. In his journal, Loy Smith wrote:

After a time I saw one of the 17th Lancers in front of me.[21] I sped on and when I got near I found that he was an officer and wore his forage cap, much to my surprise. When within a few yards of him, I said, 'This is warm work, sir.' He looked over his right shoulder at me but made no reply – his face was covered in blood and he had a very wild appearance. This officer was Captain Morris who led the 17th Lancers and behaved so gallantly. I now inclined to my right towards the centre of the valley and in another minute, lost sight of him.[22]

Morris reached the shattered corpse of Louis Nolan, realized he had fallen not far from his own lines and collapsed beside his friend.

A fellow officer commented to Evelyn Wood, then a midshipman with the Navy, 'that was a smart little affair that the Cavalry had this morning.'[23] The Charge of the Light Brigade was over in a little less than twenty minutes. The reckoning had yet to come.

Chapter Eleven
'A Mad Brained Trick'

Morris was lying beside Nolan but he was far from safe. Captain Ewart, of Raglan's staff, was told by those who returned that a staff officer was lying some way out, badly wounded. He rode down the valley and persuaded the Turks who had now reoccupied the Fourth Redoubt to lift Nolan's body, Morris and a Heavy whose jaw had been smashed. They were under an almost continuous stream of fire, however, and they dropped their burdens and ran. From the British lines, rescue was on its way in the form of James Mouat, Surgeon to the 6th Inniskilling Dragoons, and Sergeant Charles Wooden of the 17th. Wooden was not a popular man in the regiment, because he had been born in Germany. A story circulated later in the 17th that he had dismounted during the Charge rather than face the Russian guns; there seems to be no truth in that. Sergeant O'Hara of the 17th, who had done stalwart work at the guns, had helped bring Morris in from under fire. Assistant Surgeon William Cattell of the 5th Dragoon Guards wrote: 'They found a trooper trying to arrest the bleeding from the scalp. Presently some Cossacks attacked the party and the doctor, Mouat, said he had to draw his sword, which he described as "a novel experience".'[1]

The obelisk at Hatherleigh, erected in 1860, shows Morris carried in a military cloak, Mouat at his legs, Wooden supporting Morris under the arms, and a fourth figure, a bearded private of the 17th, presumably intended to be George Mansell, helping with the task. The citation on Wooden's VC (Mouat received one too) reads:

> For having after the retreat of the Light Cavalry at the Battle of Balaclava, been instrumental, together with Dr James Mouat, C.B., in saving the life of Lieutenant-Colonel Morris C.B. of the 17th Lancers by proceeding under a heavy fire, to his assistance, when he was lying very dangerously wounded in an exposed situation.

They took Nolan's letter from Morris's sabretache and put it aside for posting. One account says that Morris's letter for Amelia, found in Nolan's sabretache, was also posted, in the belief that Morris was either dead or about to die. Kinglake says that Morris and Nolan,

> who were great allies, had communicated to each other a common intention of volunteering for any special service that might be required in the course of the campaign; and they found that each of them, in anticipation of the early death that might result from such an enterprise, had written a letter which, in the event, was to be delivered.[2]

Kinglake assumed that 'counter-intelligence' was sent to Amelia to assure her that her husband was still alive. The letter forms part of the Morris Papers and on the envelope is written 'Found in Captain Nolan's sabretache on his Body after death – I think by J.M. [James Mouat]'. This is in Amelia's handwriting, as are the words 'An old letter alas!' It is addressed to Mrs Morris, Bayshill Mansions, Cheltenham, England, which seems to have been a second home for the Morrises after their marriage and a 'place of their own'. The letter itself is difficult to decipher, written as it is crossways in order to save paper and no doubt by candlelight at eleven o'clock on the night of 16 October from 'Heights above Sebastopol'. At this date, Morris had only been in the Crimea for a day at most and the date shows that this was no last-minute presentiment of doom.

> My Own Dearest,
>   I write 2 or 3 lines to tell you that the play commences tomorrow at 6 a.m., so in other words, the French guns and our own open on Sebastopol at that hour and as scaling ladders are to be in attendance I don't know what may happen, so only want to tell you that I consider you the best and most devoted wife that ever man was blessed with, and that I love you more now, I firmly believe, than I ever did in my life, and I pray that the Almighty disposer of events may soon give us a happy meeting, but if not it will I know be some consolation to you to think that I died loving you with all my heart and in a constant hope of meeting you again in a better world.
>   Adieu, my beloved one,
>   William

Mouat and Wooden laid Morris on the ground next to his brother officer, William Gordon, whose wounds were very similar to Morris's, for all he had been wearing his lance cap. John Blunt of the Consular Service, who was in the Crimea principally as interpreter and Turkish expert, saw Morris being carried back. Morris had known Blunt's uncle in India, but Morris didn't recognize Blunt. He was delirious, crying out 'Lord have mercy on my soul!'

While the surgeons did what they could for the wounded and dying, Cardigan rode to the head of what was left of his Light Brigade.

'It was a mad brained trick,' he told them, 'but no fault of mine.'

Someone from the dazed, exhausted ranks called back, 'Never mind, my lord, we are ready to go again.'[3]

Cardigan declined the offer. Rumour was later to credit him with riding down to the *Dryad* in Balaclava Harbour and having a champagne supper. In reality, he slept wrapped in a cloak near Lieutenant Maxse, his wounded ADC, and the next day he visited more of the wounded, like Billy Brittain, a trumpeter of the 17th, who was 'a most pitful case, he begged that his bugle should not be taken out of his sight.' For a while, during the Charge and immediately after it, Cardigan did indeed, in Morris's phrase to Kinglake, lead 'like a gentleman'.

Those Russian officers who told the truth were astonished by the actions of the Light Brigade. The honest Kozhukhov wrote:

> It is difficult, if not impossible, to do justice to the feat of those mad cavalry, for, having lost a quarter of their number and being apparently impervious to new dangers and further losses, they quickly reformed their squadrons to return over the same ground littered with their dead and dying. With such desperate courage, these valiant lunatics set off again.[4]

Liprandi believed the Brigade must be drunk and prisoners who were taken were questioned as to how much rum they had had. Ryzhov wrote how Lucan (who was slightly wounded in support of the Light Brigade) only escaped by the speed of his excellent horse and how he 'drunkenly swung his sabre to the right and to the left.'

Back at the lines, while the farriers shot hopelessly injured horses – Morris's Old Treasurer probably among them – and the surgeons went about their grim business in the short, autumn afternoon, a roll call was taken. Once again, as with the figures on parade in the morning, discrepancies creep in. Paget's *Crimean Journal* does not list regiment by regiment, but ranks and casualties. He therefore counts on parade 5 field officers, 16 captains, 24 subalterns, 7 staff, 51 sergeants, 25 corporals, 17 trumpeters and 528 privates, making the usually accepted 673. Curiously, he only cites 643 horses, but presumably this discrepancy occurs because the missing 30 did not belong to the Brigade. Paget's total casualties, which includes killed, wounded, prisoners and horses shot for wounds, are as follows – 1 field officer, 15 captains (the heaviest proportional casualty rate is in this rank), 10 subalterns, 2 staff, 22 sergeants, 15 corporals, 9 trumpeters and 223 privates, making a total known casualty figure of 297, appreciably less than half the Brigade. Of the horses, a staggering 460 casualties were listed, although virtually all the horses had some damage done to them. Paget himself, in riding down the valley, had had to use his sabre on riderless troop horses which, maddened with fear and relying on trained instinct, crowded in against him, threatening to crush his legs.

Colonel Whinyates in *From Corunna to Sevastopol* breaks his figures down differently, by regiment, but his total killed, wounded and taken prisoner only equals 287. Although he admits the horse figures for the 13th Light Dragoons and the 17th Lancers (likely to be higher by virtue of being in the front rank) are estimates only, his total is only 315. For the 17th Lancers, Whinyates gives the figure of 11 officers on parade in the morning and 136 NCOs and privates. Of these, 2 officers (Winter and Thomson) were killed, as were 2 Other Ranks, while 4 Officers (including Morris) and 33 Other Ranks were wounded. One officer (Chadwick) and 13 Other Ranks were taken prisoner. The number of horses lost was said to be 99.

John Smith, known in the regiment as 'Blood' or 'Fighting' Smith, testified later that he and George Mansell carried Morris off the field, 'to take him away to Balaclava hospital'. This would have been the nearest of the temporary field hospitals set up by the regimental surgeons, any one of whom may have continued Mouat's preliminary dressing once Morris was away from the firing line. A number of naval surgeons hurried to the scene too and we have no way of knowing precisely who tended him.

It was not for another three days that Morris was well enough to write to Amelia. Portal, who had ridden the Charge with the 4th Lights, wrote to his mother on 26 October:

> The number of wounds and deaths among the officers is too horrid to think of. Poor Morris ... was shot in the head [sic]. I passed by him lying on the ground when we were in full gallop, but of course could do nothing. He was found and brought in and was not quite dead, but quite out of his mind. I must write to Arthur Taylor [Amelia's brother] about him.

Of the men whom Morris mentions in his letter of 4 November, written on the troopship *Australia* bound for Scutari, some, as already mentioned, were in the Heavy Brigade. The rest were connected with the Lights.

First comes 'Capt. Nolan, 15th Hussars (K)' – an odd formality for men who according to all sources were close friends. It is by no means certain when they met, but it was probably in India in the spring of 1846 after Aliwal. Did Morris feel disgust for the dead Aide? Did he hold him responsible, as many others did then and have since, for the disaster of the Light Brigade? As always, the clever professional staff officer allows himself no comment, even in his private correspondence with his wife. It is true that writing was difficult for him at this stage: '... and close my letter (though I could go on writing for a week) as my arm is very painful and even this slight movement does harm.'

Next, Morris cites Captain Charteris, ADC to Lord Lucan. Walter Charteris was the son of Lord Elcho and Lucan's nephew. On the morning of Balaclava, he had a presentiment of death. He borrowed the handkerchief of linguist Blunt, tied his sword hilt to his wrist and doubted aloud whether he would be able to return it. When Lucan led the Heavies personally to support the Light Brigade, he was wounded in the leg by the same shell burst that killed Charteris, riding beside him. Lord Bingham, Lucan's son and also an ADC, tried to bring his cousin's body back from the valley, but he was beaten back by enemy fire and only succeeded in grabbing his sword and watch.

After Charteris, Morris lists G Lockwood, 8th Hussars. Captain George Lockwood had purchased an ensignship in the 75th Foot in July 1837 and had exchanged into the 8th Hussars as Lieutenant in May 1844. A Captain by December 1851, he had embarked on the troopship *Medora* on 27 April. Most people felt sorry for Lockwood and indeed any officer who had to endure Cardigan regularly. He had taken part in the infamous sore back reconnaissance and crept away whenever he could from the Light Cavalry to pay his devoirs to Fanny Duberly. Lockwood was a regular caller, both on board her ship, the *Star of the South*, and at Captain Duberly's quarters at Balaclava. He was not alone. Nolan was often there too, as was Cardigan. In the Charge, Lockwood had lost sight of Cardigan at the guns and rode back down the valley in search of his Brigadier. He found Lucan and asked him if he had seen Cardigan. Lucan seems to have assumed that Lockwood had missed the Charge entirely and told him the Brigade had moved down the valley some time ago. Lockwood wheeled his horse and rode back towards the guns. He was never seen again and his body was never found. The Russians denied having taken him prisoner.

Lord Fitzgibbon, also of the 8th, is next in Morris's casualty list. John, Viscount Fitzgibbon, born in 1829, the only son of the 3rd Earl of Clare, was commissioned as Cornet in March 1850. Private Hanrahan of the 8th remembered Fitzgibbon falling before the guns with 'something between a groan and a shriek'. Eyewitnesses claimed that he was hit by two bullets in the chest soon after Nolan was killed. His body was never found, but the story went that he had been captured, then sent to Siberia and that he returned to England in about 1870. Appeals were made by his family for him to come forward, but he never did. He was 5 feet 10 inches tall, with a squint in one eye and wore a monocle. Interestingly, whereas Morris's list says 'Missing' for Lockwood, it merely says 'K' for Fitzgibbon.

He then mentions Captain Maude, RHA. George Maude was typical of junior officers in all branches of the service. Brave, hard-working and efficient, he was critical in his letters home of the high command: 'The more I see of Lord Lucan and Lord Cardigan, the more thoroughly I despise them.'[5] Together with Captain Brandling, who commanded the other troop, Maude's Royal Horse Artillery had been in and out of scrapes in their support of the cavalry since the campaign began. Early on the morning of 25 October, as the

Russians were advancing to take the redoubts, Maude and his horse had been hit by a shell. He was carried back in a blanket, drenched in blood. For the rest of the day, his Battery, commanded by Captain Shakespeare, fired, withdrew, fired and advanced without him.

Cornet Clowes, 8th Hussars, is the next member of the Light Brigade in Morris's letter. George Gooch Clowes was the son of a Colonel, from Broughton Hall, near Manchester. Like an increasing number of the younger cavalry officers, he had been educated at Rugby and obtained his cornetcy in the 8th in March 1853. He embarked for the Crimea on the troopship *Wilson Kennedy* on 2 May. Mrs Duberly describes him as having the 'dignified composure of a very big dog ... noticing a very little one'. Wounded by grape shot in the Charge and his horse killed, Clowes lay as still as he could and 'played dead', but the Cossacks were spearing anything on the ground, so he got up and ran. He was taken prisoner like Morris, and like Morris found himself free, but he was weak from loss of blood and recaptured. Captain Fellowes, who replaced Morris as DAQMG when Morris left Headquarters to command the 17th, rode out later under a flag of truce with Trumpeter Joy of the 17th and bargained with the Russian officers, in French, to release Clowes and the other prisoners. This was eventually done. At the time of his letter, Morris believed that Clowes had been killed.

Cornet Riverdale Richard Glyn, of the 8th, is one of those whom no one credits with having ridden the Charge. Morris's list says Glyn was wounded, but there is no such official record and it may merely have been rumour at the time. He obtained his cornetcy in April 1852, embarked with Lockwood on the *Medora* and seems to have been made Lieutenant the day after Balaclava. Whether this was with purchase or because of the need to upgrade officers now that the Brigade was so pitifully reduced, is uncertain.

There is no doubt about Lieutenant Edward Seager of the 8th, next on Morris's list. Born in 1812, Seager was Regimental Sergeant Major of the 8th in November 1839 and obtained his cornetcy two years later. A Lieutenant by May 1843, he embarked in the *Wilson Kennedy* and both he and his horse were wounded in the Charge. For men like Seager, from the ranks, life had its disappointments in terms of acceptance. Bearing in mind that he retired in 1881 as a Lieutenant General, however, he seems to have made the most of matters and is one of a very select group to have risen so far.[6] John Harris paints an excellent picture of him: 'from the blasphemous to the pious like Seager, whose sabretache contained his wife's and his children's pictures, the hair of one of the children and his mother's gift of a prayer book and testament.'[7] Harris quotes him: 'That the Light Brigade returned ... was through the great providence of God.'[8] He had been Adjutant to the regiment (not a popular post and one often given to a man from the ranks) between October 1841 and the day of the Charge, when he received a slight wound.

Lieutenant Edward Phillips from Morris's list was twenty-four at the time of the Charge, obtaining his cornetcy in July 1851. He embarked as Lieutenant on board the *Shooting Star* on 25 April. Kinglake describes Phillips, whose horse was shot, defending himself against Russian Lancers. They broke off on a trumpet call and he and a wounded Private named Brown managed to get back to their own lines, Phillips riding bareback on a riderless mount because he could not twist its slipped saddle back into position. Morris says he was wounded, but there is no official record.

Major John Thomas Douglas Halkett was born in 1816, the son of a Scottish gentleman who was at one time Governor of the Bahamas. Educated at Rugby, he obtained his cornetcy in January 1835 and through a steady climb by purchase, was a Major by 15 March 1850. He did not get on with Paget, his commanding officer in the 4th Lights, but was generous enough to share his hip flask with him as Nolan brought the fatal order to Lucan. Like Morris a member of the Army and Navy Club, Halkett was married with two daughters. Lummis recounts the story that Halkett was wounded by a shell and as the 4th and 8th rode past he called out to them to take his money 'for the married women at home'. Parkes and Crawford of the 4th came across Halkett mortally wounded, but Cossacks drove them back and when they saw him again his body had been stripped naked except for his jacket. To the appallingly treated soldiers of the Russian army, items of uniform belonging to enemy officers (and very probably their own) were highly prized. It is odd that Halkett should have been left his jacket, however, even the undress version of which was elaborate and valuable.

Lieutenant Henry Astley Sparke, 4th Light Dragoons, was also killed in the Charge. He was twenty-six, the son of a clergyman from Norfolk and he had obtained his cornetcy in December 1846. His lieutenancy dated from October 1850. He was buried by the Russians.

Captain Thomas Hutton of the same regiment is next in Morris's list. The son of a lawyer from Lincoln, Hutton had purchased an ensignship in the 15th Foot in June 1839. A year younger than Morris, he had exchanged into the 4th Lights in September 1847 and was a Captain by April 1852. He embarked for the Crimea on the troopship *Simla* on 4 August. He witnessed the infantry's storming of the Alma and although the muster roll of his regiment states that he was at Scutari from 1 October until the end of December, definitely rode in the Charge. As he raced for the guns, he was hit in the arm and leg and thought he had lost the leg. Determined to stay with his line rather than fall out, he called out to Captain Alexander Low, commanding his squadron, 'I am wounded, what shall I do?'

'If you can sit your horse,' shouted Low, 'you had better come with us. There is no going back now. You'll only be killed.'[9]

When Paget saw him next, he had been shot in both thighs and his horse was hit no less than eleven times. Hutton was still doing stalwart execution among the Russian gunners and shared Paget's flask of rum. His charger was later destroyed when they got back to their lines and Hutton was to sail on the *Australia* (the same transport Morris took to Scutari) reaching the hospital on 29 October.

Morris's next officer was not strictly part of the Light Brigade, but Lieutenant Henry Fitzhardinge Berkeley Maxse, ADC to Cardigan. His grandfather was the 5th Earl of Berkeley and at Balaclava he was twenty-two years old. He had bought a commission in the Grenadier Guards as Lieutenant in June 1849, exchanged into the 13th Light Dragoons three years later and into the 21st Foot a month after that. Harris claims that Maxse was still in the 13th at the time of the Charge and that would certainly make sense in explaining why he was Cardigan's ADC instead of one of the Infantry Brigadiers'. Along with Mayow, Wombwell and Trumpeter Brittain, Maxse's place on the 25th was immediately behind Cardigan, apparently to his left, in front of White's squadron of the 17th. He had not been well prior to the Charge but insisted on being there. When Nolan was hit as the brigade gathered momentum, his swerving horse hit Maxse's jittery stallion, causing the animal to rear and shy. As he reached the guns, the ADC was hit in the right foot and ankle by round shot and he went down, where Wightman of the 17th rode over him. He must have held on to his horse, because he was able to ride back, using only one stirrup. He used a 'rotten old pistol' his brother had given him, but it misfired. Crippled for a few days and suffering from severe bruising, Maxse was to criticize Kinglake later for trying to whitewash Nolan. In a letter to his brother, he wrote: 'Nolan was killed close to me and Kinglake's account is *absurd* as to Nolan wanting to charge any other guns but those which he did.'[10]

Morris next refers to Lieutenant George Powell Houghton of the 11th Hussars. He was gazetted Cornet in March 1853 and sailed for the Crimea on the troopship *Trent* in May of the following year. He had been a Lieutenant for five weeks at the time of the Charge. On the morning of 25 October he was riding a chestnut charger with white stockings, not unlike Cardigan's Ronald, and like Cardigan he wore his pelisse buttoned up, not slung. About halfway down the valley, a shell splinter hit him in the forehead and he was carried back to the lines on the animal's back, probably unconscious. The similarity of appearance caused the rumour to spread that it was Cardigan who had turned back and that he never reached the guns at all. According to the articulate and intelligent Private William Pennington of the 11th, Houghton was a handsome and courteous officer who was sadly missed when he died later at Scutari on 22 November.

In the same regiment rode Lieutenant Harrington Astley Trevelyan, the son of a senior officer from Perth in Scotland. He was only nineteen at the time of the Charge, having been gazetted Cornet in October 1851. He too had sailed on the *Trent* in May. As the only available serving lieutenant that morning, he commanded the 11th's right-hand squadron. He was wounded in the left calf.

Captain John Augustus Oldham was Morris's opposite number in the 13th Light Dragoons and like him had led the front rank, but on Cardigan's right. The son of a soldier, he had purchased an ensignship with the 86th Foot in April 1842 and exchanged, via the 55th Foot, into the 13th Lights in August 1847. As a Captain, he had sailed for the Crimea on board the troopship *Mary Anne* on 19 April. His superiors, Lieutenant Colonel Charles Doherty and Major William Grove, were sick, the latter at Scutari. On 17 October, Oldham had been placed under arrest by Lucan for sending one of the 13th's sergeants across a river. The cavalry were out on a limb at this stage and the work of repulsing small Russian forays caused incidents such as this. In the Charge, his horse, like Maxse's, was difficult and the animal raced off well ahead of the 13th. Its hind legs were blown off and as Oldham scrambled to his feet he was hit by rifle fire. Witnesses reported seeing him last, wounded and bleeding, armed with sword and pistol. His body, like Lockwood's, was never found.

An error on Morris's list concerns Captain Thomas Howard Goad of the 13th. Goad had been an ensign in the 51st Foot in July 1845 and exchanged into the 13th Lights two years later. A Captain by 1850, he embarked on the troopship *Calliope* on 11 May. He had a brother, George Maxwell Goad, who was a Cornet in the same regiment. Although injured at Balaclava when his horse fell on him, Cornet Goad did not ride in the Charge, probably because his injury prevented him, and after it was all over, he searched for his brother. When Fellowes rode out under a white flag to bargain for prisoners, the Russians gave him a bloodstained note taken from Captain Goad's body. He had last been seen sitting some way out from the guns, wounded in the face. According to his friend, Lieutenant Percy Smith, the note was a bill of exchange. According to Morris's list, Goad was only wounded, although with a cornet also in the regiment, this confusion was understandable.

There was no mistake about Cornet Hugh Montgomery of the 13th. The son of a gentleman from County Antrim, Montgomery was educated at Harrow and Cambridge and was about twenty-four at the time of the Charge. He was seen in combat with six Russian Hussars. He shot four and chased the others off with his sword. On his way back, he jumped in to rescue two of his men from Cossacks. The exact cause of his death is uncertain.

The remaining officers in Morris's list are from the 17th. First comes John Hartopp, the Lieutenant who Lummis says may have ridden the Charge. According to Morris's letter, he was wounded, but it is rather odd that in the days when medals made reputations, the son of a baronet should not insist on his clasp for Balaclava, particularly since Hartopp received his Crimean medal from the Queen personally on 18 May 1855 on Horse Guards Parade. Hartopp applied for leave of absence in January and retired from the Army by sale of commission later in the year.

Captain Robert White, who had commanded the right-hand squadron of the 17th, was wounded. Like Morris, he had been heckled by Cardigan for riding too fast and forcing the pace. He fell as he reached the guns, but other than a severe wound to the leg the exact nature of White's injuries are not listed. He certainly recovered, going to Scutari the next day and home to England in January to recover fully. He was to retire as a general in 1891.

Captain Augustus Webb was less lucky. He had been hit in the shin during the Charge and had collapsed in agony after the confusion with Corporal Berryman of the 17th who, together with Sergeant John Farrell of the 17th and Corporal Joseph Malone of the 13th, were to be awarded the VC for carrying Webb from the field. He was known as 'Peck' to his friends in the regiment and at first the wound was probably not thought to be severe. When the surgeons tended him, however, the limb was amputated, certainly at speed and without full anaesthetic. He died of his wounds at Scutari on 6 November, the day, ironically, that Florence Nightingale and her nurses arrived there. He is buried in grave number 31. A lock of his hair, probably cut from his body, was woven into a locket, and is now in the regimental museum.

Captain John Winter, leading his troop in the Charge, had been the first cavalryman ashore at Gallipoli, racing through the shallows with Archibald Clevland. He was last seen alive among the guns and his wounded horse was one of the first to find its way back to the lines.

Lieutenant Sir William Gordon had very similar wounds to Morris. He had been hit five times by sabres to the head, had slumped defenceless in the saddle and had ridden through a gap at a walk between Russian soldiers who blocked his escape. His horse had been shot through the shoulders and died as Gordon was helped from the saddle. He was made Captain the following day and was described at Scutari as being the only patient 'with his head off'. He resigned his commission in 1864 and lived on until 1906, having served with distinction during the latter stages of the Indian Mutiny.

Lieutenant Thomson, the shadowy figure from Hatherleigh and younger brother of White, was killed. Morris brought the boy's diary back from the Crimea in January 1855. In a letter to Thomson's stepfather, Sir Noel Harris, Morris wrote:

> I am so sorry you gave yourself the trouble of writing to me for the very slight service I did in bringing back your poor dear son's diary. I assure you there was not a man or Officer in the Regiment who would not have done a thousand times as much for him. He is not only a great loss to his relations and friends, but to the service, as no one could have given his mind more thoroughly to his work than he did and I think I may safely say he had not an enemy in the world and everybody liked him who knew him.

Last in Morris's list comes Cornet Chadwick, who at the time was listed as 'Missing'. He had reached the guns, but his horse, weakened by loss of blood, refused to jump them. Chadwick parried the lances around him, but eventually one of them hit him in the neck and he fell off. Taken prisoner, he was one of the thirty or forty about whom Fellowes parlayed with the Russians. He was made Lieutenant the same day and exchanged two years later into the 15th Hussars and half pay.

The letter from which this casualty list is taken is dated 4 November, by which time a certain balance, albeit not complete, is creeping in to the information. Morris's first letter to Amelia was written only three days after the Charge, again from the steamship *Australia*, and bears witness to the fact that Morris was lying badly injured and being buffeted about in that parlous state for at least ten days (he arrived at Scutari on 7 November). Since it contains his first impressions of Balaclava, when the events were still fresh in his mind, it is worth quoting the letter in full:

My Own Dearest,

Here I am on my way to Constantinople [sic] with two sabre cuts in my head and one in my arm. One of those in my head is a large one [possibly the lance thrust in fact] and the other insignificant and the one in my arm would last long I think. We had a goodish fight on the 25th, the Enemy attacked us in our Position soon after daylight and commenced by carrying all the Redoubts which we had placed in the hands of the Turks and out of which the cowardly brutes ran as soon as they were attacked. The Enemy then advanced their Cavalry into the plain and advanced towards us but we charged them with the Heavy Cavalry and drove them back after a good fight. Elliot got cut a good deal over the face in the fight, but is I hear doing well. I was and had been in command of my Regiment for 2 or 3 days and tried all I could to get Lords Lucan and Cardigan to let me charge on the Russians' flanks as they came up on the Heavy Brigade but they would not, and afterwards they sent us down to charge the Enemy's cavalry flanked by 2 fires [batteries] ... so that the Light Cavalry has been nearly cut to pieces.

[A sketch follows which Kinglake says Morris drew while in bed in a Balaclava tent.]

Of the 17th there are White shot through the leg, Webb shot through the leg badly, badly shattered; Gordon cut over the head – Winter, Thompson [sic], Chadwick missing. Poor Capt Nolan was shot dead close to me – he was a gallant fellow. I went down [through the valley] amidst a storm of shots and shells without getting one. Therefore, my Wife, I think your prayers have been answered and the Lord has preserved me in the day of battle. I did pretty well and should not like to take what I gave. When I was on the ground the Cossacks came and took my watch and sword, but anyhow my Darling I felt pleased as I have commanded my Regiment in action and they cannot help making me a Brevet Major and perhaps a C.B. [Companion of the Bath] because we beat the Russians off on every side. I have had a hard fight not to be sent away from this place [the theatre of war] but the Doctor won't listen to me, as I should not be surprised if they stormed Sebastopol in a few days. I should like to see all I can, at the same time not to do anything that the Doctors tell me is decidedly unwise,

Ever, my own dearest,
Your most loving Husband,
William

While the Light Brigade buried their dead and auctioned their clothing and equipment for the widows at home, and the recriminations flew between Cardigan, Lucan and Raglan as to who had caused the Charge in the first place, Morris suffered along with the other dying and wounded the horrors of a sluggish crossing of the Black Sea. In his letter to Amelia on 4 November, we have the most accurate description of the wounds he received:

> I have two sabre cuts over the head, one a very heavy one, a sabre cut over the right arm, hitting the lower edge of the forearm [the ulna] about the centre and producing what they call a saliswitch fracture of the bone which in other words I fancy is a split, besides which my fourth rib from the bottom on the left side is broken and my right eye very extensively blackened to say nothing of sundry bumps over my nose and forehead.

Kinglake attributes Morris's survival of these wounds to his physical fitness:

> Up to the commencement of the campaign, Morris had been keeping himself in an almost constant state of high 'training'; and, by some, the possession of the bodily force that was needed for enabling him to go through what he did has been attributed in the past to that case, though the indomitable courage and determination of the man were probably his chief resource.[11]

Morris was more concerned for Webb:

> You will be grieved to hear that poor dear Webb had his right leg amputated today [presumably on board ship], he was only partially under the influence of chloroform and bore it most manfully though

he is very much reduced and weakened from his late attack of fever and I should doubt if he has stamina enough left to withstand the shock his constitution has received ... God bless you, my own Dearest, I think when I tell you about the action the other day you will have an extra kiss for me ... I have not the least made up my mind what I shall do yet, but shall I think see home if Sebastopol is taken.

The ship from Balaclava began to unload on Sunday, 6 November. The previous day, in dense fog, the grim Battle of Inkerman had been fought. Because the cavalry was crippled, it was, like the Alma, another infantry duel. Of the attacking Russian force of 40,000, the losses were 10,729 including 6 generals and 255 officers. British losses amounted to 597 dead and 1,860 wounded. The French lost 130 killed and 750 wounded. What it effectively achieved was a stalemate and both sides settled down for the winter – the Russians to add to their fortifications under Todleben and the British to suffer a Crimean winter without the comforts of an efficient supply system.

The day before Morris reached Scutari, Florence Nightingale and her first party of nurses arrived from England. There can be no doubt that the sanctity of the 'lady with the lamp' has taken several knocks recently, but she *was* a remarkable woman. The Nightingales were philanthropic and Florence received a broader education than was usual for a girl. This combination led to her insistence, which shocked and appalled her family and friends, not to mention the morally hidebound Victorian middle class, on founding a 'Protestant sisterhood, without vows, for women of educated feelings'. The fact was that nursing was not then a profession and nurses themselves were synonymous with the lower orders of women and prostitutes. Florence's attempts to make something of a sharp mind and her passionate zeal to *do* something in an age of enforced inactivity and trivial pursuits for ladies came to nothing, until the middle of October 1854, when she wrote offering her services to the War Office. It was fortunate that a family friend was Sidney Herbert, Secretary for War, and he pulled strings on Florence's behalf. On 21 October, she left London with her selected nurses – 'Miss Nightingale's Women' – and they travelled via Boulogne to Paris, then on to Marseilles. From there they travelled aboard the *Vectis*, a steam mail-packet, to Constantinople. Conditions in the Barrack Hospitals at Scutari are universally known, thanks to the heroism and obstinacy of Nightingale's nurses. 'Vast echoing corridors', wrote Mrs Woodham-Smith, 'with broken tiles and walls streaming with damp, empty of any kind of furniture, stretched for miles ... Everything was filthy; everything was dilapidated.' The barracks also contained a canteen (for the sale of liquor only), a cavalry stable and cellars where two hundred or so camp followers, 'who had been allowed by an oversight to accompany the army, drank, starved, gave birth to infants, carried on their trade as prostitutes and died of cholera.'[12]

To reach this mess, the wounded like Morris had to be lowered into rowing boats and taken to a rickety landing-stage as there was no pier. Those who could not walk (and probably at this stage Morris was advised not to) were carried up a steep slope, by overworked and careless Turkish stretcher bearers. Drunkenness was common, discipline among the troops stationed there poor. There were no shops at all until the British had arrived and around the barracks whole bazaars had been set up full of Turks, Greeks and Jews.

The medical administration of the Army was shambolic. In the field, each regiment had its own staff of surgeons (men like Mouat), assistant surgeons and orderlies. In hospital bases like Scutari, three overlapping, dilapidated and inefficient government departments jostled with each other with differing degrees of pomposity and tons of paperwork. The Medical Department itself (the Staff Corps), the Commissariat and the Purveyor's Department (medical quartermasters) worked under too many chiefs for any clarity of organization to emerge – the Secretary at War, the Commander in Chief and (inexplicably) the ordnance officer. All these departments had dwindled to a tiny staff during the 'long peace' and the constant need to cut financial corners. Mr Ward, the Purveyor at Scutari, had two clerks and three errand boys under him. In common with some of the senior officers in the Crimea, he and the Commissary General, Mr Filder, were Peninsula veterans, and the term 'Mr' is indicative of the contempt in which they were held by officers. Mrs Woodham-Smith sums them up superbly as being: 'Ill paid, despised. Not highly qualified and painfully anxious for promotion, their fear of their superior officers, especially of the military authorities, was abject.'[13] The paperwork buried them. Dr Menzies, the Senior Medical Officer at Scutari, complained to the Roebuck Committee set up to analyse the mess that was the Crimean War, that he 'had no time left for what should have been his principal duty, the proper superintendence of these hospitals.'[14] 'Their heads', wrote Miss Nightingale the following year, 'are so flattened between the boards of Army discipline that they remain old children all their lives.'[15] Ward, answering questions before the Hospital Commission while Morris was still at Scutari said, 'The patients were never so comfortable [in the Peninsula] as they are here!'[16] Some of this is a rather feeble attempt to save face, yet there is an element of truth in it. What had happened is that society, science, technology and above all, the public's perception of those things had moved on. The Army had not.

Florence Nightingale was roundly ignored by virtually all the doctors at Scutari except James McGrigor, a young man not hidebound by Army convention. Encountering opposition from her own nurses, who felt she had let them down (neither were many of them very competent), and from the doctors, who could not accept what these women were doing there, Florence patiently did nothing until the wounded from Inkerman and the cases of exposure and starvation from Balaclava began to drift in from the middle of November. Then, in desperation, with Scutari overflowing with effluent from blocked latrines, running with lice and rats and bursting at the seams with dying men covered only by their blood-stiffened greatcoats, the doctors' aloof composure cracked and Miss Nightingale was allowed to use the considerable sum of £30,000 – raised by *The Times*'s fund and her own collection – to do what the Purveyors were unable to do and provide comforts for the men. By Christmas, she had supplied 6,000 shirts, 2,000 socks and 500 pairs of drawers as well as plates, cutlery, trays, operating tables, screens, towels, soap and food. Those who saw her at work, calmly going about her appalling business, wandering the wards at night with her little Chinese lantern, were astonished. Others who did not were still suspicious – and not a little jealous – of the 'Nightingale Power' as it came to be called. Colonel Sterling, back in the Crimea, where conditions had become chaotic after the terrible hurricane of 14 November which had destroyed tents and blown horses over, wrote: 'Miss Nightingale coolly draws a cheque. Is this the way to manage the finances of a great nation? Vox Populi? A divine afflatus. Priestess Miss N. Magnetic impetus drawing cash out of my pocket.'[17]

How Morris fared in all this we can only guess. On 6 November along with the other survivors of Balaclava, he was probably given hot arrowroot and port wine, but the officers' quarters on the first floor cannot have been much better than the men's at ground level. The same latrine and fresh water problem existed (the carcass of a horse was discovered in the plumbing system) and the stench lay heavily over the whole place. He must have watched men dying from gangrene, fever and the same dysentery which was to kill him three and a half years later. After Christmas, however, he was destined to be removed.

Chapter Twelve
Home and 'Johnny Turk'

Many officers went home before Christmas. The stagnation which had arrived with the biting cold around Sebastopol had a terrible effect on morale. The wounded, like Morris, had every justification to go home, but many others applied for leave and got it, some selling out as soon as they reached England. The attitude of civilians to these men varied enormously. Cardigan, who left in November, was mobbed as a hero as a jingoistic crowd tried to pull hairs from Ronald's tail as souvenirs. His various biographers have excused his homecoming by reminding us that he was fifty-seven and bronchitic, and he had a succession of urinary infections. Lord George Paget, anxious to enjoy something of the married life he had recently embarked on, was, paradoxically, 'cut' by acquaintances in his clubs. Lieutenant Brigstocke, of the 4th Dragoon Guards, came home to Ryde in the Isle of Wight to an enormous street party organized by his mother. There is no certain record as to how Morris fared, but his returning to Scutari in the spring perhaps points to a less than happy time.

Unfortunately, the only detailed evidence for Morris's leave of absence comes from the less than reliable pen of Peter Carew, who states that Lady Carew (nee Ann Taylor) was 'in a pretty fash' and Amelia herself taken 'very queer' by news of Balaclava from George Paget:

> I grieve to tell you that poor Morris was badly wounded by a sabre cut in the head, at the head of the 17th at Balaclava. He is now in the hospital at Scutari and I fear he is in a sad way. I believe that his wife is with you [at Haccombe] so doubtless you will break it to her as gently as possible. Pray do not be too perturbed about the reports in the Times newspaper of the bad condition of the hospitals.[1]

Paget suggested that Lady Carew and Amelia should contact 'Mr Inman, the shipowner', who was arranging visits of 'social families to the seat of war'. Such an idea would be unthinkable today, but the Crimea (and many other mid-century theatres of war) were full of TGs (travelling gentlemen) and their ladies who, in the firm misconception that war was a pretty and chivalric business, descended on entrenched armies in hordes. Walter, Lord Carew, was horrified: 'Constantinople, which is full of Turks and mangy curs is no place for a pack of women,'[2] but his sensibilities did not allow him to stop them; nor did he go with them. His little daughter Bessie seemed to sum up the ladies' views when she said they could not leave 'poor Uncle Willie alone in that dreadful place'.

Accordingly, on 15 December, Lady Carew, Amelia, little Bessie and Annette, Lady Carew's French maid, caught Inman and Company's 1,500-tonne paddle steamer, the *City of Glasgow*, at the East India Docks and set off, at £5 per head, for what was to be a two-week voyage. By this time, Amelia had received a letter which contains Morris's only reference to Florence Nightingale:

> My improvement, I do believe, is mainly due to Miss Nightingale and her ladies. Although they only arrived on the 4th [sic] they have verily created order out of what was nothing less than chaos, Miss Nightingale is the guiding light; the other ladies are worthy, but stars of a dimmer radiance.[3]

The voyage was delightful – luncheon at twelve, dinner at four, the Captain, according to Bessie, 'a shaggy sort of man with enormous whiskers'. The ladies played deck croquet and charades and Lady Carew and Annette were both seasick. Although one of Portal's letters home (Robert Portal was the great-uncle of Peter Carew) states that Morris had gone home from Scutari with his wife and is dated 21 December, this is clearly incorrect, because the party did not reach Malta, where they picked up mail, until 27 December. It was quite hot, wrote Bessie, and 'Mama and Aunt Amelia are able to do their crewel-work on deck.' Annette caused a minor fire by hanging some of her mistress's fol-de-rols too near one of the engines. Paget's wife had joined them en route, and by 2 January Paget had been reunited with her. The ladies wore thick veils and the soldiers 'shouted lustily at us', says Bessie – they believed them to be harem women. They stayed at Lord William Paulet's enormous house on the shores of the Bosphorus while Amelia went immediately to the hospital.

Morris's leave of absence, 'given at the Horse Guards' on 16 January 1855 and signed by James Simpson Deputy Adjutant General (DAG), ran from 4 January to 10 May 'on account of Wounds – when he is to join the Depot'. There was a New Year's Ball held at the British Embassy in Constantinople, where Lord and Lady Stratford de Redcliffe presided. Bessie had not yet 'come out', so she and Annette watched from the Minstrels' Gallery. As soon as a ship was available, the Morris party went home. The Morris Papers contain the passport granted under the auspices of Alexander Turnbull, the British Consul in Marseilles:

> We request all Town Governors, group Commanders, Naval and
> Army officers and all those who need to be requested ... to allow to
> pass freely from Marseilles to London, Captain Morris, Officer of
> the Army, H.M. British subject, accompanied by his wife, Mrs
> Morris ... and to accord him aid and protection in the case of
> emergency.

There is little information concerning Morris's convalescence at home.
Presumably, he went with Amelia to Hatherleigh, although his appointment as
Deputy Adjutant General at the Horse Guards in February would have
necessitated his being in London on a daily basis, so perhaps they used
Cheltenham as their nearest base and took a town house. He was now Major
Morris, the brevet rank having been given to him on 12 December while still at
Scutari. On 7 February he received a letter at the Cheltenham address of
Bayshill Mansions from Cox and Company, his agents, whereby he was paid
£266. 2s. 11d. less Income Duty £15. 10s. 6d., 'as a gratuity of one year's pay
in consideration of the Wounds received by you at Balaclava on 25th October
last.'

At the end of March, Morris received a letter from the Cavalry Depot at
Brighton (where the remnants of the 17th Lancers were still stationed)
enquiring, as part of a quarterly process, whether he intended to purchase
another promotion. There were likely to be other promotions and gratuities in
the wind for a hero of the Charge, which had already gone down in legend, and
Morris did not reply to the request. What was uppermost in his mind was the
Crimea. Now he only had second-hand accounts, Russell's articles in *The Times*
and rumours that no doubt filled the smoking rooms of the Army and Navy
Club. Almost certainly, he intended to go back as soon as he was well enough.

The problem of Morris's wounds is complicated. All modern accounts
which deal with his death talk in terms of sunstroke caused by a silver plate
having been fixed to his skull at some time after the Charge. Contemporary
accounts state unequivocally that Morris died of dysentery and it is likely that
the silver plate theory leading to sunstroke merely presents a more romantic
image. I have found no contemporary allusion to the plate at all and the medical
thinking of the time can be found in G H B Macleod's *Notes on the Surgery of
the War in the Crimea*. The book makes it clear that head wounds were treated
very conservatively. Macleod cites a number of case histories, but there is no
mention of Morris. Certainly, operations of this sort were known – the ancient
Egyptians had practised them – but they were highly dangerous, and
recognized to be so in an age (the 1850s) when a far greater scientific awareness
was dawning. Macleod wrote:

> The teaching of all was to lead us to wait; to purge the patient
> thoroughly; to remove only such pieces of bone as could be got at

with forceps and which were quite detached and loose; to bleed, if need be, locally and even generally; to use cold applications when there was a fear of inflammation; to enjoin perfect rest, not only to the body generally, but, if possible, to give repose to the special senses also, by isolating the patient ... to enforce the lowest diet, and to continue all this treatment for a long period, even after all danger seems past.[4]

How much of this was obtainable in the sick transports across the Black Sea and at Scutari was of course very open to question. An operation of the type Morris would have had to undergo could not have been carried out either at one of the Balaclava field hospitals or at Scutari. This leaves us with the possibility that it was carried out in England. Again, we have no contemporary references to it. James Simpson, the Deputy Adjutant General, wrote on behalf of the Army Medical Board to Morris on 6 January (while Morris was probably still on his way home), asking him to 'attend at the Office ... No. 13, St James's Place, between the hours of one and two on Wednesday or Friday next, for special examination, in order that a report may be made upon your state of health, for his Lordship's consideration.' How well Morris was during his four months at home and whether he had time to have a plate inserted in his skull and to recover from it, we do not know. Robert Portal, who had remained with his regiment in the Crimea and was to do so until the war was over, was astonished that he should go back to the front. At the end of April he wrote to his mother:

I did not think he would have come out again, as last year he ran so many risks, both from the climate and from the enemy, that people generally supposed he had had quite enough of it. However, he seems determined to gain himself a name out here, if possible, or die in the attempt. I wrote him a letter when the bombardment [of Sebastopol] began, directing it to the Club [Army and Navy], and have also written him another one now that it is over, both of which letters, I have little doubt, would be interesting to his wife ... I am glad you have at last made acquaintance with Mrs Morris and Miss Taylor.

The Miss Taylor referred to here was Amelia's little sister, Eliza, whom Portal married in the summer of 1856. Four days after this letter, Portal wrote to his sister: 'I never thought Morris would come back, although he did say he should; how poor Mrs Morris must feel it, though I know she bears up against it in the most wonderful manner possible.'

Before he left England, Morris received a royal command:

The Lord Steward is commanded by Her Majesty to invite Major Morris, 17th Lancers, to Dinner on Monday the 2nd April at Eight O'Clock precisely.

Frock dress was to be worn, and although no record exists from Morris or Amelia, he certainly went, for on 2 June, Henry Clifford, an unassuming young officer in the Rifle Brigade who was to win the VC, wrote home from the *Tamar* off Scutari:

> I saw a Capt. Morris yesterday, you have perhaps seen his name in the papers. He behaved most splendidly in the unfortunate charge at Balaclava, and was badly wounded in the head with a sabre cut, had three ribs broken and side very much torn, with a thrust from a lance and his right arm cut to the bone by a sword. No one thought he would live, but he is well enough to walk about now, tho' looking very ill and after spending a few months in England has come out here again.
>
> The Queen asked him to dine and spoke to him very kindly. He came out with me in the *Ripon* and I thought him such a very fine fellow. I was so glad to see him.[5]

Eight months after Balaclava, Morris was back, but he had gone via Scutari, where Amelia says in her sketchy two-page biography of him, probably written years later, he was sent 'to superintend and command the remounts'. This appointment was to run from April and a second paper in Amelia's hand explains that this was specifically to supervise cavalry embarkation. But all was not well and Clifford's comment about Morris looking ill was a result of a bout of fever. Portal wrote from Balaclava on 18 May when it was 95 degrees in the shade:

> Some of our officers here give a very bad account of Morris. They say he is very 'flighty' and when they left was in bed with a very bad fever, which seemed to be taking a dangerous turn. I really cannot conceive what could induce him ever to come out again to this country, where he already nearly lost his life twice before. I should have thought that his wife's influence might have stopped him.

On 25 May he wrote that Morris 'is very bad with fever', but at Constantinople. Whether he had been moved or whether this was 'shorthand' for Scutari is uncertain.

On 5 May, Morris had received a letter from General Airey:

> I was glad to hear from you and I hope you are pretty sound. Lord Raglan wishes you to remain at Scutari until the cavalry remounts have passed up – of course receiving your allowance of £2 per diem. When that is over you can come and join the Department again and I shall be very glad to see you.

There is little doubt that Airey's sentiments were genuine. Like all the high command in the Crimea he had recently come under fire from all sides – the press and parliament and, via both, the people. At the end of January the redoubtable John Roebuck, radical MP for Sheffield, had moved a resolution in the Commons that a Select Committee be set up to enquire into the condition of the Army before Sebastopol and the conduct of the associated government departments. The pacifist Prime Minister, Lord Aberdeen, resigned, 'with such a whack,' wrote Gladstone, 'they could hear their heads thump as they struck the ground', as the government fell with him.

Aberdeen's replacement was the even more redoubtable Lord Palmerston, 'this terrible milord', who five years earlier had sent a fleet in support of one British subject and threatened war against an entire nation. In his seventies, deaf and hesitant of speech, he was still formidable, passionately concerned for British prestige abroad and intimately acquainted with the Army, as he had been Secretary at War for nearly twenty years. The Queen hated him, but neither Lord Derby nor the diminutive Lord John Russell could form an alternative ministry, so Palmerston it had to be. He was, in his own words, 'l'inevitable'. Both he and Lord Panmure, whom he appointed Secretary at War, had little time for the Army above regimental level and they slated the Staff openly for lack of co-ordination and decision-making. Panmure – 'the bison' – wrote to Raglan privately in February demanding that he change his senior staff officers, especially Airey. A chief of staff (the same Lieutenant General James Simpson who had recently written to Morris) was on his way. Panmure told him to report on all staff officers and weed out the weak ones – Airey and Estcourt being the primary targets, 'that knot of incapables', as Palmerston called them, adding the civilian Filder at Scutari to the tangle. The attack, as Christopher Hibbert points out,[6] was unmerited and perhaps Raglan deserved better, but even the Queen was now baying for blood, agreeing with Panmure about the brevity and unhelpfulness of Raglan's despatches. In the event, the baying died down and both Airey and Estcourt stayed where they were. Even so, it had been a difficult time for Airey and he must have welcomed Morris warmly when he arrived in August.

James Simpson, a sensible, sympathetic Scotsman, wrote from the Crimea that Raglan and his Staff were much maligned and he found incompetence nowhere:

They are a very good set of fellows – civil and obliging to everyone who comes ... and I must say I never served with an army where a higher feeling and sense of duty exists than I remark in the General Staff Officers of this army. It pervades all ranks, except among the low and grovelling correspondents of the Times.[7]

On 4 August Morris, bored with the inactivity, wrote to his sister Emma. She had written to him with news of his brothers Cholmley and Wessie at the Cape, and he was 'very glad you like my wife. She is a good woman I assure you, always trying and thinking beforehand what she can do for someone or other.' Emma had recently had a party which she had 'managed famously' and her mother 'did the honours capitally'. Morris in a rare moment of wistfulness envied Cholmley his little girl, Nellie:

he says it is the best tempered little thing in the world ... I am horribly bored by being kept down in this place and all I can do I have done to get up to the Front without avail. The reports are very conflicting. Some people say an attack is to take place at once and others that there is to be none and that the French can sap up to the ditch of the Russian works and so make what is called a lodgement [a temporary defensive work on a captured part of the enemy positions]. I think a general attack should be avoided if it possibly can [there was not to be a renewed allied bombardment of Sebastopol until 17 August as a preliminary to unsuccessful attacks largely by the French in September]. We have regularly lost the summer before that place and our General Officers instead of getting better as the war goes on are getting worse, if all accounts are true and the French are getting to hold them very cheap.

This sort of comment is rare for Morris. The careful Staff Officer, loyal, steadfast, is letting his hair down here in an uncharacteristic attack on the High Command. Raglan was dead (worn out with effort and constant attacks from home, he had fallen prey to cholera in July) and Morris did not know Simpson. It began to look as though another fruitless winter would set in. 'I have only one horse and a pony,' he wrote, 'and I care very little about riding in this country, the ground about here is so hard for it.' Emma's pony was worn out and Morris lamented that he was not able to choose a replacement himself. In his absence, he suggested Jack Russell, still the hunting parson, Mr Fortescue (his brother-in-law of Fallapit, Devon) or Amelia's brother Fitz, as likely providers of a good mount.

Even though Morris had missed most of the horrors of the winter, he must have noticed immediately the changes when he arrived at Balaclava. In February the agents of *The Times*'s fund had arrived and brought with them 1,000 tons of supplies. Huts were erected everywhere, the road was improved and at last made passable the six and a half miles between camp and harbour. Hampers from Fortnum and Mason arrived for the officers and there was so much surplus clothing that some of the men were selling it for drink. Somerset Calthorpe on the Staff asked a sentry if he was comfortable. 'I should be, sir,' the soldier replied, 'if I hadn't got so many bloody clothes on.' Mrs Seacole, the jolly mulatto from Jamaica, opened her hotel and gangs of navvies built a railway. It is this atmosphere of levity and hope that photographer Roger Fenton recorded from his airless little wagon after his arrival on 9 March. There was even some fraternization in the trenches between the British and the Russians. Perhaps there was time for Morris to enjoy the flowers – the primroses, violets, paeonies and crocuses – that grew in abundance on the wooded slopes towards Kadikoi, but if there was, it was relatively short-lived. Morris, now elevated to Brevet Lieutenant Colonel, was attached to the Turkish Contingent.

This appointment, although it was to result in the award of the Order of the Medjidie in the following year, cannot have pleased Morris very much. The Turkish Army was universally recognized as a shambles by the British and both they and the Russians held the Turks in mutual contempt. No one had forgotten their hasty evacuation of the redoubts on the morning of Balaclava and the scavenging 'Johnny' Turk was treated accordingly, kicked like a dog by Englishmen and Frenchmen alike. Henry Clifford wrote in January 1855 that he felt increasingly sorry for them and cites the case of one Turkish soldier driven to theft by abject poverty, who was lashed twenty-five times in front of the British officer whose gloves he stole, received another twenty-five in front of the Pasha, yet another before his colonel and a final twenty-five in front of his comrades. The officers were rather better, especially the dignified and cultured Omar Pasha, who according to Nigel Kingscote, Raglan's ADC was 'a capital fellow. Quite different to the Turks in general, hates all display ... He is a sporting looking fellow and sits well on his horse in a plain grey frock coat and long jackboots, he is fond of horses,'[8] and as such, of course, was likely to endear himself to the British officer. In fact 'Omar' was not a Turk, but a Greek-speaking Croat named Michael Lettas. Fenton's photographs of Turkish troops, such as those surrounding Ismail Pasha, show well-armed and equipped men in fezzes and colourful jackets. It was the Bashi Bazouks with their bare-breasted concubines that gave the Turks their worst reputation. They were irregular cavalry and Major Ewart of the 93rd Foot described them in June 1854:

> They were wild-looking fellows, each man dressed and armed according to his own fancy. Some had long lances and all had two or three pistols and a knife, besides a sword, whilst several carried a flag ... [They were] sadly in want of instruction in drill and discipline.[9]

This view of the Turkish army as a ramshackle, inefficient organization, bent on looting and pillage, is an oversimplification. The Turks had been fighting off the Russian advance since the autumn of 1853 along the Danube and they had conducted some excellent defences. At Eupatoria later, they were again to do themselves more than justice. But in the Crimea, they did not shine. Their officers were often, like Omar Pasha himself, 'foreign' mercenaries who brought European disciplines and skills to bear in order to rise quickly in the Sultan's service. Morris may well have been able to converse with these men in English or French, but otherwise an interpreter would have been essential and these were plentiful.

The Turkish Contingent itself comprised eight cavalry regiments, sixteen infantry and six artillery units. The officers were European but the men Turkish. It is likely that Morris retained his AQMG uniform as he was still officially serving in that capacity. His commission, dated 30 January 1856 and signed by Panmure, appointed Morris 'to have the local rank of Colonel in Our Army in Turkey while serving with the Turkish Contingent Force' and ran from 15 January. By this time, Morris was at Kertch.

The town of Kertch lay on the eastern coast of the Crimean peninsula guarding the narrow straits into the Sea of Azov. A plan of it, drawn up by Major Crease and Captain Ord of the Turkish Contingent Engineers in November 1856 shows a medium-sized town complete with mosque and Greek Orthodox cathedral dominated on the Bay of Kertch by the ramparts of Fort Paul. There were 2,600 Russian sailors and Black Sea Cossacks there under the command of Lieutenant General Baron Wrangel.

In May 1855 while Morris was ill with fever at Scutari, an allied expedition had set off to capture Kertch with a view to damaging Russian supply lines from the mainland and to open the Sea of Azov to allied shipping. The idea was British, one of the last positive actions of Lord Raglan, and the force, some 15,000 strong, was led by Sir George Brown and the French General Forey. The original expedition on 2 May was called off hours after sailing, when Napoleon III, now able to interfere directly with his generals because of the newly erected telegraph system, ordered Canrobert to 'attack the enemy externally', which meant in practice a renewed offensive against Sebastopol, the Mackenzie Heights, Alushta and Simferopol. It was this lunatic order which prompted Canrobert's resignation and the instalment of the slovenly looking Pelissier as French commander. On 22 May, Pelissier ordered the Kertch expedition to go ahead in defiance of the Emperor.

It was one of the most successful operations of the war. Wrangel had orders not to give battle. Gorchakov, now Russian Commander in Chief, believed that the Allies intended to seal off the Crimean peninsula entirely, which would have ended the war at a stroke. Wrangel destroyed as much of his artillery as he could. Once into the Sea of Azov, the allied gunboats destroyed the Russian naval squadron they found lurking there, but all further attacks were merely minor raids on fishing villages or merchant ships. One hundred guns were captured, thousands of tons of corn and flour destroyed, Russian steamers sunk, factories destroyed and arsenals blown up. A French garrison was left behind to continue the occupation.

Morris says little of his time at Kertch. At Great Torrington in September 1856 when a banquet was held in his honour, he said: 'There we never had anything but a few skirmishes with the Cossacks; still it was very hard work. I held a very important position which I hope I discharged to my superiors' satisfaction.'

One glimpse of the very hard work is available, in a letter written by Morris to General Sir William Codrington KCB, since November, with Simpson's resignation, Commander in Chief in the East. It was 14 January 1856:

> l have the honour to submit for your Excellency's consideration that it would be of the greatest advantage for the defence of Kertch that two floating batteries or six gunboats armed with heavy guns ranging 2,500 or 3,000 yards be placed in the bay so as to sweep the valleys to the north and south of the town and also to prevent the enemy from establishing his batteries on the ridge of ground to the north of the town called Windmill Hill on which if he once succeeded in establishing himself the town would be no longer tenable.
>
> I have consulted my chief engineer as well as the commanding officer of artillery and they both agree in thinking that the floating batteries or gunboats would enable us to defend the place even against a regular siege as the whole force might then be employed to repel any attack on the west side.
>
> Should your Excellency concur on these opinions I trust you will apply to the Admiral at Balaclava to send the batteries or gunboats with as little delay as possible as there is no saying how long the sea will remain free from ice.

The imperiousness of this letter would indicate that it was in fact from Major General Vivyan, commanding at Kertch, dictated by him to Morris and with Morris's experience and recommendations; such work was beyond the normal capacity associated with the office of the AQMG. Here Morris remained until some time in July 1856. His final pay certificate, valid until 28 August, allowed him £2. 8s. 6d. a day, plus servants' allowance at 9 shillings, field allowance at £1, £30 for his chargers and £25 for passage. And Morris duly signed the slip: 'I acknowledge I have no further claims on the British Government for service in the Turkish Contingent.'

He must have been one of the last British officers to leave the Crimea. Back in November of the previous year, Sebastopol had at last fallen and the allies entered to find Todleben's magnificent fortifications in ruins. In February the peace conference opened in Paris and an armistice was signed in the Crimea. The official end of the war came on 27 April. Not before time, William Morris went home.

Chapter Thirteen

Mutiny

Morris's second homecoming from the Crimea was a great deal happier than his first. He had sailed in July 1856 and by one of those quirks of fate had missed the letter from the Horse Guards appointing him Assistant Adjutant General of Corfu, the 'garden of the Gods', a mountainous little island off Albania whose valleys produced oranges, olives, figs and vines. The letter, written by W F Foster, the Deputy Adjutant General, and dated 5 July is in the Morris Papers:

> Sir,
>
> I have the honour by direction of the Field Marshal Commanding in Chief to acquaint you that Her Majesty has been graciously pleased to appoint you to serve as Assistant Adjutant General to the Brigade of the three Regiments in the Ionian Islands.
>
> You will therefore proceed to that station with as little delay as possible to assume your duties, reporting yourself on arrival to the General Officer Commanding.

In the event, Morris reached England and was ordered to take up the same post but at the Curragh camp in Ireland. He was now a decorated soldier and at the height of his success. In June 'Le Lieutenant Colonel William Morris Aide Quartier Maitre General' had been appointed Chevalier of the Legion d'Honneur. The French lost no time in cashing in on the Entente Cordiale which now existed. The firm of Leotar, sculptors of Paris, contacted Morris without delay.

> Colonel,
>
> Knowing of your noble sympathies for His Majesty the Emperor I am writing to offer you, if you are agreeable, a copy of the statuette of His Majesty with these immortal words on the pedestal, according to your choice:

1. 'The Alliance between England and France has been soaked in the glorious blood of Alma, Balaclava, Inkerman and the Malakoff' – Napoleon.
2. 'Lieutenant Colonel William Morris, Assistant Quarter Master General is appointed Knight of the Imperial order of the Legion of Honour' – Napoleon.

If you are satisfied with the statuette of the Emperor I would be honoured to present you subsequently with the bust as for the statuette of the famous Colonel Morris, the hero of Balaclava, in his 17th Lancers uniform. This little statuette can be offered as a handsome conversation piece, a noble and glorious family memento.

It is not recorded whether Morris bought either. He was already Brevet Lieutenant Colonel, of course, and had served in the capacity of full colonel at Kertch. The French honour was duly recorded in the *London Gazette* of 4 August:

The Queen had been pleased to give and grant unto the undermentioned officers and men in Her Majesty's service her Majesty's royal licence and permission that they may accept and wear the Insignia ... of the Imperial Order of the Legion of Honour ... which His Majesty the Emperor of the French has been pleased to confer upon them as a mark of His Imperial Majesty's approbation of their distinguished services before the enemy during the late war.

He was in good company. On the Staff James Airey (son of the QMG), George Mayow (unattached, AQMG who had ridden in the Charge with Morris) and Arthur Hardinge (AQMG, Coldstream Guards, who was Morris's best man) all received the award, as did James Mouat MD, CB, who had pulled Morris from under fire at Balaclava. In the cavalry, Morris's friend Alex Elliot, ADC, 5th Dragoon Guards, Brevet Major William de Cardonnel Elmsall (who, like Elliot, had charged with the Heavies), Rodolph de Salis of the 8th Hussars, Alexander Low of the 4th Lights, and in Morris's own regiment, Captain Sir William Gordon, Bt., and Trumpeter John Brown were all made Knights of the Order.

As for his CB, the warrant dates from 5 July 1855:

Whereas we have thought it fit to nominate and appoint you to be an ordinary Member of the Military Division of the Third Class or Companions of the our said Most Honourable Order of the Bath, we do by these presents grant unto you the dignity of a Companion of our Most Honourable Order.

The local, as opposed to international, accolade came on 6 September 1856 at a banquet at Great Torrington, a few miles to the north of Hatherleigh. It stirred Edward Capern, a Devon poet, to rush into print with verses similar to those composed for Cardigan and other Balaclava heroes.

Hail to thee! Hail to thee! Champion of Liberty!
Fresh from the field of his struggle and pain,
Hail to thee, Hail to thee 'Bold son of chivalry',
Hail to the land of the Hero again.

Seven more excruciating verses followed before Morris, amid tumultuous applause, buckled on the sword presented to him by the assembly. Although Messrs Wilkinson's ledgers are difficult to decipher, it is likely to have been Arthur, Amelia's brother, who actually commissioned the weapon. The sword was completed on 2 June 1855. It is typical of such presentation swords, especially for cavalry officers, of the Mameluke type with ivory grips and gilded quillons and scabbard mounts. It is listed as Sword No. 6021 and the maker's name on the blade is Henry Wilkinson, Pall Mall, London. The inscription on the blade reads:

To Major William Morris, from his friends and neighbours, in the North of Devon, to replace his sword, lost when he was severely wounded, in command of the 17th Lancers, at the glorious Charge of the Light Cavalry at Balaclava, October 25th 1854.

The sword was bought by subscription organized on an exclusively local basis by G Braginton Esq., the Mayor of Torrington, while Morris was still Captain, and despite the honours and rank elevation that followed (they did manage to have 'Major' inscribed on the blade in time) the original idea was adhered to that only a few local friends should be involved in the presentation. At the Globe Hotel, Great Torrington, on the afternoon of Saturday, 6 September the presentation took place and the sword was given to Morris by Sir Trevor Wheler, Bt. in his capacity as the most distinguished soldier present – a veteran of Waterloo. Apparently, the spread was impressive, 'comprising as it did every delicacy of the season and reflecting the highest credit on the resources of Mr Wills, the landlord of the Globe.' Wheler took the chair and among the guests were Colonel Buck, MP for North Devon, Major Macartney and Captain Arnold of the 17th, and a number of local gentlemen, including the redoubtable Jack Russell, who had ridden with Morris when Morris was a boy.

The toasts were 'The Queen', 'Prince Albert, the Prince of Wales and the rest of the Royal Family', 'The Lord Lieutenant of the County' and 'The

Duke of Cambridge and the British Army', all accompanied, of course, in true Victorian loyal tradition by cheers and 'three times three'.

Morris, amid deafening cheers, thanked them all for their kindness and the honour done to his profession. He thanked the county too for sending out provisions to the Crimea. His health was then drunk. 'We are assembled here today,' said Wheler,

> to congratulate that gallant officer on his safe return to his native shores and are desirous of placing on record the deep sense we entertain of the zeal and gallantry he has shown on all occasions when his services have been required by the country ... It is but small testimonial, but I hope you will accept it [the sword], and do us the honour to wear it – [cheers] – for I do sincerely believe that if the British cavalry had to give this sword to one of their officers more deserving than another, though there might be great difficulty in making their selection, their unanimous verdict would be 'Give it to Colonel Morris, the bravest of the brave.'

And amid 'immense cheering' the band struck up 'See, the Conquering Hero Comes!'

Morris, 'who was evidently labouring under considerable emotion', according to Woolmer's *Exeter and Plymouth Gazette*, replied with thanks and outlined the events that had brought him to this point in his career, much of which has been quoted already above. Of Balaclava, Morris said:

> I looked up the line on either side and it did my heart good to see each man gathering his horse up and pressing down his cap just as if he was going to take a fence [loud cheers] ... Gentlemen, I have been promoted and rewarded by Her Majesty for my services, while other men more deserving than myself have either lost their lives or owing to unfortunate circumstances have gained nothing. I have been favoured by Providence in many escapes, for I must say that I do not attribute them to my own exertions, but to the hand of Providence ... I mean, as long as I am capable, to devote myself to the profession which I have taken up; to make myself as far as possible a master of its details, both theoretically and practically; and any time that I have – any leave I get – I hope to spend it among you [cheers]; and should Providence permit me to become an old man past active service, I hope to end my days among my kind and excellent friends in North Devon. But whatever be my lot ... rest assured that this day will never be effaced from my memory ... gentlemen, from the very, very bottom of my heart, I thank you.

It was Jack Russell who then read Capern's poem, a copy of which was presented to everyone in the room by L P Pridham of Bideford, as a small tribute from the town. George Trewman, Esq., of Hatherleigh then spoke for the parish and his colourful phrases reveal a totally unknown side of Morris and one for which no other evidence exists. He had known Morris from boyhood:

> He showed his prowess in the field at the tail of the fox, urged on by his tutor and friend [presumably Russell]. *In electioneering matters* he had been engaged with their friend who invariably evinced energy, activity and perseverance [my italics] ... His blood had mingled with the soil of Hindoostan ... [and he was] one of that gallant band who drew forth the emphatic expression from one of their French allies 'C'est très magnifique, mais il n'est pas la guerre!' ... He had spoken of their hero – a soldier and a gallant one – a master of his profession – enthusiastic and persevering; he would now direct their attention for a moment to a most amiable woman – one worthy in every respect to be a soldier's wife; who dropped not a tear at war's alarms; but by her firmness gave strength to the soldier's mind and from the depth of her affection administered comfort to him in the hour of sickness.

Trewman proposed the health of Mrs Morris – 'May she and her husband enjoy many years of health, peace and felicity' – and the band struck up again.

In keeping with time-honoured tradition, still observed by the bride at wedding suppers, Amelia Morris relied on her husband to reply. He agreed with the company that she was a truly good soldier's wife. He had never seen a tear in her eye in parting for the seat of war but 'I am perfectly certain that her lips were full of prayers for my safety.'

With all the euphoria and no doubt liquid refreshment of the occasion, some irregularity had crept into the proceedings vis-à-vis the toasts. Wheler hastily remembered the Navy and the local clergy, for whom the Reverend W W Karslake replied, well remembering how as a boy, Morris had had to forgo a hunt, 'until he had mastered a Greek play which his father had desired him to read.'

Colonel Buck rose next, annoyed with himself in all this talk of glory that he was only a 'feather bed soldier' (an officer in the Devon militia) and had volunteered to go anywhere at the outbreak of recent hostilities and suggested to Palmerston in the Commons his regret that Englishmen's services were ignored while 'foreigners [the King's German legion] who had disgraced their colours and the service' were sent out to the Crimea. It was now that Buck, whether through drink or some sense of genuine injustice, singled out Cardigan for attack. A similar dinner had been held at Leeds for the former commander of the Light Brigade some days earlier (although of course he had returned from the Crimea for good ten months before) and Buck could not resist making the obvious comparisons between the Noble Earl and Morris: 'It was necessary for that noble lord to use and give some explanation of his conduct during the war – an explanation which [Colonel Buck] did not consider to be sufficient.' Morris had no need to defend himself; 'no one had ventured to throw a stone against him … the country had suffered from the system of favouritism which had placed men in positions they were not qualified to fill.' Morris by his ability and apt qualifications was pre-eminently suited to fill such posts. The day ended shortly before nine.

It was a day of happiness and triumph. But one man who had not been invited was not pleased. Lord Cardigan followed the activities of officers of his Brigade with the peevish behaviour of a sadistic schoolmaster. In May he had forced his way uninvited into the wedding celebrations of Bob Portal of the 4th Lights, who had married Amelia's younger sister. Palmerston was guest of honour and the 4th provided a guard at the church porch. Only Walter Carew seemed to enjoy Cardigan's company, both of them more than merry on champagne.

Already, however, rumours, some of them silly, most of them insulting, were beginning to fly concerning Cardigan's conduct in the Crimea. They were to culminate in the absurd accusation in 1863 by Somerset Calthorpe that Cardigan had not reached the guns at Balaclava at all. In the meantime, Cardigan heard of Buck's speech, and, stinging from *The Times*'s rebuke that his view of the Charge was a 'falsification of history' as expressed in a speech he had made at Leeds, decided to take action. He wrote to Buck on 18 May and the Colonel replied two days later. Cardigan replied again on 25 May, making it clear he was not satisfied with Buck's explanation that he had been partially misreported, nor could he see that Morris had anything to complain about. It was typical of Cardigan to miss the point – Morris was not complaining. Of Morris's promotion to Assistant Adjutant General at the Curragh, Cardigan found this 'a much more agreeable way of obtaining promotion than by paying £40,000. This proves that Officers in the service do not obtain promotion by money alone,' and Morris's silence on the Charge was obviously because 'he never having been attacked by anonymous libellers had no ground for entering into any defence of his conduct.'[1] The quarrel between Cardigan and Buck reached the national press, the Cardiganite *Morning Post* sneering at those who attacked him by claiming that he rode so far ahead of the Brigade that his enemies perhaps could accuse him of trying to defect to the Russians! But Buck was small fry and Cardigan was soon diverted in a more lethal quarrel over reputations with Lord George Paget.

If the events described at Great Torrington marked the pinnacle of Morris's success, there was one attempt in which he had failed. On 15 April 1856, while still at Kertch, he had written to Lucan:

My Lord,

I have the honour to request that you will be pleased to forward to the Military Secretary, Horse Guards, my claim to the Victoria Cross.

The newest and highest decoration for bravery in the field had been instituted by the Queen in January of the same year. It was a Maltese cross, $1^1/_2$ inches across, with the crown surmounted by a lion and with the legend 'For Valour' on a scroll. The metal was to be from the guns captured at Sebastopol and for the Army, the ribbon was of crimson. Its first recipient was a naval officer, Midshipman Lucas, backdated as it were to 1854. A total of sixty-four medals were awarded for the Crimea, among them Surgeon Mouat and Sergeant Wooden, who had dragged the wounded Morris from the field at Balaclava. The medal was awarded for 'conspicuous bravery or devotion to the country in the presence of the enemy'.

It is difficult to explain Morris's actions with regard to the VC. So few of these medals have been granted (the eleven in one day for the defence of Rorke's Drift in the Zulu War remains a record, despite two World Wars) that the institution has assumed a sanctity of its own and the mere thought now of a man nominating *himself* for it seems a sacrilege. On three other counts, however, the request can be seen in proportion. First, it was a new award and a certain means of promotion. The zealous professional Morris probably saw it as such. Second, the obtaining of medals was very important to soldiers, officers in particular. Even the most unassuming demanded them and were mortified if they were not received. Third, the decision to award the VC or not is a particularly arbitrary one; there are those who said then and those who say now that Morris should have obtained the medal. Judging by the rough citation written by Sir George Brown supporting Captain Clifford's claim in the Crimea, he did *far* less than Morris.

In support of his claim via Lucan to the Horse Guards, Morris recounts the events of the Charge:

When my regiment came in front of the Russian Hussars I considered it necessary to close with the enemy thirty-five or forty yards ahead of the men, calling on them to follow me. I ran my sword through the body of one of the enemy and was then surrounded and cut down, falling off my horse – Captain Sir William Gordon 17th Lancers who saw me at the time can corroborate this statement.

As soon as I became sensible, I got up from the ground and went a little way to the rear when I was met by four or five Cossacks against whom I defended myself for some time with my sword, receiving a lance wound in the head and giving them several cuts in return, but was taken prisoner at last and went towards the enemy for about twenty yards when seeing two loose horses coming I called out to Sir George Wombwell who was also a prisoner to catch a horse and ran off myself to do so, but the horse knocked me down and I saved myself by running back where the enemy shot was falling very thickly and into which the Cossacks would not follow me. I there caught a horse but he was shot dead under me before I had gone far and I had to walk back.

As well as citing Gordon and Wombwell in this account, Morris submitted the affidavits of seventeen men of the 17th Lancers in October 1856 to substantiate a claim that either Lucan or his superiors at the Horse Guards seem to have dragged their feet over. All of them cite Morris's leadership and the acts of heroism he performed that day.

What is interesting to historians of the Charge is the new evidence these affidavits bring to light, published here for the first time. Of the seventeen signatories, there are five men – John Collin, Samuel Hunscott, Joseph Alexander, George Smith and George Mansell – who swear they rode the Charge, whereas Canon Lummis, still the Light Brigade authority, does not mention them as having done so. A sixth man, John Shearingham 'probably' (according to Lummis) rode the Charge – his affidavit for Morris confirms this. Whether the reader accepts the usual 673 sabres for the Charge or Whinyates's more cautious 661, we must now add six more.

These affidavits were collected by TSM Ranson of Morris's troop and sent in a covering letter from Portobello Barracks on 17 October:

> Sir,
>   I beg to acknowledge the receipt of your letter bearing date 16th October/56. I herein enclose to you statements of NC officers and men relative to Balaclava Charge. I have been as quick about it as possible as it took some little time to collect the evidence. Hoping sir that it is to your satisfaction.

Judging by the speed with which Ranson and the others had complied, Morris must indeed have been a popular officer.

But popularity does not win medals and his application was rejected. In an undated letter, Morris wrote:

> Many thanks for your letter relative to the Victoria Cross. I am sorry His Royal Highness [the Duke of Cambridge] thinks I am not entitled to it but it cannot be helped and I trust if any staff is sent to the troops going out to India that my wish for active employment may be brought to the notice of the Duke of Cambridge in order that I may have another chance of trying for the Victoria Cross.

His passion for action, his quest for opportunities to reach the heights of professionalism were this time to prove fatal. From the sense of this letter, it must have been written after May 1857 when the Mutiny at Meerut made it an urgent necessity to send troops to India.

In the meantime in the October of 1856, Morris took up his post as Assitant Adjutant General at the Curragh and it is likely that Amelia went with him. Morris was no stranger to Ireland, of course, having served there with the 17th in the late 1840s. The Curragh, in County Kildare, was a gently undulating tract of open grassland six miles long and two wide, thirty-two miles south-west of Dublin. Its link with the British Army dates from the Crimean War, when a small permanent camp was established in 1855. When Morris got there, it was still a new venture and as its administrative supremo, he played his part in making it into the largest and most important garrison and training establishment in Ireland. Only four documents have survived in the Morris Papers which relate to this period. The first is a letter from Morris to Lord Lucan, dated 30 October 1856, a time when he was still ardently pushing his claim to the VC:

> I saw by the papers that you had come over to Ireland [Lucan owned estates in Mayo and elsewhere] but I do not know your direction beyond Castlebar which I fancy will find you. If you are in Ireland and have a fancy to see the Curragh camp, I can give you an indifferent shakedown and mount you for the Field Day.

Lucan had come under ferocious attack ever since his recall in the spring of 1855. Accused of ineptitude and even cowardice in not leading his Division personally, he demanded – and was refused – a court martial. Yet the British Army and the British people had a way of forgiving and forgetting. He was now Colonel of the 8th Hussars and in the next ten years would be made General, Gold Stick and Colonel of the Life Guards. Whatever history thinks of him, he was Morris's ultimate superior in terms of Balaclava and as he had gone to Cureton in the 16th for a testimonial, so now he turned to Lucan to support his claim to the VC. As we have seen, it did him little good, and bearing in mind the *public's* attitude towards Lucan in 1855–6, it is hardly surprising. There must have been those in higher places who felt the same.

The other documents relating to Morris and the Curragh are official returns from the Division stationed there, filled in by Morris's hand. Here he met men who had served in India, like Colonel Walter Unett, who had led a squadron of the 3rd Light Dragoons hacking their way through a dense mass of Sikh infantry at Chillianwalla as Morris had done at Aliwal. He was slashed across the back and shoulder, hit in the ribs and loins but was back in the saddle by February of that year to lead his squadron at Gujurat, which did something to restore General Gough's wavering reputation. It is interesting that General

Airey's final comment on the Charge of the Light Brigade was reputedly, 'These sort of things will happen in War. It is nothing to Chillianwallah.'[2]

And Morris also met old friends like Charles Doherty of the 13th Light Dragoons, prevented by sickness from riding the Charge. Also with the 13th by this time was the ubiquitous Evelyn Wood, who had served with the Navy in the Crimea and was to serve under Morris in India with the 17th Lancers. He was bored by the long Mess dinners at the Newbridge Barracks – the General was a 'two-bottle man' – but elated by the professionalism of Morris and saw in him a man after his own heart:

> Colonel Morris ... had studied at the Senior Department Sandhurst and greatly added to the interest of our military exercises by the schemes he gave us to work out. We refought many actions of Frederick the Great and some of Wellington's Peninsula battles, which induced reading, and served to weaken, if not to break down the Mess rule of 'No shop' at table.
>
> Colonel Morris was however ahead of the generals and after he had pointed out that the Horse Artillery should have advanced previous to a charge [no doubt he remembered the farce at Balaclava] and come into action against the troops to be attacked, we were startled by the generals' decision that the Horse Artillery should have charged the cavalry.[3]

We cannot tell from the sparse returns in the Morris Papers how he felt about paperwork, but the much-decorated, much-lauded Lieutenant Colonel, anxious for action, anxious to 'try again for the Victoria Cross', cannot have felt he had found his niche. In December 1856 John Reynolds, who had probably known Morris at the Horse Guards the previous year, wrote to him: 'I am glad you like your present berth. But nothing I fear would quite satisfy a fellow like you but being in the midst of hard knocks.' Morris's niche in history was being prepared for him, thousands of miles away at his old stamping ground with the 16th Lancers – Meerut.

On the hot afternoon of Sunday, 10 May, a mutiny broke out among the Sepoys of the Bengal army at the barracks there. Hugh Gough, son of the 'Tipperary' General of the Sikh Wars, was one of the first on the scene 'of the most wild and awful confusion ... huts on fire ... sepoys dancing and leaping frantically about, calling and yelling at each other and blazing away in the air ... a maddened crowd of fiends and devils.' The troopers of the 3rd Cavalry broke into the jail and released imprisoned comrades. Someone – apparently a Moslem butcher – grabbed a Mrs Chambers, the pregnant wife of an officer, and hacked her to pieces. At Meerut, at Delhi and at Cawnpore, the Sepoys ran amok and in later years the British built a monument at Cawnpore to the women and children who died in the 'house of martyrdom'. It was to be a shrine and a tangible reminder of indelible mistrust. Fifty or more women and children were herded into a single room and there hacked to death with swords. White troops first on the scene were sickened by the sight – blood sloshing around their spurs and long tresses of hair hanging from gashes where the sharp tulwar blades had bitten into the walls and timbers.

When William Howard Russell of *The Times* reached India early in 1858 he spoke of horror and bestiality on both sides. The rebels, guilty or not, mutineers or not, were tied to the mouths of cannon and blown apart, their souls as well as their bodies shattered and lost forever.

Yet in February 1856, Lord Dalhousie, the retiring Governor General, wrote to the Queen:

> The guns are announcing from the ramparts of Fort William that Lord Canning has arrived. In an hour's time he will have assumed the Government of India. Lord Dalhousie will transfer it to him in a state of perfect tranquillity. There is peace, within and without. And although no prudent man will ever venture to predict the certainty of continued peace in India, yet Lord Dalhousie is able to declare, within reservation, that he knows of no quarter in which it is probable that trouble will arise.

How could Dalhousie have been so wrong? And why was it that for the second time in the prosperous 1850s the smug complacency of the Victorians could be shattered by events so far away?

First, the increasing westernization of India under successive Governors General took over not only land (as with Ellenborough in the Punjab), but also organization and administration. Roads were built, railways and canals. Schools were established and a postal service introduced. Increasingly, the language of the government centres at Bombay, Delhi and Calcutta was English. 'You can well imagine', wrote *The Times* in June 1857, 'the effect on the quick, suspicious temper of a Hindoo of all that is passing in India. Everything around him is in a state of change.'

Second, a new type of man, both from the Honourable East India Company, via its public school, Haileybury, and from the officer ranks of the Indian Army, was to be found in the subcontinent. The old 'Indian officers' who spoke Hindi, and *knew* the Indians under their command and loved them as their children, were being replaced by public school boys who expected the men to learn English. And already they brought their wives with them to rebuild little Cheltenhams and Leamingtons in the cantonments of India, alienating themselves and their menfolk from the Indians, increasingly sending their children away to school in England.

Third, both the caste and the religion of the native were compromised by the muscular Christianity and fierce bigotry of the British. Brahmin and Lascar, at distant ends of the rigid caste system, found themselves banded together under British officers, civil and military. The oldest and most respected Nizam could only hope to be a Risaldar or Havildar (NCO) in the Company's armies. And the British expected them all to cross the Kala Pani, the Black Water, to serve in Burma and even, it was at one time mooted, the Crimea, which would have meant an appalling loss of caste. Hindu, Moslem and countless sects were dumped into regiments and battalions.

In the Bengal army particularly, trouble was brewing. Since 1853 no officer had been allowed to punish his men with more than five days' drill. This was felt to be progressive by some and a sign of weakness by others. The Bengal army was split between Brahmins and Rajputs. Three-fifths of the Sepoys (infantrymen) were Hindu; most Sowars (cavalrymen) were Moslem. There had been four minor mutinies in this army since 1842, caused in part by the ratio of white officers to native troops being allowed to fall dangerously low. The system of 'lapse' introduced somewhat arbitrarily by Dalhousie stole the Indian princes' lands from them and caused an immediate discontent.

Two other factors remained. This was 1857, exactly a century after Robert Clive's victory at Plassey and the infamous Black Hole in Calcutta. Rumours spread that the ghost of Suraj-ad-Dowlah, Clive's opponent, would return to drive the interlopers out. And in this year of 1857 the British issued the infamous cartridges for the new Enfield rifle. These had to be bitten before insertion and rumours spread that they were smeared with beef fat or pig grease. Even though these cartridges had been withdrawn before May 1857, the damage was done. As J H Stocqueler wrote in his *History of the British Army* in 1871, 'Now the Hindoo worships the cow and the Mohamedan abhors the hog – two powerful reasons why they should not be called upon to touch the rifle cartridge, much less apply it to their lips.'[4]

This was not a nationalist uprising. Even within the mutinous 3rd Bengal Cavalry, Captain Craigie's troop remained loyal throughout the Mutiny and the other Presidency armies, those of Bombay and Madras, were totally unaffected. It was this very loyalty and the pacifying influence of 'Clemency' Canning which helped end the Mutiny relatively quickly.

Even so, three native rulers in particular took advantage of the blow to the outnumbered British: Nana Sahib, who had probably sanctioned the outrage at Cawnpore; the Rani of Jhansi, a redoubtable female ruler whose sexual excesses were built up out of all proportion by the more salacious Victorian newspapers; and the cunning Tantia Topi, against whom the 17th Lancers were directed.

'The Sepoy has time to brood', warned *The Times*, 'over imaginary wrongs and to suspect that he is subjected to cunning temptations.'

Chapter Fourteen

Flowers at Poona

On 2 September 1857, the 17th Lancers received orders for India. Less than a week later they had increased their six troops to ten and obtained 132 volunteers from other regiments, notably the 3rd, 4th and 13th Light Dragoons, the 11th Hussars and the 16th Lancers; four of the five regiments of the Light Brigade were represented. Did any of the volunteers of the 16th remember 'Slacks', the eager young Lieutenant from eleven years before?

Morris had wasted no time in applying for a posting with the 17th. On 23 September, from the Adjutant General's office in Dublin, Sir Richard England wrote:

> With reference to previous correspondence I have now the honour by desire of the General Commanding to request, pursuant to an application from the Officer Commanding the 17th Lancers [Benson] that Brevet Lieutenant Colonel Morris may be ordered to join that Corps in Dublin as early as possible.

On 28 September, a letter reached Morris from the Commander of the Forces Office, Royal Hospital, Dublin, promoting him. 'Captain and Brevet Lieutenant-Colonel Morris, C.B. to be Major without purchase' backdated to 17 September. And on the same day from the Horse Guards:

> Sir,
>
> Having submitted to the General Commanding in Chief your letter of the 15th Instant, I am directed by His Royal Highness to acquaint you in reply that the time you spent at Scutari from the date of your promotion to the Brevet rank of Lt. Colonel, as Superintendent of Cavalry Disembarkation, and the time you were employed as Deputy Quartermaster General to the Turkish Contingent will be allowed towards the period required to qualify you for the rank of Colonel.

Morris was therefore a supernumerary Major by the time the 17th formed its depot on 1 October. In terms of *army* rank, he was on a par with Henry Roxby Benson, now commanding the 17th. Benson, a former alumnus of St John's College, had obtained a cornetcy in the 17th in January 1840 and by a series of purchased promotions sailed out to the Crimea in January 1855. In Lawrenson's and Morris's absence and with the death of Willett, Benson assumed command and obtained his lieutenant colonelcy in September 1856.

The regiment was moved now by rail, on 6 October, to Cork, where they embarked on Brunel's SS *Great Britain*. The ship sailed, Morris having bade farewell to his ever stoical Amelia, on 8 October, and they put in to refuel at Cape Verde Island and the Cape of Good Hope. It must have been a vastly different undertaking for the 17th after their departure for the Crimea from Portsmouth in the April of 1854, the regiment divided then into five sailing vessels. This time the journey – a far greater one, of course – took seventy days. It must have seemed different to Morris too. In 1842 his voyage out had taken eight months.

At the Cape, he was able to meet his brothers, Cholmley and Westcott. At the end of November, Cholmley wrote to Emma that his children, Willy and Nellie, had met their uncle for the first time and that he looked well and was not in the least altered.

On 17 December, the Deaths reached Bombay, the East India Company's Presidency in Central India. They had suffered one death, of a Private, from heart disease. As Benson had gone ahead of the *Great Britain* with the Riding Master, the Veterinary Officer and four rough riders by overland route, it is likely that Morris commanded the regiment on the voyage. The 17th were disembarked in two divisions and on 19 and 21 December moved up to Campoolee in the foothills of the Bhore Ghauts and then on to the more comfortable cantonments at Kirkee, which they reached on Christmas Eve and Boxing Day. Here, it was a matter of waiting until suitable horses could arrive. The lesson of not carrying horses on board ship had been learned and it made sense. Over the next weeks, as the new year arrived, quantities of remounts arrived from Bombay – Arabs, Syrians, Walers and Capes. As each squadron was properly mounted, so it set out to bring the last of the Mutineers to heel.

With the 17th at Kirkee was Lieutenant Evelyn Wood. By March two squadrons were mounted and he requested that Benson allow him to join Sir William Gordon's troop in which he was to lead the first squadron against Tantia Topi. Wood was rightly impressed by Gordon but he became ill with neuralgia at the end of March. He was living in Morris's house, which Morris shared with Major Learmonth. In the bungalow, Wood had a bed and bath for a nominal rent. He was mugging up for a forthcoming examination in Hindustani for an interpreter's post and it was now, to cheer Wood up, that Morris told him of his exploits against the Sikhs at Aliwal.

Colonel Morris noticed that I was depressed and asked me the reason. After condoling with me, he invited me to come out into the garden, as he just received a sword, made by Messrs. Wilkinson of Pall Mall, designed on the model of a sword used most effectively by Colonel Clarke of the Scots Greys at Waterloo; but Colonel Morris, who was the Champion swordsman in the Army, believing in the advantage of a light weapon, had ordered his sword to be made lighter, which Messrs. Wilkinson did, but declined responsibility, fearing that if struck by another sword, it might break. He struck the trunk of a mimosa tree with the sword three times with as much force as he was capable of exerting and then examined it, handing it to me, saying, 'You may trust your life to it', and utterly refused to allow me to decline the present.[1]

That March, the *London Gazette* carried the news of the Turkish order of the Medjidje and the Queen's permission for her officers to wear it. Morris received the Third Class of the Order. The document, in Ottoman Script, bears the tughra, the imperial cipher of Sultan Abdul Mejid and confers on

the Colonel, an officer of the English Army, Morris by name, who accompanied my Imperial Armies in the late war in the Crimean region, in honour of his devoted and self-sacrificing conduct and display of courage and zeal in battle, and in recognition of services rendered, an Imperial Order of the Medjidje, Third Class.

The First Class was the lowest and the Fifth, jewelled, the highest.

Lord George Paget complained in his *Crimean Journal* that only two of the Light Brigade – Alexander Low of his own regiment, the 4th Lights, and John Douglas of the 11th Hussars – received the honour and accused the Sultan of meanness. However, both Morris and George Mayow, who had ridden the Charge, received it, so Paget is being less than accurate. The following month, Morris was again taken away from the 17th, this time to act as Assistant Adjutant General at Mahableshwar, the pleasant hill station that served Bombay and Poona. This move was perhaps a blessing in disguise, at least at first, because May was abnormally hot in Kirkee and there were deaths among the non-commissioned officers of the 17th. The Field Officers of the regiment were frequently at Mahableshwar and must have seen a lot of Morris, now on the staff of Sir Henry Somerset.

It was from here that Morris wrote what was probably his last letter home. Ironically, it is full of references to Hatherleigh, as though he was homesick. Had he, after all, had enough of soldiering? Had he abandoned any hope of the VC? Gordon's troop had ridden out after Tantia Topi to earn undying fame. Should it have been Morris's troop? On 24 May he wrote to his sister:

Don't you think you could persuade the 'Mayor and Corporation' of
Hatherleigh that it would be for their interest, as well as for the
interest of the town, if they were to make a racecourse of
Hatherleigh Moor; it must not be less than two miles long. I will give
£20 towards it; Mr Oldham and Mr Mallett might Subscribe, or at
least give their sanction, as some encouragement to the breeding of
horses is sadly wanted in the neighbourhood and I am sure Mr
Madge of Stockley will help. I would give stone for bridging over the
gullies. I made a racecourse at Kirkee which only cost £15 and there
are four or five bridges in it.

There are references to the fact that the lambing season at Fishleigh had not
been a good one. He turns then to Mahableshwar and two of his earliest loves
– horses and flowers:

This is a very pretty place, but too much confined to suit me, and I
would much rather stand the heat of the plains and have my gallop,
though the temperature here is as pleasant as possible, neither hot
nor cold, and the flowers are lovely; all English flowers grow well,
and the wild flowers are beautiful ... We go to Poona on the 1st June.

A telegram to this effect had arrived, by courtesy of the Honourable East India
Company's Electric Telegraph, on 8 May: 'Join Headquarters at once and let
me know the day you will arrive here that I may send to meet you.'
     What more of this correspondence reveals is that Amelia Morris came out in
June to spend some time with her husband, although there are no details
whatever of her journey. Their time together was short, because towards the
end of June, Morris was taken ill with dysentery. The story of his death is taken
up by Archdeacon John Reynolds in a letter to his wife:

Next day, Friday – I went to see a sick officer of the 17th lancers –
Col. Morris who was Assistant Adjutant General of Queen's Troops
under Col. Greathead. I think I told you of him – he was, strange to
say, of my own College, as was Col. Benson. His wife came out only
a month ago hoping to have a little peace and quiet, even in India,
having been denied the same ever since her marriage owing to the
Russian War at Balaklava – Col. Morris led the 17th Lancers in that
memorable Light Cavalry Charge and was dreadfully wounded in
the retreat – the latest mail brought us news that the Victoria Cross
has been given to the surgeon who went out and attended to Col.
Morris's wounds, as he was bleeding to death under fire – thereby
saving his life. Poor Mrs Morris on hearing of her Husband's state,
went out immediately and under God nursed him to health again,

but alas! only to lose him now. The liking I had for him seemed reciprocal for he asked me when expecting his wife if I would share my house with him. I could not do so as Sir J. Leith was coming to me. He afterwards went to Mahableshawar with Mrs M. and the dysentery came on which never left him.

The form of the disease was likely to have been the bacillary type. Its symptoms included fever and frequent painful stools containing blood, pus and mucus. It was usually contracted by eating or drinking contaminated substances. The incubation period is about a week and the onset is sudden, with fever, headaches, vomiting and diarrhoea. Morris had passed this way before, for the symptoms of the cholera he contracted at Varna were in many ways similar. Then he had shaken it off while others had died. Now he was not to be so lucky. 'I saw Mrs Morris twice on Friday,' Reynolds continues,

but neither time could I see him. But the next day I went to see Col. Morris again, earnestly praying that God would be with me during the interview – and it was deeply interesting – the more so from the noble and soldierly spirit of the dying man whom I addressed. And there was *nothing* of human pride or self-approval, no-one could be more humble or more penitent. I can only tell you that I was more thankful and happy about him, though I knew that life was ebbing fast – and though I could not but share freely in the tears which his poor wife was shedding – as he earnestly asked for mercy for his Saviour's sake, I left to meet him again, I hope, in a happier world. By the Bishop's advice I wrote to Venton [the Poona Senior Chaplain] asking him to call and see Col. Morris and explaining my own visits. On Monday morning I heard of Col. Morris's death. At twelve o'clock on Sunday Venton had called to see him, but he was all but insensible. Next day, a brother clergyman kindly consented to relieve me of a funeral which set me at liberty to attend the funeral at Poona.

The *Poona Observer* of Monday, 12 July, as well as reporting movements of the rebels under Tantia Topi, carried the story:

We deeply regret to have to record the death in the Neutral Lines at Poona last night of Major (Brevet Lieutenant-Colonel) William Morris CB of HM's 17th Lancers, only a few days since appointed Deputy Assistant Adjutant General of Her Majesty's Forces; from dysentery. Colonel Morris was a most distinguished officer and his death is much regretted by all those who had the pleasure of knowing him ... The remains of Colonel Morris will be interred at

Poona this evening with military honours and the Brigadier commanding the division has requested that every officer off duty will attend the funeral to pay the last respect to the memory of this brave and veteran officer.

Reynolds was there:

It was a grand gathering of the military all in full dress – the officers being ordered to attend – the Lancers were there from Kirkee. The firing party (300 men) being from the 33rd Foot. All the Royal Artillery and the Commander-in-Chief. I knew it would rain so provided myself with an umbrella and stood at the grave beside Mr Venton who read the service. Long before the troops all got into the churchyard down came the rain and drenched us all to the skin. Opposite me stood the widow, poor thing, as calm and enduring as flesh and blood could be, she had stood by him and nursed her gallant husband when nearly hacked to pieces in the Crimea, she had followed him to India – and now she would even see the grave close over him. She stood leaning on Commodore Wellesley and Colonel Greathead. Seeing that they had no umbrella immediately the rain began to fall I sent mine by the clerk which I hoped served to keep her dry.

When Gambier Parry wrote his biography of Reynell Taylor in 1888 he spoke of death – 'the scythesman at the elbow' – of every man. The scythesman had caught William Morris at Poona on 11 July and all that was left of him was lowered into the muddy little churchyard that an alien faith had built on hostile soil. The 17th Lancers went home without him.

On the black-edged paper the mid-Victorians used to mourn their dead, Samuel Field, Vicar of Hatherleigh, wrote to Jane Morris on 17 August:

I cannot resist the feeling which influences me to assure you how sincerely I condole with you under the painful bereavement you have experienced. I sincerely grieve for the loss you have sustained of a son so affectionate and attentive to his widowed mother, so kind and anxious to promote the interests and happiness of the members of his family circle.

It may tend to comfort you in your distress to be assured that the loss of your gallant son is lamented as a public calamity. Short has been his course but it has been marked and filled up by noble exploits and deeds of valour, which have procured for him the meed of grateful esteem and commendation. And as his military career was most honourable, so he has fallen in his country's cause deservedly and universally respected and deplored. I trust and believe that you will be aided and supported to bear this trial by the highest consolation of true religion; yet even this may prove at least some mitigation of your sorrow under this affliction that you have given a son to your country who has contributed to its glory and defence.

May we my dear friend amidst our trials, bow submissively to the Divine Will and be favoured with the Divine Presence; and in meek resignation say 'It is the Lord, let Him do what seemeth Him good.'

The War Office in October were rather colder towards Amelia:

Madam,

The Secretary for War having submitted to the Queen your application of the 23rd September 1858, I have the satisfaction to acquaint you by his direction, that Her Majesty has been graciously pleased to grant you a pension of £70 a year, being the rate allowed for the widow of a Major, the same to commence from the 12th Day of July.

Such was the esteem from official channels for a husband and son who had contributed to the 'glory and defence' of his country.

Relatives, brother officers and friends were more forthcoming. It had been a double loss for Amelia, for her mother had died earlier in the year. Reynell, who felt the double loss nearly as keenly, wrote of Morris as 'a soldier and a Christian to the backbone', 'a type of what a man ought to be'. In the church at Poona, a tablet was erected to Morris's memory. On it is this inscription carved below the Death's Head and scroll:

Sacred to the Memory of
William Morris
of Fishleigh, Devon
Brevet Lieut Colonel and Major
Her Majesty's 17th Lancers
Commander of the Most Honble Order of the Bath
Knight of the Legion of Honor
3rd Class of the Imperial Order of the Medjidie
Deputy Assitant Adjutant General
Of HM Forces Bombay
Who departed this life the 11th July 1858 at Poonah
Aged 37 years
This Tablet is erected
By his Brother Officers

> As a mark of their esteem for his character
> As a friend and a distinguished Soldier
>
> Maharajpoor   Sobraon
> Budiwal   Balaklava
> Aliwal   Sebastopol
>
> To them who by patient continuance in well-doing seek for glory
> and honour and immortality, eternal life – Romans II Chap, 7 ver

At home in Hatherleigh, Jack Russell, Samuel Hooper, Samuel Field, George Braginton and many other men of North Devon put their hands into their pockets to pay for the erection of a monument to the man whom they had honoured so recently at Great Torrington. 'That this Meeting', wrote Hooper,

> of the inhabitants of the native parish of the late lamented Col. Morris CB and others of his friends and admirers, deeply sympathises with his bereaved widow, who in a distant land devotedly ministered by his couch of suffering.
>
> That this Meeting desires respectfully to convey to Mrs Morris of Fishleigh, an expression of condolence on her bereavement of a son of whom she might justly be proud, since his gallant deeds had won national admiration and the meed of the Sovereign's commendation.
>
> That this Meeting sympathises with the other relatives of the late Col. Morris, in the loss of one who was an honour to all with whom he was connected by the ties of blood and even of neighbourhood and who, had he not been cut off in the prime of life, by a malady induced by an insalubrious climate, would have doubtless further distinguished himself, and with prolonged life, have attained a very high position in his profession.

Ninety-one names, together with their subscriptions, bought the 'lasting monument to his memory' which still stands on Hatherleigh Moor. Apart from the local clergy, Field and the Karslakes, the local landowners were there – Braginton, Oldham, the Mallets. From the 17th Lancers, Major Macartney and Captain Arnold were represented, and squires, officers and MPs abounded.

On its erection in 1860, the result was reported in Morris's obituary in *Woolner's Gazette* of Exeter. The monument was designed by the sculptor E B Stephens and was made of granite by the Exeter firm of Easton. It is 50 feet high and its base 10 feet square, showing Morris being carried off the field at Balaclava by Mouat, Wooden and Mansell.

> The portraits are said to be excellent likenesses ... the 'Death or Glory' (the badge of the regiment) on the arms of the sergeant who

carries the wounded officer is a singular and touching commentary on the whole scene.

The east facet records the battles in which Morris fought, and the north:

To the Memory of
Lieut. Col.
William Morris CB KLH
Major 17th Lancers
Born at Fishleigh in this county
Decr 18th 1820
Died at Poona Bombay
July 11th 1858

The article concludes:

Whilst the warrior is sleeping peacefully in his Eastern grave, the monument – so creditable to the patriotic spirit of the North Devon men and to the genius of the artist – will tell more powerfully than words the story of his valour and posterity will learn how chivalry and goodness in youth and heroism and patriotism in manhood, were honoured in Devonshire in the year of grace 1860.

*****

As time passed memories faded of William Morris. By the time Lady White-Thomson gave her husband's lecture at the school at Hatherleigh in 1902, the ranks of those who had ridden with them both were thinning. Colonel Lawrenson of the 17th Lancers was dead, and so was Alexander Learmonth who had shared a bungalow with Morris at Kirkee. John Hartopp too was gone. And Henry Benson. White-Thomson himself had only months to live. Of the officers who had ridden the Charge, only Gordon and Morgan had a few years left to them, both men retired now to their respective estates. Only one of Morris's three brothers was alive – Montague.

Morris's second brother Cholmley had succeeded to the Fishleigh and Inwardleigh estates in 1860, and his third brother Westcott too was dead. Of his five sisters, only Juliana Mary, still a spinster, was alive in 1902 and it was from her that the letters came from which White-Thomson quoted.

William Morris's army career spanned eighteen years, from the time he first took ship at Gravesend bound for Meerut until he died quietly on the Sunday afternoon in the Neutral Lines at Poona. That the career began and ended in India is a fitting reminder of the days of Empire. It was men like Morris who made the Empire what it was and it does not find much favour today. A great deal of water has passed under the bridge and the world that Morris knew and many of the values he stood for have gone.

Had he lived longer, had Providence given him the time he asked for in his speech at Great Torrington, had every happiness attended the union of William and Amelia, as Sir Trevor Wheler had hoped, he would have become a crusty old general and would probably, like Evelyn Wood, have written his own memoirs in several volumes.

As it is, Morris left very little. One of the correspondents in the research for this book was General Taylor, descended from Amelia's family, and he said that soldiers' families do not keep mementoes – they have neither room nor time. All that remains is a handful of letters, some medals, a regimental squad book and two swords. Morris was not a great writer of letters. He kept no journal. He was a man of action, too busy with his life to think in terms of recording it for posterity. This dearth of source material creates its own enigma, like a photograph too faded to see, a letter too worn to read. Something of Morris can be caught still, walking under the trees at Fishleigh or standing on the rich, red earth of Hatherleigh Moor. The monument, although repaired by the 17th/21st Lancers in 1963, is again showing signs of its age and the ravages of the North Devon winds.

It is never enough. Morris was not a colourful eccentric like Cardigan; he did not, like Paget, leave a detailed account of the Crimean campaign. Yet it is against the Charge of the Light Brigade that Morris's career must be set. It was that insanely heroic twenty minutes for which he had been trained and which had shaped his life. Were it not for that, he would be quite unknown, like hundreds of other young officers of the nineteenth-century British Army.

What makes Morris out of the ordinary is that he was the most experienced man in the Light Brigade – a professional in the world of the 'noble amateur' which dominated military society in the Victorian period. It is perhaps a sad reflection on that society that in the end his advancement was due to his dogged courage, his sense of duty and the power of his sword arm – valuable possessions it is true, but innate and not remotely connected with the professionalism for which he longed. At Great Torrington he asked for time to be allowed to reach the heights of his profession and those who heard him saw in his own success the march of education and progress in the Army. In the year of his death, the Staff College proper was opened at Sandhurst and despite the continued shortcomings of that institution, it at least began to create officers, in Cromwell's phrase, 'who knew what they fought for and loved what they knew.' In the year before his death, a Parliamentary Commission had looked into the purchase system which threatened to perpetuate the very amateur spirit which Morris loathed. Because of the forces of self-interest and tradition, it was to be another fourteen years before that system disappeared. Morris would have approved.

One last thing can be gleaned from the mementoes of William Morris – his fatalism. From his falling into the Cam while at university, through cholera and fever at Scutari, to the wounds of the Charge and the onset of dysentery at Poona, we have a man strangely fated to suffer. 'Those whom the Gods love, die young.' Was it chance that Amelia Morris came out to India in the summer of 1858? Did Morris have a presentiment that he was going to die? This may be too fanciful, too romantic a picture. I cannot believe he wanted to die in bed. As his friend John Reynolds had said, he was a man only happy among hard knocks; he sought medals, he sought action. And if these things are not fashionable today, then perhaps ours is a world sorrier for it.

In his fifth volume of *The Invasion of the Crimea*, Kinglake writes what is in effect an obituary of Morris:

> He was much thought of in our army as a valorous and skilled officer, and with so high a reputation for straightforwardness and accuracy, that once, when a general officer imprudently ventured to put himself in conflict with Morris upon a matter of fact, there was a smile at the 'impar Congressus', no one who knew Morris consenting to imagine it possible that he could be the one who mistook.[2]

More than all the patriotic rumblings of the poet Edward Capern and the Victorian platitudes and eulogies from other contemporaries, I think the Pocket Hercules would have been most touched by that.

Notes

Chapter 1: The Morrises of Fishleigh

1. There is of course no Clenelly in Caernarvon. It is possible that William Morris Senior confused Caernarvon with Carmarthen (though this is unlikely) and that Clenelly is Llanelli. Alternatively, there are a number of possibilities of mis-spellings in Caernarvon itself – perhaps Llaneilian-yn-Rhos.
2. Morris Papers. Unless otherwise attributed in a note, all quoted passages come from the Morris Papers.
3. Colonel Thomas Pride (d. 1658) was a regicide who rose rapidly through the New Model Army, won fame at Naseby in 1645 and prevented 140 Members from taking their seats in the Commons because of the feared rapprochement with the king.
4. The names Montague and Cholmley became incorporated into the Morris family and have been preserved to the present.
5. Ironically, bearing in mind the attitude of the eighteenth-century Anglican establishment to the 'dangerous' Methodist revival, Christ Church was the college of John Wesley in the late 1720s. It has produced ten Prime Ministers in its history. One of them, Robert Peel, had gone down three years before William Cholmley arrived.
6. Hatherleigh Parish Records, Devon Record Office, Exeter.
7. E Gambier Parry, *Reynell Taylor* (London: Kegan Paul and Co., 1888).
8. *Dictionary of National Biography* (1971), p. 464.
9. *A Memoir of the Reverend John Russell* (London: Richard Bentley and Son, 1878), p. 28.
10. Ibid., p. 29.
11. Sir Robert White-Thomson, *A Memoir of Lieutenant Colonel William Morris* (privately printed, 1902, no page numbers).

Chapter 2: Schola Cantabrigiensis

1 In Morris's last years his commanding officer in the 17th Lancers, Colonel Benson, was a Johnian; so was John Reynolds, the chaplain who was with him shortly before he died.
2. Bungaree Garrick was an Australian bare-knuckle boxer who took his name from the Aborigine chief who sailed the world with the explorer Matthew Flinders.
3. Hermione Hobhouse, *Prince Albert: His Life and Work* (London: Hamilton, 1983), p. 63.
4. White-Thomson, *Memoir of Lieutenant Colonel Morris*.

Chapter 3: The Scarlet Lancers

1. Quoted in James Lunt, *16th/5th The Queen's Royal Lancers* (London: Leo Cooper, 1973), p. 12.
2. J. MacMullen, *Camp and Barrack Room; or the British Army As It Is, by a late Staff Sergeant of the 13th Light Infantry 1846*, quoted in the Marquess of Anglesey, *A History of the British Cavalry 1816–1919*, Vol. 1 (London: Leo Cooper, 1973), p. 115.

3. The historian of the Crimean War, A W Kinglake, puts a rather different spin on the phrase, however: 'when specially asked whether Lord Cardigan had led "quietly", Morris answered, "Quite so; just as it ought to be – in short like a gentleman" – an expression from his lips conveying "much", so says the narrator of the converstion "to anyone who knew him".' A W Kinglake, *The Invasion of the Crimea*, Vol. 5 (London: William Blackwood, 1877), p. 262.
4. Quoted in Lunt, *16th/5th The Queen's Royal Lancers*, pp. 12–13.
5. Ibid., p. 13.
6. Ibid., p. 33.
7. Quoted in ibid., p. 33.
8. Ibid., pp. 33–4.

Chapter 4: 'A Bloody War and a Sickly Season'
1. White-Thomson, *Memoir of Lieutenant Colonel Morris*.
2. Anglesey, *History of the British Cavalry*, Vol. 1, pp. 102–3.
3. A McKenzie Annand (ed.), *Cavalry Surgeon: The Recollections of Deputy Surgeon-General John Henry Sylvester, Bombay Army* (London: Macmillan, 1971), p. 38.
4. MS of George Tookey, 14th Light Dragoons 1846–8, quoted in Anglesey, *History of the British Cavalry*, Vol. 1, p. 143.
5. Quoted in Lunt, *16th/5th The Queen's Royal Lancers*, p. 43.

Chapter 5: Crossing the Sutlej
1. Edwin Mole, *A King's Hussar, being the Military Memoirs for Twenty-Five Years of a Troop Sergeant-Major of the 14th (King's) Hussars* (London: Cassell and Co., 1893), p. 43.
2. Parry, *Reynell Taylor*.
3. Quoted in Anglesey, *History of the British Cavalry*, Vol. 1, p. 257.
4. Trooper John Pearman, 3rd Light Dragoons, quoted in Anglesey, *History of the British Cavalry*, Vol. 1, p. 267.
5. Quoted in ibid., p. 263.
6. Ibid., p. 267.
7. Lunt, *16th/5th The Queen's Royal Lancers*, p. 44.
8. Quoted in ibid., p. 45.
9. Smith quoted in ibid., p. 46.
10. Quoted in Anglesey, *History of the British Cavalry*, Vol. 1, p. 266.
11. The Queen's Lancers Museum, Stafford.
12. White-Thomson, *Memoir of Lieutenant Colonel Morris*.
13. Ibid.
14. Ibid.
15. Sir Evelyn Wood, *From Midshipman to Field Marshal*, Vol. 1 (London: Methuen and Co., 1906), p. 120.
16. H Moyse-Bartlett, *Louis Edward Nolan and His Influence on the British Cavalry* (London: Leo Cooper, 1971), p. 213.

Chapter 6: The Deaths
1. Quoted in Cecil Woodham-Smith, *The Reason Why* (London: Constable, 1957), p. 87.

Chapter 7: The Staff College and Amelia
1. A R Godwin-Austen, *The Staff and the Staff College* (London: Constable and Co., 1927), p. 43.
2. Ibid., p. 47.
3. Ibid., p. 54.

Chapter 8: The Crimea

1. Kinglake, *Invasion of the Crimea*, Vol. 1, p. 49.
2. Frances Duberly, *Journal Kept During the Russian War: from the Departure of the Army from England in April 1854 to the Fall of Sebastopol* (London: Longman, Brown, Green and Longmans, 1856), p. 26.
3. Joachim Murat, Grand Duke of Berg and King of Naples, was the son of an innkeeper from Gascony. He rose under Bonaparte to become a Marshal of France by 1804, and as commander of the Reserve Cavalry, was one of the legendary horsemen of history. He could have had the petulant Cardigan for breakfast.
4. Duberly, *Journal*.
5. Ibid.
6. *Punch*, Vol. XXVII (1854).
7. All correspondence from Robert Portal is contained in the Morris Papers.
8. *Punch*, Vol. XXVII (1854).
9. Duberly, *Journal*, p. 82.
10. Norman Dixon, *On the Psychology of Military Incompetence* (London: Cape, 1976).
11. G A Embleton, *The Crimean War 1855–56* (London: Almark, 1975), p. 20.

Chapter 9: 'Damn Those Heavies'

1. Terry Brighton, *Hell's Riders: The Truth about the Charge of the Light Brigade* (London: Viking, 2004).
2. Quoted in Nicolas Bentley (ed.), *Russell's Despatches from the Crimea* (London: Panther, 1970).
3. Bentley (ed.), *Russell's Despatches*.
4. Ibid.
5. Ibid.
6. Later to be misquoted by Henry Newbolt among others as 'the thin red line', the term became synonymous, even after the formal adoption of khaki for service dress in 1898, with the heroism, tenacity and sheer professionalism of the British infantry soldier, holding his own against impossible odds throughout the Empire.
7. Marquess of Anglesey (ed.), *Little Hodge: His Letters and Diaries of the Crimean War* (London: Leo Cooper, 1971), p. 44.
8. Bentley (ed.), *Russell's Despatches*.
9. Albert Seaton, *The Crimean War: A Russian Chronicle* (London: Batsford, 1977), p. 147 (my italics).
10. Bentley (ed.), *Russell's Despatches*.
11. Philip Warner (ed.), *The Fields of War: A Young Cavalryman's Crimea Campaign* (London: John Murray, 1977), p. 75.
12. Anglesey (ed.), *Little Hodge*, p. 75.
13. Ibid., p. 75.
14. Warner (ed.), *Fields of War*, p. 75.
15. Anglesey (ed.), *Little Hodge*, p. 75.
16. Ibid., p. 75.
17. Wood, *From Midshipman to Field Marshal*, Vol. 1, p. 49.
18. Warner (ed.), *Fields of War*, p. 78.
19. Woodham-Smith, *The Reason Why*, p. 178.
20. Kinglake, *Invasion of the Crimea*, Vol. 5, pp. 174–5 (my italics).
21. Quoted in John Harris, *The Gallant Six Hundred* (London: Hutchinson, 1973), p. 189.
22. Donald Thomas, *Charge! Hurrah! Hurrah!* (London: Routledge and Kegan Paul, 1974), p. 236.
23. James Wightman, 'One of the Six Hundred', *19th Century Magazine*, May 1892.

24. Thomas, *Charge! Hurrah! Hurrah!*, p. 237.
25. Kinglake, *Invasion of the Crimea*, Vol. 5, p. 178.
26. Thomas, *Charge! Hurrah! Hurrah!*, p. 237.
27. Kinglake, *Invasion of the Crimea*, Vol. 5, p. 176.
28. Quoted in Thomas, *Charge! Hurrah! Hurrah!*, p. 237.
29. Quoted in Woodham-Smith, *The Reason Why*, p. 178.
30. L E Nolan, *Cavalry: Its History and Tactics* (London: Thomas Bosworth, 1854), p. 63.
31. Woodham-Smith, *The Reason Why*, p. 137.
32. Kinglake, *Invasion of the Crimea*, Vol. 5, p. 179.
33. Kinglake, *Invasion of the Crimea*.
34. Ibid.
35. Ibid., p. 178.
36. Bentley, *Russell's Despatches*.
37. Warner (ed.), *Fields of War*, p. 171.
38. Anglesey (ed.), *Little Hodge*, p. 81.
39. Ibid., p. 97.
40. Warner (ed.), *Fields of War*, p. 76.
41. Ibid., pp. 91–2.
42. Ibid., p. 117.
43. Ibid., pp. 115–16.

Chapter 10: 'A Smart Little Affair'

1. Harris, *The Gallant Six Hundred*, p. 193.
2. Quoted in ibid., p. 193.
3. Kinglake, *Invasion of the Crimea*, Vol. 5, p. 192.
4. Quoted in Harris, *The Gallant Six Hundred*, p. 193.
5. Ibid.
6. Adkin's guilty four are Lord Raglan, Lord Lucan, Lord Cardigan and Captain Nolan, all of whom combined, with a mixture of ineptitude, to destroy the Light Brigade. Mark Adkin, *The Charge: Why the Light Brigade Was Lost* (London: Pimlico, 2000).
7. Nolan, *Cavalry*, p. 320.
8. Quoted in Harris, *The Gallant Six Hundred*, p. 204.
9. Quoted in Thomas, *Charge! Hurrah! Hurrah!*, p. 242.
10. Bentley (ed.), *Russell's Despatches*.
11. Harris, *The Gallant Six Hundred*, p. 206.
12. George Wombwell, Letters in The Queen's Royal Lancers Museum.
13. Wightman, 'One of the Six Hundred'.
14. Maxse Papers, West Sussex Record Office.
15. Quoted in Brighton, *Hell Riders*, p. 130.
16. Quoted in ibid., p. 138.
17. Kinglake, *Invasion of the Crimea*, Vol. 5, pp. 255, 254.
18. Ibid., pp. 255–6.
19. Ibid., p. 256.
20. Quoted in Brighton, *Hell Riders*, p. 180.
21. This was clearly written with hindsight as Loy Smith could not have known from Morris's uniform that he was in the 17th.
22. George Loy Smith, *A Victorian RSM* (Tunbridge Wells: Costello, 1987), p. 140.
23. Wood, *From Midshipman to Field Marshal*, Vol. 1, p. 49.

Chapter 11: 'A Mad Brained Trick'

1. Quoted in Adkin, *The Charge*, p. 206.
2. Kinglake, *Invasion of the Crimea*, Vol. 5, pp. 323–4.

3. Quoted in Harris, *The Gallant Six Hundred*, p. 251.

4. Seaton, *The Crimean War: A Russian Chronicle*, p. 171.

5. F S Maude, *Letters from Turkey and the Crimea* (printed for private circulation, 1896).

6. The most impressive, of course, is William Robertson, who enlisted as a Private in Morris's old regiment, the 16th Lancers, in 1877 and was a Field Marshal by the outbreak of the First World War. It must be said however that Seager's rise was probably more difficult, if not so high, in that he was doing it in the era of purchase and against astronomically wealthy officers.

7. Harris, *The Gallant Six Hundred*, p. 206.

8. Quoted in ibid., p. 255.

9. Quoted in ibid., p. 224.

10. Quoted in ibid., p. 260.

11. Kinglake, *Invasion of the Crimea*, Vol. 5, p. 32.

12. Cecil Woodham-Smith, *Florence Nightingale* (London: Penguin, 1955), p. 171.

13. Ibid., p. 114.

14. Ibid., p. 116.

15. Ibid., p. 117.

16. Ibid., p. 118.

17. Ibid., p. 134.

Chapter 12: Home and 'Johnny Turk'

1. Quoted in Peter Carew, *Combat and Carnival* (London: Constable, 1954), p. 93.

2. Ibid.

3. Quoted in ibid., p. 95.

4. G H B Macleod, *Notes on the Surgery of the War in the Crimea, with Remarks on the Treatment of Gun-shot Wounds* (London: 1858), p. 217.

5. Henry Clifford, VC, *His Letters and Sketches From the Crimea* (London: Michael Joseph, 1956), p. 168.

6. Christoper Hibbert, *The Destruction of Lord Raglan* (London: Penguin, 1961), p. 301.

7. General Simpson quoted in Hibbert, *Destruction of Lord Raglan*, p. 302.

8. Kingscote quoted in Lawrence James, *Crimea 1854–56: The War with Russia from Contemporary Photographs* (New York: Van Nostrand Reinhold, 1980), p. 130.

9. Ewart quoted in James, *Crimea 1854–56*, p. 136.

Chapter 13: Mutiny

1. Quoted in Thomas, *Charge! Hurrah! Hurrah!*, p. 286.

2. Quoted in ibid., p. 269.

3. Wood, *From Midshipman to Field Marshal*, Vol. 1, p. 155.

4. J H Stocqueler, *A Familiar History of the British Army* (London: Edward Stanford, 1871), p. 129.

Chapter 14: Flowers at Poona

1. Wood, *From Midshipman to Field Marshal*, Vol. 1, p. 120.

2. Kinglake, *Invasion of the Crimea*, Vol. 5, pp. 324–5.

Select Bibliography

Adkin, Mark, *The Charge: Why the Light Brigade Was Lost* (London: Pimlico, 2000).

Anglesey, Marquess of (ed.), *Little Hodge: His Letters and Diaries of the Crimean War* (London: Leo Cooper, 1971).

——, *A History of the British Cavalry 1816–1919*, 2 vols (London: Leo Cooper, 1973, 1975).

Annand, A McKenzie (ed.), *Cavalry Surgeon: The Recollections of Deputy Surgeon-General John Henry Sylvester, Bombay Army* (London: Macmillan, 1971).

Bamfield, Veronica, *On the Strength: The Story of the British Army Wife* (London: Charles Knight and Co., 1974).

Barbary, James, *The Crimean War* (London: Puffin, 1970).

Barthorp, Michael, *British Cavalry Uniforms since 1660* (Poole: Blandford Press, 1984).

Bentley, Nicolas (ed.), *Russell's Despatches from the Crimea 1854–1856* (London: Panther, 1970).

Blair, Rev. David, *The Universal Preceptor* (London: Sir Richard Phillips and Co., 1820).

Bolitho, Hector, *The Galloping Third: The Story of the 3rd The King's Own Hussars* (London: John Murray, 1963).

Bond, Brian, *The Victorian Army and the Staff College 1854–1914* (London: Eyre Methuen, 1972).

Brereton, J M, *The Horse in War* (Newton Abbott: David and Charles, 1976).

Brighton, Terry, *Hell Riders: The Truth about the Charge of the Light Brigade* (London: Viking, 2004).

Calthorpe, Somerset, *Cadogan's Crimea* (London: Hamish Hamilton, 1979).

Clifford, Henry, VC, *His Letters and Sketches From the Crimea* (London: Michael Joseph, 1956).

David, Saul, *The Homicidal Earl* (London: Little Brown and Co., 1997).

Dress Regulations 1846 (London: Arms and Armour Press, 1971).

Duberly, Frances, *Journal Kept During the Russian War* (London: Longman, Brown, Green and Longmans, 1856).

Featherstone, Donald, *All for a Shilling a Day* (London: New English Library, 1973).

——, *At Them with the Bayonet* (London: New English Library, 1974).

——, *Weapons and Equipment of the Victorian Soldier* (Poole: Blandford Press, 1978).

Fenwick, Kenneth (ed.), *Voice from the Ranks* (London: William Heinemann, 1954).

Ffrench Blake, R L V, *The 17th/21st Lancers* (London: Hamish Hamilton, 1968).

Godwin-Austen, A R, *The Staff and the Staff College* (London: Constable and Co., 1927).

Grey, Elizabeth, *The Noise of Drums and Trumpets* (London: Longman, 1971).

Harris, John, *The Gallant Six Hundred* (London: Hutchinson, 1973).

——, *The Court Martial of Lord Lucan* (London: Severn House, 1987).

Haythornthwaite, Philip, *The Colonial Wars Source Book* (London: Arms and Armour Press, 1995).

Heath, Ian, *The Sikh Army 1799–1849* (Oxford: Osprey, 2005).

Hibbert, Christopher, *The Destruction of Lord Raglan* (London: Penguin, 1961).

Hichberger, J W M, *Images of the Army* (Manchester: Manchester University Press, 1988).

James, Lawrence, *Crimea 1854–56: The War with Russia from Contemporary Photographs* (New York: Van Nostrand Reinhold, 1980).

Kinglake, A W, *The Invasion of the Crimea*, 9 vols (London: William Blackwood, 1877).

Knight, Ian, *Go To Your God Like A Soldier* (London: Greenhill Books, 1996).

Loy Smith, George, *A Victorian RSM* (Tunbridge Wells: Costello, 1987).

Lummis, William and Wynn, Kenneth, *Honour the Light Brigade* (London: J B Hayward and Son, 1973).

Lunt, James, *Charge to Glory* (London: Heinemann, 1961).

——, *16th/5th The Queen's Royal Lancers* (London: Leo Cooper, 1973).

Mason, Philip, *A Matter of Honour* (London: Penguin, 1976).

Mollo, Boris, *The Indian Army* (Poole: Blandford, 1981).

Mollo, John and Boris, *Into the Valley of Death* (London: Windrow and Green, 1991).

Moyse-Bartlett, H, *Louis Edward Nolan and His Influence on the British Cavalry* (London: Leo Cooper, 1971).

Newark, Peter, *Sabre and Lance* (Poole: Blandford Press, 1986).

Nolan, L E, *Cavalry: Its History and Tactics* (London: Thomas Bosworth, 1854).

Punch, Vol. XXVII (1854).

Seacole, Mary, *Wonderful Adventures of Mrs Seacole in Many Lands* (Oxford: Oxford University Press, 1988).

Seaton, Albert, *The Crimean War: A Russian Chronicle* (London: Batsford, 1977).

Stocqueler, J H, *A Familiar History of the British Army* (London: edward Stanford, 1871).

Thomas, Donald, *Charge! Hurrah! Hurrah!* (London: Routledge and Kegan Paul, 1974).

Thornton, Edward, *The History of the British Empire in India* (London: W H Allen, 1845).

Tylden, Major G, *Horses and Saddlery* (London: J A Allen, 1980).

Warner, Philip (ed.), *The Fields of War: A Young Cavalryman's Crimea Campaign* (London: John Murray, 1977).

——, *The British Cavalry* (London: James Dent and Sons, 1984).

Wood, Sir Evelyn, *From Midshipman to Field Marshal*, 2 vols (London: Methuen and Co., 1906).

—— , *Winnowed Memories* (London: Cassell, 1918).

Woodham-Smith, Cecil, *Florence Nightingale* (London: Penguin, 1955).

——, *The Reason Why* (London: Constable, 1957).

Index